DATE			

-94

D1265153

BAKER & TAYLOR

Environmental Problems in the Shortage Economy

NEW HORIZONS IN ENVIRONMENTAL ECONOMICS

General Editor: Wallace E. Oates, *Professor of Economics,*
University of Maryland

This important new series is designed to make a significant contribution to the development of the principles and practices of environmental economics. It will include both theoretical and empirical work. International in scope, it will address issues of current and future concern in both East and West and in developed and developing countries.

The main purpose of the series is to create a forum for the publication of high quality work and to show how economic analysis can make a contribution to understanding and resolving the environmental problems confronting the world in the late 20th century.

Environmental Problems in the Shortage Economy

The Legacy of Soviet Environmental Policy

Ann-Mari Sätre Åhlander

Lecturer in Economics
Mid Sweden University,
Östersund, Sweden

Edward Elgar

Published by

Edward Elgar Publishing Limited
Gower House
Croft Road
Aldershot
Hants GU11 3HR
England

Edward Elgar Publishing Company
Old Post Road
Brookfield
Vermont 05036
USA

British Library Cataloguing in Publication Data

Ahlander, Ann-Mari Sätre
Environmental Problems in the Shortage
Economy: Legacy of Soviet Environmental
Policy. – (New Horizons in Environmental
Economics Series)
I. Title II. Series
333.70947

Library of Congress Cataloguing in Publication Data

Åhlander, Ann-Mari Sätre, 1957–
Environmental problems in the shortage economy: the legacy of
Soviet environmental policy / Ann-Mari Sätre Åhlander.
192p. 23cm. — (New horizons in environmental economics)
Includes bibliographical references and index.
1. Environmental economics—Soviet Union. 2. Environmental
policy—Soviet Union. 3. Soviet Union—Environmental conditions.
4. Environmental economics—Former Soviet republics. 5. Former
Soviet republics—Environmental conditions. 6. Forest policy-
-Soviet Union. I. Title. II. Series.
HC340.E5A38 1994
333.7'0947—dc20
94–20272
CIP

ISBN 1 85898 056 9

Printed in Great Britain at the University Press, Cambridge

Contents

Contents

List of Tables

Acknowledgements

In completing this book I would like to start by expressing my sincere thanks to my supervisor Professor Peter Bohm. His sharp and constructive criticism has contributed considerably in improving the quality of this work and has made the hypotheses and arguments clearer. I also wish to cordially thank the participants of Peter Bohm's Research Seminar Group and other friends and colleagues at the Department of Economics at Stockholm University. I would like to mention Ing-Marie Andréasson, Iftekhar Hossain, Kjell Jansson, Hans Lind, Kurt Lundgren, No-Ho Park, and Roger Pyddoke in particular, and thank them for their helpful comments at various stages of this work.

Special thanks are due to Professor Konstantin Gofman and his colleagues for kindly receiving me at the Central Economic and Mathematical Institute in Moscow. I am especially grateful to Konstantin Gofman, Kseniya Lvovskaya, Leonid Dunaevsky and Geli Motkin for many valuable discussions and for giving me all possible assistance in my research. For their courtesy, time and information, I sincerely thank Professor Ivan Voevoda, Tatiyana Babenko and their colleagues at the Institute of Economics and Organisation of Industrial Production in Novosibirsk.

I would also like to express my special thanks to Professor Stefan Hedlund for his valuable criticism, encouragement and insightful comments. I am indebted to Professor Tomasz Zylics, Hans Aage and Susanne Oxenstierna for their critical reading and valuable comments on the whole manuscript. Thanks are due to Chris Davis, Mimi Turnball, Thomas Sterner and Professor Anders Åslund for their help while I was working on this book.

I am grateful for the financial support from the Department of Economics at Stockholm University, the Swedish Royal Academy of Sciences and Karin Koch and Hugo Lindberg's Travel Scholarship.

Most of the Soviet material for the study was collected during my visits to Birmingham (1986 and 1988), Glasgow (1988), Moscow (1987, 1988 and 1991), Novosibirsk (1988) and Tallinn (1988).

I am grateful to Tim Taylor for correcting my English and I would also like to take this opportunity to sincerely thank everyone else who has assisted me with this book. Finally, I thank my family for their patience with me during my busy periods.

Foreword

This is a study of the effects of the Soviet shortage economy on the environment and the use of natural resources. It was written mainly before the demise of the Soviet Union and deals only with the Soviet system. In many ways this system is still functioning as it used to.

When this study was started back in the mid-1980s documentation of the environmental problems was difficult to come by. Since then, however, quite a lot of information has been published. However, no analysis of the interrelation between the environmental problems and the economic system seems to have been made. This study attempts to fill this gap. Most of the data and material in this book has a terminal date of 1990. Nevertheless, it is an up-to-date work as from 1990 to 1993 the environmental policies and their effects have changed very little.

Ann-Mari Sätre Åhlander

1. Introduction

The Soviet Union has never been a mass-consumption society and has therefore not 'suffered' from some of the drawbacks of a Western lifestyle such as disposable packaging, plastic articles and bleached paper. Instead, neglect and inefficiency appear to have been the main causes of environmental degradation. Alarming reports show that environmental disruption is considerable. There have been reports from various places in the Soviet Union of high frequencies of lung, intestinal and skin diseases, and increased infant mortality. Heavy industry within residential areas in many of the Soviet densely populated centres is thought to have contributed to these serious illnesses.[1]

There have been reports from various parts of the Soviet Union that pollution has led to the depletion of fish stocks and devastation of forests. Forest depletion and the extraction of natural resources have also caused major environmental problems. Likewise, accidents, and gigantic projects conceived to take advantage of real or imaginary 'economies of scale', have had serious consequences for the environment and people living there.

The environmental situation has been causing increasing alarm in recent years. Despite ambitious environmental programmes, there was a general backlog of measures aimed at preserving the environment, which tended to increase rather than decrease. Neither the means nor the incentives for the introduction of these measures were likely to be provided in the short run.

There are two aspects to this backlog. On the one hand, there has been an accumulation in the quantity of measures. About 25 per cent of emissions of pollutants into the air and 75 per cent of the emitted waste water from stationary sources were improperly purified or untreated, while forestry regeneration activities were still at a very low level.[2] On the other hand, there was also a problem of quality. The waste water which was subject to purification, for instance, generally went through only the first stage of treatment, mechanical purification. The quantity aspect was largely a matter of priorities, while the quality aspect was more related to the general functioning of the Soviet economic system.

There were two rather different aspects to environmental disruption in the Soviet Union. On the one hand, there was environmental deterioration and waste which was connected with the exploitation of natural resources, and on the other hand there was the environmental pollution caused by industrial production, agriculture, road transport and other human activities. These could in a sense be seen as separate problems with their own separate causes. The current study, however, seeks a common denominator behind both these aspects.

1.1 AIMS OF THE STUDY

When explaining environmental disruption, both Western and Soviet studies have stressed the importance of factors common, at least in kind, to both planned and market economies. In both systems, a rather obvious factor leading to environmental disruption is the general emphasis on production; that is, success has been measured mainly in terms of gross national product (GNP), from which environmental degradation is not subtracted. Given this priority to material production, in order to develop a better understanding of what kind of phenomenon environmental disruption was in the Soviet context, the emphasis will be on factors which have distinguished the Soviet economic system. An initial aim will therefore be to give an account of the type of environmental disruption which characterised the Soviet economic system. It can be seen that there are two important problems which were specific to the Soviet economic system. The first problem concerns the ineffectiveness of environmental programmes in the sense that plans have been typically under-fulfilled. Environmental technology has been of a poor standard, quality of purification has been low, and there has been a shortage of environmental equipment in relation to plans. The second problem has been the general mismanagement of natural resources, which were wasted and destroyed on extraction.

In an attempt to explain these problems, this study views the Soviet economy as one of a shortage economy, characterised in addition by a low priority to environmental protection. This perception of the Soviet economy emphasises the role of producers as well as the importance of planners' priorities in the explanation of economic phenomena. The shortage economy approach to be used offers an explanation of the ineffectiveness of environmental programmes as well as of the mismanagement of natural resources. It is compatible with the explanations offered in other Western studies which emphasise the importance of the priority of material production. It especially highlights why the priority of material production appears to have been particularly detrimental to the Soviet economic system. Environmental programmes were more likely to suffer from the general shortage of resources as these were allocated primarily to other tasks. In order to provide support for the impact of shortages on the performance of environmental programmes the theoretical analysis is supplemented with empirical data. Against the background of this explanation of environmental disruption in the Soviet Union, changes in environmental policy under Gorbachev will be discussed. It will be shown that the environmental policy in the Gorbachevian reform programmes did not indicate that the problems were addressed successfully.

2

To gain further insight into the impact of the shortage economy on the management of natural resources, this study focuses on a case study of the use of forestry resources, a vital input into the Soviet economy. One reason for studying the use of forestry resources is that it gives an illustration of how the interests of production, particularly under Stalin, came to dominate those of environmental conservation, in this case regeneration activities. Another reason is that we do not have to take into consideration ethnic conflicts which play an important role in the case of water resources. As forestry is mainly a Russian economic problem the analysis is not complicated by conflicts between different nationalities, and past colonial behaviour. Third, there was only one main forestry user, Minlesprom, and as forestry resources are relatively much easier to quantify than other natural resources it is easier to verify the assumed relationship between behaviour and deterioration of resources. The effect of changing priorities within forestry will be analysed, and in this context also the effect of Gorbachev's reform package will be investigated.

In order to understand the shortage model it is best to view it as a description of an economy that experienced a transition from a system of flexible prices to a 'repressed inflation' disequilibrium state, such as the Soviet Union in the 1930s and Eastern Europe in 1945–53.[3] The behavioural pattern of enterprises was formed during this early stage of economic development when managers were under continuous pressure from the authorities to increase output and fulfil over-ambitious plans.

The case study of forestry resources provides an example of how central planners created a system which permitted and even promoted waste and destruction of natural resources. It gives an illustration of how the strategy for development based on sheer expansion had led to a dead end. It illustrates how the Stalinist priority on growth had become embedded in institutions which impeded attempts by central decision-makers to change the strategy for development. In addition it provides an example of how the institutions, which were once created to effectively impose the central priorities, developed their own objectives and resisted any change that could jeopardise their interests.

1.2 OUTLINE OF THE STUDY

Chapters 2 and 3 discuss the serious environmental situation in the Soviet Union and its causes. Chapter 2 tries to identify a pattern for the environmental disruption in the Soviet Union. This chapter sets the stage for this study. Chapter 3 reviews and discusses Soviet and Western approaches to economic analyses of the environment. In Chapter 4, various approaches to analysing resource allocation and economic development in centrally planned economies are discussed, along with the relevance of these approaches for explaining environmental disruption in the Soviet Union.

Against the background of this discussion, the analytical approach to be used in the present study is built up. Chapter 5 then applies this approach in order to study the performance of environmental programmes. Chapter 6 investigates the effects of changes in environmental policy in the *perestroika* programmes under Gorbachev.

Chapters 7 to 9 contain a case study on the use of forestry resources. The interconnection between the shortage economy and central forestry policy is discussed in Chapter 7. In Chapter 8 the behaviour of the timber procurement enterprise in the shortage economy is studied. The effect of priority changes within the forestry sector is analysed in Chapter 9 and Chapter 10 presents some conclusions.

NOTES

1 See Chapter 2.
2 *Narkhoz* (1990), pp. 248 and 251.
3 Davis and Charemza (1989).

2. The Environmental Situation in the Former Soviet Union

Many facts suggest that environmental disruption in the former Soviet Union has been considerable. There have been reports from various places within the Soviet Union of the depletion of fish stocks, oil and chemical spillage, leaks of radioactivity and outbreaks of food poisoning. According to the State Committee for Environmental Protection, Goskompriroda, the ecological situation in an area the size of Western Europe has been unsatisfactory, while in a considerably smaller area which is still larger than Scandinavia, conditions were characterised as so severe that irreversible changes in nature have taken place.[1]

By 1990, some 80 per cent of all diseases were said to be related, either directly or indirectly, to environmental factors.[2] 'Only' 23 per cent of Soviet children under the age of seven have been diagnosed as 'practically healthy', no more than 20 per cent of younger school-children were deemed to be 'absolutely healthy', while the corresponding figure for older school-children was 14 per cent.[3] Studies indicate that the prevalence of nervous disorders, allergies and illnesses of the intestinal tract among children has more than doubled since the 1970s, from eight to 20 per cent.[4] Figures on public health which were especially alarming, came from the industrial regions of the Urals, southern Siberia, the Aral Sea basin and parts of the Ukraine.[5]

Besides the general increase in illnesses, environmental pollution has also given rise to previously unknown diseases. In 1986, in the Ukrainian city of Chernovtsy, 200 children began to lose all or most of their hair.[6] Medical tests failed to identify the causes of the disease. In 1988–89 similar cases of balding were registered in Zaporozhe in the Ukraine, in Zlatoust in the Urals, in Moscow and in Biisk in Siberia.[7]

In this chapter an attempt will be made to identify a pattern for the environmental disruption in the former Soviet Union. The aim here is to give an account of the type of environmental disruption which characterises the Soviet economic system. It is argued that the Soviet strategy for development has guaranteed that the economies of scale of central planning have been used against the environment rather than to protect it. Problems with definitions and the reliability of data together with the lack of trend data tend to suggest that this account will be only fragmentary and thus unsuitable for international comparisons.

5

2.1 THE ENVIRONMENTAL SITUATION IN GENERAL

This section gives a brief general account of the environmental situation in the Soviet Union in the late 1980s as presented in Soviet official statistics. Some official statistics on various aspects of resource management and on emissions of waste and pollutants have been available since the mid-1970s. The statistical yearbook *Narodnoe khozyaistvo SSSR* has, for example, published data on emissions into the atmosphere since the early 1980s. By the end of the 1980s, however, the availability of such data had become both richer and more detailed. Three major documents have been issued in an attempt to make up for the previous decades of neglect. One report was released in 1989, by Goskompriroda,[8] and in the same year a special volume of environmental statistics was published by Goskomstat, the main statistical administration.[9] These were the first non-classified official documents devoted to assessing the state of the natural environment in the Soviet Union. The third, which was the most policy-oriented, is by Aleksei Yablokov.[10]

Many problems of definition and reliability arise in connection with data of this kind.[11] Definitions are vague and the purpose of publishing such data has often been more political than scientific. Although this changed to some extent as a result of environmental *glasnost*, many problems remained. The tradition of using vague definitions and unclear formulations which could be interpreted to fit political purposes was not easily changed. A lack of time-series data made adequate analysis very difficult.

It is worth noting that with respect to water pollution, all three of the above-mentioned documents agreed that the situation had deteriorated. But when it came to pollution of the atmosphere, the first two contradicted Yablokov's pessimistic account, arguing that there had actually been an improvement, in spite of an increased use of natural resources. Who is right is hard to determine.

In the Goskompriroda report the ecological situation was described as unsatisfactory in 290 regions covering 16 per cent of Soviet territory or an area equal to that of Western Europe.[12] In 1988, about one-fifth of the Soviet population (60 million people) lived within this territory.[13] This area was subdivided into three categories using a system of environmental mapping.[14] The first category comprised that of 'slightly affected areas' (*prostye arealy*), areas that were principally affected by one single form of environmental degradation or natural resource exhaustion. Included in this group were waters that had been affected by pollution or exhaustion, such as the Azov Sea, the Black Sea, the White Sea, part of the Caspian Sea, Lake Onega and Ladoga. Agricultural lands accounted for a large proportion of this category on which overgrazing, intensive cultivation and deforestation from logging operations had led to changes in the chemical composition of the soil, wind erosion, desertification, and compacting of the topsoil. Together they were significant enough to cause a noticeable decline in the productivity of the land. Other characteristic examples were disruption from mining operations, and degradation and overcutting of forests. About ten per cent of the former territory of the Soviet Union fell into this category, located chiefly in northern Kazakhstan and the Black Earth region.

The second category referred to areas with transitional damage (*perekhodnye arealy*). Degradation in these areas had reached the point that even under favourable circumstances the local environment would take decades, maybe even centuries, to recover. In some of these areas, such as the Aral Sea region, the threat to human health was serious. This group, covering about three per cent of the total territory, included many lakes and rivers, which had been turned into sewers, but also parts of the Black Earth region and Moldavia, which had suffered massive damage from overcultivation and overapplication of agrochemicals.

The final category, that of 'seriously affected areas' (*slozhnye arealy*), was characterised by environmental degradation which had either reached or passed the point of irreversible change. Heavy industrial concentrations in conjunction with major mining operations accounted for the bulk of this group, which covered 3.3 per cent of the territory of the former Soviet Union, an area larger than Scandinavia. Areas that were particularly affected included the Donbass in the Ukraine, the Kuzbass in Siberia and the eastern Urals, together with many other densely populated centres.

2.2 AIR POLLUTION

This section outlines the problems of air pollution and relates them to the Soviet economic system. Air pollution has been quite severe in all major industrial areas of the former Soviet Union. The situation was extremely serious in the Donbass and the Kuzbass, the central and southern parts of the Urals, certain areas of Central Asia, some places in the Far East, and in the north European parts of Russia. The most important stationary sources of air pollution were power and heating plants, iron and steel industries, oil extraction and the metal, petrochemical and chemical industries (see Table 2.1).[15]

Even though industrial production in the Soviet Union has been at a comparatively low level, the priority given to heavy industry, which was a major contributor to pollution, and the low level of environmental technology might explain why industrial pollution was substantial. As heavy industry constituted a higher share of industry in the Soviet Union than in Western market economies, this in itself implied that pollution per unit of industrial production was likely to be higher in the Soviet Union. The power and heating plants were primarily located in the oil- and gasfields. Coal power stations with high emissions of air pollutants were situated in the Donbass, Kuzbass, Ekibastus and Karaganda regions and at some other places in the northern and eastern parts of the Soviet Union. The combustion of coal resulted in surrounding areas being covered with grey dust.

Table 2.1:   *Emissions of pollutants by various industrial branches (as a percentage of the total air pollution by Soviet industry, which was an aggregated measure where different pollutants were added in tons).*

	1977	1988
Power and heating plants	43.0	32.1
Iron and steel works	15.0	16.8
Oil extraction and petrochemical industry	11.0	14.6
Other metal industry	8.0	9.6
Chemical industry	3.2	2.7
Construction materials industry	3.3	3.4
Pulp and paper plants	2.6	2.3

Sources: Weissenburger (1988); *Doklad...* (1990), p. 51; *Okhrana...* (1989), p. 80.

Iron works constituted important sources of air pollution in the Donbass, Kuzbass, the Urals, Moscow, Leningrad, Volgograd, Odessa and Baku. The industrial centres for the production of steel situated in the Ukraine, the Urals, Kazakhstan and in western Siberia were important contributors to the air pollution in these areas. Extraction of oil gave rise to air pollution in the Urals, Baku, Groznyi and other places around the Caspian Sea and in eastern Siberia. Moldavia, Belorussia, the Ukraine, the south-eastern parts of the former RSFSR, and some places in Central Asia were the areas which had suffered worst from the chemical industry emissions.

Emissions of air pollutants exceeded established health norms in all industrial areas. In 103 industrial cities, where there is a total population of 50 million people, emissions exceeded norms by ten times or more.[16] In sixteen cities during 1988, the recorded levels of air pollution were more than 50 times that of the standard.[17] The fact that so many Soviet cities exceeded health norms is not in itself unusual, when seen in an international perspective. What is remarkable, however, was the fact that such norms were exceeded by ten times or more.[18] In 1988, Soviet scientists also produced a list of 68 cities, with a combined population of about 40 million people, where the air was 'especially dangerous for human habitation'. Included on that list were Novosibirsk, Kemerovo and Barnaul in the Kuzbass as well as many other cities in Russia and the Ukraine which are usually associated with the heavy industrialisation drive.[19] In addition to this the Ministry of Health suggested the inclusion of another fifteen cities that had high rates of illnesses.[20] There have been reports from various places in the Soviet Union that illnesses due to air pollution have been increasing.[21] High occurrences of lung diseases for instance, have been registered in Dnepropetrovsk and Donetsk in the Ukraine and in Murmansk and Karabash.[22] On 21 July 1989, air pollution in Omsk caused the city soviet executive committee to declare a state of emergency.[23]

Inquiries from Volgograd indicated a strong correlation between air pollution and high occurrences of miscarriages, and intestine and skin diseases.[24] In Erevan, high emissions of poisonous substances from a chemical plant were thought to explain the high rate of illness in the area. Cases of leukaemia had, for instance, increased many times during the last 15 years.[25] In Armenia, air pollution in cities has been linked to a dramatic increase in infant mortality and to a high incidence of congenital defects among new-born babies.[26] Reports from Baku stated that due to the high level of air pollution the rate of illnesses had increased by ten per cent.[27]

High emissions of air pollutants were also thought to have caused an increase in the occurrence of lung diseases in the Urals.[28] In an alarming report from the city of Ufa researchers detailed the accumulated effects of air pollution from the more than 400 industries in the city.[29] According to them, the factory smoke often appeared as a thick fog inside the flats. Pollution was thought to have caused a situation whereby it was unhealthy to drink tap water or eat fruit and vegetables from the private allotments in the city. A number of heavy industries situated in the middle of the city in the residential areas were also stated to be the cause of a particularly high occurrence of illnesses, especially among children. The practice of having child-care centres within the factory areas, contributed to the seriousness of illnesses.[30]

There have been reports from various places about the forest die-back due to air pollution.[31] In Lithuania, the high concentration of chemical industry has damaged vast areas of forest.[32] On the Kola Peninsula the surrounding forests have been badly damaged by the metal industry in Murmansk. The *taiga* around Bratsk and Kansk-Achinsk, the conifers around the car-producing city of Togliatti in the Urals, at Sverdlovsk and Chelyabinsk and in the Ukraine were considered to be threatened as well. The forests around Nikel, Norilsk, Krasnoyarsk and Irkutsk have been especially affected by air pollution.[33]

Statistics presented by Goskomstat indicate that annual emissions from stationary sources decreased by 23 per cent between 1980 and 1990.[34] This reduction was chiefly attributed to the conversion of oil- and coal-fired power plants into natural gas.[35] The development of city heating systems and the closing of enterprises would also have contributed to the reduction of pollution.[36] According to a state official at Goskompriroda, one important aim of the Soviet energy policy was that the planned conversion from oil- and coal-fired power plants to nuclear power plants would reduce air pollution.[37] The official policy was that by increasing the use of nuclear power at the expense of oil and coal, one source of certain pollution would be substituted by the minor risk of a serious one.

In 1975 the emissions from stationary sources into the air amounted to 77 per cent of total emissions, and by 1988 this had fallen to 63 per cent.[38] This downward trend might partly be explained by the expansion of automobile traffic. As purification devices for exhaust fumes from motor vehicles were virtually non-existent, increased road transport meant that automobile-generated emissions had increased in relation to the total air pollution. In the years 1981–88, in 361 cities, automobile-generated emissions were the main source of air pollution.[39] In 1988, 73 per cent of the emissions of air pollutants in Moscow were attributed to emissions from motor vehicles.[40] In that same year, 1988, Goskomstat stated that the total amount of harmful emissions into the air from motor vehicles and stationary sources amounted to 97.5 million tons.[41] By adding to this the exhaust fumes from boats, airplanes, diesel locomotives, and stationary sources of air pollution located in non-urban areas the total reached well over 100 million tons. However, it is not known how well the existing equipment for measuring emissions was actually working.

According to Yablokov, only about half of the enterprises in the country causing air pollution had any form of pollution control facilities.[42] Existing devices, moreover, were often ineffective and frequently turned off at night.[43] Monitoring performance was also complicated by the fact that the required equipment for measurement was often completely absent.[44] Pollution-control technology was at a comparatively low level. Purification plants suffered from inefficient and untested designs, poor workmanship, low capacities for the jobs assigned them, and inadequate maintenance.[45] An investigation by *Izvestia*, for example, reveals that a significant proportion of the equipment to reduce air pollution in the Donbass failed to function, while those devices that did work were incapable of filtering out the most toxic gases.[46]

A figure of 100 million tons might thus be taken merely as a lower limit of the probable total emissions into the air over the Soviet Union in 1988. This rough figure can be compared with those of ECE and OECD, according to which total emissions into the air in the USA amounted to 141 million tons in 1980, and 130 million tons in 1985. The corresponding figures for Western Europe were 70 and 64 million tons respectively.[47]

One problem with such a comparison is not only the uncertainty concerning measurement and the efficiency of cleaning, but also that up until 1986 the official Soviet statistics did not account for the different pollutants separately. According to Soviet official statistics, the total amount of air pollution in 1990 from stationary sources amounted to 55.7 million tons (see Table 2.2).[48]

About 60 per cent of the total emissions into the air from stationary sources in the Soviet Union occurred in the former RSFSR (see Table 2.2). The cities with the highest emissions are shown in Table 2.3. The situation appears to have been most severe in Norilsk up in the north, the centre of an important mining district with deposits of nickel, cobalt and copper. It was primarily the enrichment industry, with highly sulphurous fumes, which created the severe air pollution in the area.[49] The rich deposits of gas in the area made it desirable to build up this kind of energy-intensive industry there.

Table 2.2: Emissions of substances from exhaust fumes into the air in the differerent Union republics in 1982–90 (in thousands of tons).

	1982	1985	1990
SSSR	65,700 (75)	69,800 (76)	55,700 (78)
RSFSR	41,600 (74)	42,300 (76)	34,100 (77)
Ukraine	12,900 (73)	12,300 (74)	9,400 (76)
Kazakhstan	4,400 (83)	6,200 (82)	4,700 (86)
Uzbekistan	1,500 (65)	1,500 (65)	1,300 (69)
Belorussia	1,500 (68)	1,400 (68)	1,200 (77)
Azerbaidzhan	978 (45)	887 (53)	2,100 (28)
Turkmenistan	445 (31)	700 (30)	500 (44)
Estonia	722 (92)	640 (93)	600 (93)
Georgia	576 (51)	491 (55)	400 (54)
Moldavia	505 (82)	483 (82)	400 (86)
Lithuania	474 (76)	480 (77)	400 (83)
Armenia	239 (77)	246 (74)	200 (81)
Kirgizia	225 (80)	225 (83)	200 (84)
Latvia	257 (66)	204 (71)	200 (68)
Tadzhikistan	149 (77)	125 (80)	100 (82)

Note: The figures in the brackets indicate the proportions of total emissions which have been subject to purification.

Sources: *Narkhoz* (1986), p. 386; *Soyuznye Respubliki – Osnovnye Ekonomicheskie i Sotsialisticheskie Pokazateli* (1991), pp. 131–2.

The second highest level of air pollution occurred in Novokuznetsk, in the Kuzbass area (see Table 2.3). The emissions might primarily be attributed to the thermal power stations which have been constructed in the coal-mining district near the city. The presence of power plants further made it advantageous to locate energy-intensive industries there, such as metal works for aluminium and zinc, which also contributed to a large extent to the pollution in the area. The emissions of air pollutants in Magnitogorsk and Nizhnii Tagil in the Urals might primarily be attributed to the iron and steel industries, but the chemical industry was also an important source of pollution here. Pollution from the burning of coal in Ekibastus has covered the steppe for many kilometres around the station with grey dust.[50]

Table 2.3: Emissions of substances from exhaust fumes into the air in population centres in the RSFSR in 1985–90 (in thousands of tons).

	1985	1988	1990
Norilsk	2,568	2,344	–
Novokuznetsk	1,001	833	572
Ekibastus	1,336	744	–
Magnitogorsk	903	849	791
Nizhnii Tagil	682	641	–
Omsk	529	440	–
Angarsk	509	431	–
Chelyabinsk	444	427	392
Moscow	397	312	273
Ufa	391	304	260
Krasnoyarsk	339	259	244
Novosibirsk	232	235	–
Volgograd	365	228	207
Sankt Petersburg	253	236	193
Groznyi	343	298	238
Perm	251	193	152
Barnaul	209	184	–
Saratov	195	187	–
Kuibyshev	173	147	–
Kemerovo	166	122	95
Togliatti	135	126	–

Sources: Narkhoz RSFSR za 70 let (1987), p. 429; *Narkhoz* (1991), pp. 274–5; *Okhrana...* (1989), pp. 22–5.

Air pollution in the Ukraine amounted to just under 20 per cent of the total emissions of air pollutants in the Soviet Union (Table 2.2). The most severely affected were, apart from the Donbass area, Kerch, Kharkov, Odessa and the capital itself, Kiev (Table 2.4).

Kazakhstan's share of the total air pollution in the Soviet Union increased from less than seven per cent in 1982 to just over nine per cent in 1986. Emissions were mainly located in the eastern parts of the republic. A comparison between the emissions from stationary sources in the capitals of the 15 republics showed that the emissions were highest in Baku in

Azerbaidzhan and second highest in Moscow (see Table 2.5). The level of air pollution in these cities well exceeded that of the other capitals. They were however less badly affected than the most polluted cities in the former RSFSR and the Ukraine (compare Tables 2.3–2.5).

Table 2.4: Emissions of substances from exhaust fumes into the air in population centres in the Ukraine in 1985–90 (in thousands of tons).

	1985	1987	1988	1990
Krivoy Rok	1,314	1,290	1,253	–
Zhdanov	–	786	–	–
Kerch	–	375	–	–
Dnieprodzerzhinsk	370	337	296	268
Dniepropetrovsk	354	321	296	–
Makeevka	375	319	307	–
Zaporozhe	302	287	267	246
Kommunarsk	369	251	243	188
Donetsk	208	194	178	171
Kremenchuk	175	186	168	–
Lisichansk	121	132	131	–
Enakievo	137	121	115	–
Odessa	125	107	88	81
Kiev	99	94	71	53

Sources: *Narodnoe Khozyaistvo Ukrainskoi SSR* (1987), p. 404; *Okhrana...* (1989), pp. 125–7; *Narkhoz* (1991), pp. 274–5.

To sum up, one characteristic feature of air pollution problems in the former Soviet Union is that several types of ecological stress had been concentrated in certain regions. The strive towards rapid industrialisation meant that huge industrial complexes for the exploitation of local resources were created in these regions, mainly located in Russia and the Ukraine. These industrial areas were densely populated, high levels of air pollution thus affected a large proportion of the population. The policy of locating heavy industry within residential areas and child-care centres within factory complexes contributed to the high occurrence of illnesses.

Table 2.5: Emissions of substances from exhaust fumes into the air in the capitals of the Union republics in 1985–90 (in thousands of tons).

	1985	1988	1990
Baku (Azerbaidzhan)	515 (43)	425 (48)	1,394 (24)
Moscow (RSFSR)	411 (62)	317 (62)	273 (61)
Minsk (Belorussia)	116 (62)	111 (64)	102 (64)
Kiev (Ukraine)	99 (64)	70 (73)	55 (79)
Bishkek (Kirgizia)	89 (86)	74 (86)	64 (87)
Erevan (Armenia)	76 (36)	52 (44)	43 (33)
Tashkent (Uzbekistan)	62 (48)	50 (66)	39 (53)
Alma-Ata (Kazakhstan)	54 (74)	47 (77)	39 (78)
Kishinev (Moldavia)	49 (43)	32 (55)	26 (58)
Tblisi (Georgia)	46 (31)	43 (37)	39 (37)
Tallinn (Estonia)	44 (82)	40 (84)	69 (73)
Riga (Latvia)	47 (80)	37 (75)	50 (45)
Dushanbe (Tadzhikistan)	34 (91)	30 (94)	21 (94)
Vilnius (Lithuania)	25 (47)	33 (35)	33 (34)
Ashabad (Turkmenistan)	21 (39)	7 (64)	6 (66)

Note: The figures within brackets indicate the proportion of total emissions which have been subjected to cleansing.

Sources: Narkhoz za 70 let (1987), p. 615; *Narkhoz* (1988), p. 573; *Narkhoz* (1991), p. 274.

2.3 WATER SHORTAGE AND WATER POLLUTION

In this section an attempt is made to distinguish the type of water quality problems which are specific for the Soviet economic system. Pollution has been severe in the Caspian Sea, the Black Sea, the Azov Sea, the Aral Sea and Ladoga, as well as in the Volga, Dniepr and Don (see Table 2.6).[51] Particularly alarming, however, was the increasing pollution of smaller water sources in the southern Ukraine, the Urals and in western Siberia.[52] The pollution of Lake Baikal has received a lot of attention due to its uniqueness.[53]

The main culprits were the pulp and paper industries, the steelworks and metalworks, and the chemical industry.[54] In some areas agriculture was the main source of water pollution. An important reason for agriculture having an increased impact on the environment was the accelerated use of mineral fertilisers and pesticides.[55] Apart from industry, agriculture and road transport, waste water from households was an important source of pollution.[56]

Table 2.6: Emissions of untreated waste water into seas and rivers in the
Soviet Union in 1985–90 (in millions of m^3).

	1985	1987	1988	1990
The Caspian Sea	3,582	7,821	11,160	13,050
The Black Sea and Lake Azov	3,586	3,724	5,550	7,522
The Baltic Sea	2,573	2,648	3,350	3,762
Lake Baikal	124	107	–	–
Ladoga	265	360	–	–
Volga	2,419	6,720	9,950	10,819
Dniepr	933	870	1,430	1,988
Don	471	788	1,470	1,597
The Ural river	40	40	125	111
Ob	1,951	–	2,660	3,017
Enisei	1,126	–	1,240	–

Sources: Narkhoz (1988), pp. 570 and 574; *Narkhoz* (1989), p. 247; *Narkhoz* (1991), p. 271.

The official figures presented in Table 2.7 indicate that water pollution increased in the period 1985–90. In 1988, the Soviet Union was, according to Goskomstat, able to treat only 30 per cent of its sewage adequately to meet established sanitary norms. A further 50 per cent was improperly purified, while the remaining 20 per cent was dumped into the water untreated.[57] Scattered facts suggest that purification facilities were often ineffective.[58] Many large cities, including Dnepropetrovsk in the Ukraine, Baku and Riga, the Latvian capital, did not have any sewage treatment facilities at all.[59]

Since the official statistics included only such waste water as passed through communal treatment facilities, many factories that discharged their waste directly into rivers and streams were excluded. What should also have been included were the various forms of illegal dumping, together with accidents and spontaneous runoff in connection with storms.[60]

According to Gofman and Motkin, accidents alone accounted for about 20 per cent of pollution.[61] In 1987, in Armenia, for example, accidental emissions of waste water took place at individual enterprises at the all-Union Ministries of Mineral Fertiliser, Chemical Industry, Nonferrous Metallurgy, and at the Armenian Ministry of Agriculture. In the Ukraine such emissions occurred at enterprises belonging to the all-Union Ministries of Chemical Industry, the Coal Industry, the Petroleum Industry, the Ferrous Metallurgy Industry, and at the Ukrainian Ministries for Construction and Agriculture. Accidental emissions of waste water also occurred at a number of enterprises in Estonia and Azerbaidzhan, particularly at enterprises at the Azerbaidzhanian Ministry of Petroleum Industry.[62]

Table 2.7: Emissions of untreated and inadequately treated waste water in the different Union republics in 1985–90, (in millions of m³).

	1985		1988		1990	
USSR	16,200	(58)	28,485	(30)	33,564	(23)
RSFSR	11,900	(54)	24,024	(16)	27,799	(10)
Ukraine	1,300	(78)	2,436	(62)	3,198	(51)
Azerbaidzhan	445	(28)	348	(42)	303	(51)
Uzbekistan	419	(68)	349	(58)	292	(65)
Georgia	341	(45)	322	(49)	229	(38)
Lithuania	331	(21)	333	(27)	349	(22)
Kazakhstan	279	(54)	340	(45)	345	(43)
Armenia	177	(67)	301	(51)	212	(56)
Latvia	251	(32)	254	(30)	251	(31)
Estonia	198	(58)	202	(60)	246	(52)
Moldavia	42	(84)	89	(69)	91	(70)
Belorussia	90	(89)	67	(93)	104	(90)
Tadzhikistan	59	(76)	93	(69)	101	(66)
Kirgizia	12	(94)	15	(92)	43	(75)
Turkmenistan	1	(95)	0	(100)	1	(91)

Note: The figures within brackets indicate the proportion of water that has been treated adequately to meet established sanitary norms.

Sources: *Narkhoz* (1988), p. 569; *Narkhoz* (1989), p. 247; *Soyuznye Ekonomicheskie i Sotsialnye Pokazateli* (1991), p. 134.

In 1988, accidental emissions of waste water occurred in Alma-Ata, Krasnodarsk, Odessa, Beltsakh in Moldavia and Pervoyralsk. Accidental emissions of harmful substances were further reported from Karaganda, a number of Georgian towns, from oil fields in Azerbaidzhan and from the food industry in Moldavia.[63] According to Goskompriroda, in 1989 there were about 2,000 serious environmental accidents in the Soviet Union.[64]

The effect of water pollution has been highly correlated with the supply of water. By Western standards, the industrial use of water has been disproportionately high in the Soviet Union. This is an important reason why many cities and towns have had problems with their water supply, which has sometimes affected the quality of the drinking water.[65] The increased use of mineral fertilisers and pesticides was particularly alarming in areas with water shortage, regardless of whether this was natural or had been caused by an overuse of available water resources.[66]

The uneven distribution of water resources further aggravated the problems of water supply. About 75 per cent of the Soviet population, and around 70 per cent of all industries were to be found in areas that together accounted for only 16 per cent of renewable water resources.[67] Consequently the government has taken great measures to redistribute water supplies, efforts which have led to massive environmental disruption around reservoirs and canals.[68] Hydropower programmes, for example, exploited a large part of the country's available water assets. According to Goskompriroda, the reservoirs at Bratsk, Krasnoyarsk and Ust-Ilimsk had become filled with 3.6 million cubic metres of floating wood debris, producing large concentrations of phenols.[69]

Another consequence was the swamping and waterlogging of surrounding lands, which served to reduce the flow of water into the rivers, and thus hampered the self-purification of the waterways. The flow of water in the Volga had, for example, been substantially reduced.[70] Irrigation further contributed to reducing the flow of water.[71] According to Yablokov, it had come to the point where a drop of water which could once have travelled from its upper reaches down to the Caspian in a month and a half, would need a year and a half to cover the same distance.[72]

Water shortage has been a serious problem in most agricultural regions. The water resources within the Ukraine were estimated to be less than two per cent of the total amount of water in the Soviet Union.[73] The shortage of water in the Ukraine, combined with the intensive irrigation of agriculture, had caused problems with groundwater resources, which in some instances became polluted.[74] What was very serious, for instance, was the fact that the drainage systems in the Dniepr were threatening the quality of the drinking water in the southern Ukraine.[75] The Dniestr, which supports Odessa with drinking water, was also severely polluted, mainly because the water treatment facilities in towns along the river did not function properly.[76]

The water shortage in Central Asia is due to the fact that agriculture there has used up 75 per cent of the Soviet Union's total water supply for agriculture. Even though problems of water shortage were a known fact back in the early 1960s, the use per hectare has been disproportionately high, even by Soviet standards. The highest consumption has been in Turkmenia.[77] The use was often difficult to control as water meters were missing.[78] In traditional Stalinist fashion, rather than reducing the use of water, efforts have been made to increase supply. As research was concentrated on preparations for the big river diversion project, little has been done to combat problems of water quality. Purification of waste water was uneven,[79] and the monitoring of the pollution of ground water and surface water by agriculture has been neglected.

The most serious problems were those of the Aral Sea region, the whole existence of which has been threatened by the desiccation of the Aral Sea. The high-target plans for cotton production placed high demands on irrigation.[80] Limiting the flow of the Amu-Darya and Syr-Darya and the deteriorating quality of these waters have caused a situation that may well turn out to be practically irreversible. The soil in the area has been heavily salinated. Untreated waste water which was high in mineral content was used for drinking, causing high morbidity levels in the area. Alarming reports of an increased infant mortality, and increased occurrence of hepatitis and other infectious diseases in Uzbekistan and Kazakhstan have been attributed to the deteriorating quality of the drinking water around the Aral Sea.[81]

Similar problems were facing Lake Balkhash, the Caspian Sea, the Black Sea, and Lake Issyk-Kul.[82] It was thought that the high use of water in the northern Caucasus was the reason why the Azov Sea was experiencing salination.[83] The water level has been falling in Lake Issyk-Kul and in Lake Balkhash. It is further reported that water pollution of the Moldavian agriculture in combination with the water shortage have caused problems with the quality of drinking water within the republic.

To sum up, one characteristic feature of Soviet water quality problems has been that it was the combination of water shortage and water pollution that made the situation serious. The disproportionately high industrial use of water caused problems with the water supply in many cities and towns, and affected the quality of drinking water. Similarly, the intense irrigation of farm land, the building of gigantic hydropower stations and the large-scale measures expended by central leaders to redistribute water supplies have aggravated problems of water supply.

2.4 NATURAL RESOURCE USE

Another important problem has been that of erosion.[84] The problems have largely been connected with the traditional habit of cultivating vast open fields with no shelter belts, but erroneous cultivation methods, overgrazing and disregard for rotation patterns also played a part. In addition, large-scale irrigation of arid and semidesert regions has led to salinisation of the soil and contamination of the ground water.[85] Soviet use of agricultural machinery has further added to the problems of erosion. In 1988, six times as many tractors were produced in the Soviet Union as in the United States,[86] and according to Goskompriroda, the big, heavy tractors were one of the principal factors contributing to soil degradation. According to Goskompriroda, rain and melting snow have washed away some 1.5 billion tons of topsoil annually.[87] Erosion has been a particularly serious problem in the Black Earth region, that is above all in the Ukraine and in southern Russia. Other trouble spots were Moldavia, Caucasus, and Central Asia.[88]

Fertilisers and pesticides have become important environmental pollutants.[89] Although agricultural production per capita has been low in the Soviet Union by Western standards, the use of fertilisers, herbicides and pesticides is relatively high. One explanation has been the habit of measuring success in terms of gross output. The use of fertilisers, herbicides and pesticides was regulated in plan targets which had to be fulfilled. While Soviet fertiliser production in 1960 was less than half that of the United States, by 1988 the Soviet Union produced more than 37 million tons, which was nearly twice as much as the United States.[90]

The use of pesticides especially affected the quality of food and public health. Goskomstat reported that, in 1988, around ten per cent of the examined food produce failed to meet the government's safety regulations.[91] According to Yablokov, the contamination rate was much higher. He reported that in some areas of the country up to 50 per cent of the foodstuffs were contaminated with pesticides in 1987. One-third of produce tested that year contained levels of pesticides which were hazardous to health. Forty-two per cent of baby foods also contained dangerous levels of pesticides.[92]

Natural resources have been wasted and destroyed.[93] The exploitation of natural resources has also had serious effects on the environment. Extensive oil and coal extraction has for instance destroyed vast areas in the Urals, land which could otherwise have been used for agriculture or other purposes.[94] The use of air and water as recipients of industrial emissions and municipal waste provides an example of a more direct negative influence on the environment.

Vast areas of forest land were flooded during the construction of the hydropower plants at Bratsk, Ust-Ilimsk, Sayanoshushenk and Boguchansk.[95] Millions of hectares of valuable agricultural land were destroyed during the building of water reservoirs.[96] Agricultural land in the Ukraine was flooded or salinated during the construction of the Danube–Dniepr canal.[97] Oil production has been another cause of pollution and waste of natural resources. Oil which was lost during the extraction process has been an important source of pollution of earth, lakes and rivers.[98]

An additional example of environmental disruption caused by the extraction of natural resources may be taken from Estonia. In the northern part of the country there were rich deposits of phosphorite ore. This was transformed into phosphorous fertiliser which was then used in Soviet farming. The negative consequences of both mining and enrichment processes have been amply documented.[99]

Some losses of other raw materials may be attributed to deficiencies in the transporting system. It has for instance, been reported that losses of mineral fertiliser, cement, timber, coal and iron often occur during transportation. An audit conducted by Gosplan reveals that 11 per cent of all fertilisers never reached the field because of transport and storage problems.[100]

According to Yablokov, about 30 per cent of pesticides were lost on their way to the field.[101]

2.5 CONCLUSIONS

Many facts suggest that environmental disruption in the form of air pollution, water pollution and exhaustion of natural resources in the Soviet Union has been considerable. Available figures suggest that water quality has deteriorated, while air pollution development is ambiguous. The expanded use of nuclear power at the expense of coal and oil might have contributed to the decrease of air pollution. According to Soviet official statistics, the most seriously affected areas, where irreversible changes in nature have taken place, include the huge industrial centres of Donbass in the Ukraine, the Kuzbass in Siberia, and the eastern Urals.

One distinguishing feature was that in the Soviet Union the environment has been sacrificed without achieving the same high standard of living as Western countries. Environmental disruption in the West seems to have been an inevitable consequence of industrial and agricultural development which was for a long time neglected or allowed time to reach critical levels. Although industrial production in the Soviet Union has been at a comparatively low level, the priority on heavy industry, which was a major contributor to pollution, and the low level of technology for environmental protection explains why industrial pollution has been substantial. The creation of massive industrial complexes in some regions and the high population density in these areas meant that a large proportion of the population was exposed to high levels of air pollution. The policy of building houses next to the factories contributed to the greater degree of exposure. The high industrial and communal use of water led to difficulties with water supply, which contributed to increased problems of water quality.

Although agricultural production per capita was relatively low in the Soviet Union, the use of mineral fertiliser, herbicides and pesticides per unit of agricultural produce was relatively high as their use was regulated in plan targets which had to be fulfilled.

In Western market economies the high frequency of automobiles meant that road transport was a major source of pollution. Although the age of mass motoring had not arrived in the Soviet Union, automobile-generated pollution was substantial because of poor engines, poor fuel and the lack of purification devices for emissions. In industrialised Western countries, households were important contributors to environmental disruption through their use of energy, disposable packaging, plastic articles and paper. The lower level of consumption in the Soviet Union meant that packaging in light industries was a rarity and the use of paper was at a very low level. Although the flush toilet in the Soviet Union was not widely used in urban housing, the low technological level of sewer systems ensured that waste water from households had a substantial impact on the environment.

Problems of reliability of data made it difficult to know how serious the environmental situation in the Soviet Union really was in terms of sickness rates and other effects. What made the situation especially serious was that measures taken to protect the environment appeared to be largely ineffective. While environmental *glasnost* led to an increasing worry about environmental problems, the backlog of measures aimed at preserving the environment tended to increase rather than decrease. This meant that the environmental problems entered a vicious circle and the situation could not easily be changed within the framework of the traditional Soviet economic system. The same applied to the use of natural resources. As regards oil, coal and timber, the situation had become particularly serious for the national economy as the point when it was no longer possible to increase production by mobilising additional resources appeared to have already been reached.[102]

Another conclusion to be drawn from this chapter is that the potential economies of scale of central planning in the case of the Soviet Union were not used to serve the environment. On the contrary, the enormous economies of scale of the Soviet economy were used against the environment. Rather than mobilising resources to protect the environment, they were mobilised to combat the environment and change it in order to facilitate the fulfilment of politically determined production targets. In the case of agriculture, for example, in order to save output targets, more land was used and fertilisers were brought in. As this caused weed infestation, herbicides were used. Then pesticides were used against harmful insects. In the case of water, when available water resources were depleted as a result of gigantic hydropower programmes, great efforts to redistribute water supplies were undertaken. Thus, dams were erected, channels were constructed and rivers were diverted.

There were many examples of how politically determined production targets caused irreversible changes in the environment. The most famous example was perhaps how the centrally established cotton policy pursued in Central Asia, which placed heavy demands on irrigation, led to the desiccation of the Aral Sea. Another example was how the high targets for industrial production led to the creation of huge industrial regions with high concentrations of pollution.

NOTES

1   *Doklad...* (1990), pp. 100–101.
2   Yablokov (1990), p. 8.
3   *Doklad...* (1990), p. 116.
4   *Doklad...* (1990), p. 117.
5   Ibid.

6   Yablokov (1990), p. 9. See also Mikhailisko and Tovstink (1988), pp. 1–5.
7   Yablokov (1990), p. 9.
8   *Doklad...* (1990).
9   *Okhrana okruzhayushchei sredy i ratsionalnoe ispolzovanie prirodnykh resursov v SSSR. Statisticheskii sbornik*, Goskomstat SSSR, Moskva, 1989.
10 Yablokov (1990). Aleksei Yablokov is Boris Yeltsin's adviser on environmental matters. The report was originally prepared for an international conference, Ecology-89, held in Gothenburg, Sweden, in August 1989. Subsequently, a digest was published in English, under the same title, in the journal *Environmental Policy Review*.
11 Some of these are discussed in Altshuler and Golubchikov (1990).
12 *Doklad...* (1990), p. 100.
13 This figure does not include territory affected by the Chernobyl accident (*Doklad...* (1990), p. 102).
14 Doklad... (1990), pp. 100–102.
15 Weissenburger (1984), Teil I, p. 19. See also *Okhrana...* (1989), p. 88; *Doklad...* (1990), p. 51.
16 *Doklad...* (1990), p. 17; Yablokov (1990), p. 3.
17 *Doklad...* (1990), p. 21; Yablokov (1990), p. 3.
18 Peterson (1990b), p. 8.
19 *Ekonomika i Zhizn*, No. 4, 1989, p. 18; *Trud*, 5 July 1989, p. 1; *Doklad...* (1990), p. 124; Peterson (1990b), pp. 8–9.
20 *Trud*, 5 July 1989.
21 *Sotsiologicheskaya Industria*, 21 March 1989. See also Feshbach and Friendly (1992) for the connection between environmental deterioration and health problems in the Soviet Union.
22 *Sotsiologicheskaya Industria*, 29 September 1987; *Pravda*, 21 April 1988.
23 *TASS*, 2 August 1989.
24 *Pravda*, 18 April 1988.
25 Fuller (1987), pp. 1–2.
26 Ibid. See also Fuller and Mikaeli (1987), p. 2.
27 Fuller and Mikaeli (1987), p. 2.
28 *Pravda*, 21 April 1988.
29 *Pravda*, 2 December 1987.
30 *Pravda*, 2 December 1987; *Literaturnaya Gazeta*, 9 December 1987; *Pravda*, 20 January 1988.
31 Medvedev (1991).
32 *Izvestiya*, 27 October 1987.
33 *Vestnik Statistiki* (1991), No. 6, pp. 57–9.
34 *Okhrana...* (1989), p. 83; *Narkhoz* (1991), p. 273.
35 Peterson (1990a), p. 7.
36 Ibid.
37 Sergei Kutukov, Goskompriroda, personal interview, Moscow, 15 March 1991.
38 Weissenburger (1984), s. 19; *Doklad...* (1990), p. 51; *Okhrana...* (1990), p. 83; Yablokov (1990), p. 3.
39 *Byullentin...* (1990), p. 28.
40 *Okhrana...* (1989), pp. 23 and 26.
41 *Okhrana...* (1989), p. 83.
42 Yablokov (1990), p. 3.
43 Ibid.
44 *Pravda*, 18 April 1988.
45 Turnball (1990). For examples of the ineffectiveness of equipment in 1987 and 1988, see *SSSR i Soyuznye...* (1988), pp. 115, 303, 369, 403 and 556; *SSSR i Soyuznye...* (1989), pp.115, 205, 308 and 369; *Pravda*, 16 May 1987; *Sotsialisticheskaya Industriya*, 21 July 1987; and *Sotsialisticheskaya Industriya*, 16 February 1988.
46 Peterson (1990b), p. 7.
47 SCB, *Miljöstatistisk Årsbok*, 1986–7.

48 Of this, emissions of heavy metals amounted to 12 million tons while those of gaseous and liquid substances was equal to 44 million tons, of which sulphur anhydride constituted16 million tons, nitric oxide 5 million tons, and carbon monoxide 13 million tons (*Narkhoz* (1991), p. 273).

49 *Pravda*, 11 March 1989.

50 *Izvestiya*, 22 October 1987.

51 *Pravda*, 16 June 1987; *Ekonomicheskaya Gazeta*, No. 43, 1987; *Izvestiya*, 11 October 1988; *Vestnik Statistiki*, No. 6, 1988; *Ekonomicheskaya Gazeta*, No. 27, 1988, *Sotsialisticheskaya Industriya*, 16 February 1988, *Sotsialisticheskaya Industriya*, 17 January 1989; *Sotsialisticheskaya Industriya*, 9 February 1989.

52 *Pravda*, 12 December 1987; *Izvestiya*, 9 January 1988; *Sotsialisticheskaya Industriya*, 1 March 1989.

53 *Izvestiya*, 6 January 1985; *Pravda*, 12 January 1987; *Pravda*, 11 March 1987; *Pravda*, 10 May 1987; *Pravda*, 22 June 1987; *Pravda*, 20 July 1987; *Sotsialisticheskaya Industriya*,14 August 1987; *Izvestiya*, 16 October 1988; *Izvestiya*, 30 October 1988; *Komsomolskaya Pravda*, 27 November 1988; *Izvestiya*, 4 May 1989.

54 *Doklad...* (1990), p. 53.

55 *SSSR i Soyuznye Respubliki...* (1988), p. 164; *SSSR i Soyuznye Respubliki...* (1989), p. 114; Khazanov (1990), p. 22; *Izvestiya*, 15 September 1987.

56 In 1988, Soviet industry produced 52 per cent of all waste water, while agriculture accounted for 34.5 per cent and 13 per cent was caused by communal sewage (*Doklad...* (1990), p. 45).

57 *Okhrana...* (1989), pp. 62 and 77–9. See also *Byullentin...* (1990), p. 14.

58 *Pravda*, 16 May 1987; *Pravda*, 5 June 1987; *Sotsialisticheskaya Industriya*, 21 July 1987; *Sotsialisticheskaya Industriya*, 23 February 1988; *SSSR i Soyuznye...* (1988), p. 332; *SSSR i Soyuznye...* (1989), pp. 115, 205, 308 and 369. For details about Lithuania on this matter, see Idzelis (1983), pp. 296–7. According to Fuller and Mikaeli (1987), not a single purification plant on the Caspian Sea had begun functioning effectively by 1987.

59 *SSSR i Soyuznye Respubliki...* (1988), pp. 46, 115 and 461.

60 See also Peterson (1990c), p. 16.

61 Gofman and Motkin (1991).

62 *SSSR i Soyuznye...* (1988), pp. 115, 303, 369, 403, 494 and 556.

63 *SSSR i Soyuznye...* (1989), pp. 18, 115, 172, 205, 242 and 309.

64 *Izvestiya*, 28 January 1990.

65 *Izvestiya*, 4 May 1988.

66 *Izvestiya*, 15 September 1987.

67 Peterson (1990c), p. 14.

68 For examples, see *Sotsialisticheskaya Industriya*, 14 January 1987; *Pravda*, 21 April 1987; *Sotsialisticheskaya Industriya*, 23 September 1987; *Izvestiya*, 1 October 1987; *Sotsialisticheskaya Industriya*, 3 October 1987, *Sotsialisticheskaya Industriya*, 16 October 1987; *Pravda*, 27 July 1987; Gerner (1988); Marples (1988); *Sotsialisticheskaya Industriya*, 18 February 1989.

69 *Doklad...* (1990), p. 54.

70 *Izvestiya*, 20 September 1988; *Sotsialisticheskaya Industriya*, 17 January 1989.

71 *Sovetskaya Rossiya*, 16 August 1989.

72 Yablokov (1990), p. 3.

73 Boiko (1987), pp. 59–65.

74 *Sotsialisticheskaya Industriya*, 16 February 1987.

75 Marples (1988).

76 *Izvestiya*, 21 August 1988.

77 Sheinin (1987), pp. 11–15; *Narkhoz* (1988), p. 245.

78 Bystritskaya and Mikhura (1983), pp. 123–5.

79 The low emissions and high percentage of purification in Central Asia are partly explained by the low density of sewer systems. Similarly, the low percentage of purification in the Baltic republics is partly due to a high frequencey of sewer systems.

80 From 1970 to 1988, the area of irrigated land in Central Asia and southern Kazakhstan grew by 3.2 million hectares, which represents an average of 180,000 hectares each year (*Narkhoz* (1989), p. 473).

81 For further details about the serious environmental situation in the Aral Sea region, see *Novyi Mir*, No. 5, pp. 182–241, 1989, 'Aralskaya katastrofa'; *Pravda*, 7 September 1987; *Ogonek*, No. 1, 1988; *Sotsialisticheskaya Industriya*, 1 February 1989; Turnball (1990), Chapter 3.

82 *Pravda*, 5 June 1987; *Pravda*, 16 June 1987; *Izvestiya*, 4 July 1987; *Ekonomicheskaya Gazeta*, No. 43, 1987.

83 *Pravda*, 26 August 1987.

84 See *Vestnik Statistiki*, No. 11, 1991, p. 65 and Hedlund (1990), pp. 61–3.

85 *Doklad...* (1990), p. 115.

86 *Narkhoz* (1989), pp. 676–7.

87 *Doklad...* (1990), p. 68. See also *Okhrana...* (1989), p. 93.

88 *Okhrana...* (1989), p. 8; *Doklad...* (1990), p. 69; Yablokov (1990), p. 5.

89 Yablokov (1988).

90 *Narkhoz* (1989), pp. 674–5; Peterson (1990d), p. 10.

91 *Okhrana...* (1989), p. 101; *Okhrana Zdorovya v SSSR* (1990), p. 180.

92 Yablokov (1990), pp. 4–5. See also Peterson (1990d), p. 12 and Wolfson (1989).

93 For examples, see *Ekonomicheskaya Gazeta*, No. 19, 1986; *Pravda*, 1 May 1987; *Sotsialisticheskaya Industriya*, 17 December 1988; *Sotsialisticheskaya Industriya*,23 February 1988; Mamin (1992).

94 Peterson (1990d).

95 *Doklad* (1990), p. 47; *Literaturnaya Gazeta*, 25 January 1988.

96 Peterson (1990d).

97 *Sotsialisticheskaya Industriya*, 2 October 1987.

98 *Pravda*, 15 March 1988.

99 See further Ignats (1988).

100 Peterson (1990d), p. 10.

101 Yablokov (1990), p. 5.

102 See Tretyakova (1991) and Chapter 7 of this book.

3. Approaches to Economic Analysis of the Environment

In the previous chapter an attempt was made to give a general account of the environmental situation in the Soviet Union. It was found that the huge economies of scale of the centrally planned economy, in the case of the Soviet Union, had been used to combat and change the environment. Further, the serious environmental situation this policy had caused could not easily have been changed in the traditional Soviet economic system. The aim of this chapter is to provide a comprehensive explanation of environmental disruption in the Soviet Union.

In both Western and Soviet literature, two main approaches can be distinguished when explaining environmental disruption in the Soviet Union. One sees the problems as a result of a failure of the system, while the other sees them as a result of a conscious policy of neglect. This distinction can appear to be exceedingly fine. For analytical purposes it is nevertheless important. These two approaches will be discussed in Section 3.1.

Similarly, two main approaches to the economic analysis of environmental disruption can be identified. The different explanations to environmental disruption offered by Soviet and Western scholars are due partly to different perceptions of the Soviet economy. What appears to be the most common approach in the literature is to view the problems as the result of some kind of divergence from an ideal model. An alternative is to see them as a part of the general functioning of the Soviet economy. These two approaches will be discussed in Section 3.2. Then, in Section 3.3, conclusions are drawn from the findings of this chapter and the approaches of the present study are specified.

3.1 EXPLANATIONS FOR ENVIRONMENTAL DISRUPTION

3.1.1 A Failure of the System?

Many Western as well as Soviet approaches indicated that the lack of appropriate methods for evaluating environmental disruption might have contributed to an explanation of the environmental problems within the

Soviet Union. One frequent interpretation of environmental disruption within the Soviet Union has been that it is the result of a failure of the Soviet economic system. The centre had in effect not managed to incorporate the environment into the planning process. It had failed to evaluate the revenues and costs of preventing environmental disruption. In fact, most publications on the environment by scholars from the three best-known economic institutes at the Soviet Academy were, in one way or another, concerned with the problems of evaluation. For analytical convenience it is appropriate to distinguish between two rather different aspects of this approach; evaluation for planning and evaluation for pricing.

Some academic works have been concerned with the basic valuation problems at the planning stage, indicating that the problems were due to imperfections in the planning mechanism. That is, planners had failed to plan for the environment and the use of natural resources. Gregory and Stuart have seen the problems of valuation as a breakdown of valuation.[1] If planners were not aware of appropriate resource valuations, including the costs of environmental disruption, they would have been unable to allocate resources in a rational manner even if they had desired to do so.[2] A similar idea has been forwarded by Lvovskaya.[3] According to her, an important explanation of the poor results of environmental expenditures was that resources were allocated on a central level on the basis of the 'branch principle', which meant that resources were distributed through the ministerial hierarchies rather than directly to regions or cities.[4] As the ministries themselves decided upon the allocation of environmental expenditures, measures would not necessarily have been taken in the worst polluted parts of the Soviet Union. This in effect meant that measures would have been largely ineffective because they were not geared to the most heavily affected cities or towns.[5] In contrast to market economies which to a considerable degree are coordinated by the flow of price information among market agents, the Soviet economy was coordinated by flows of quantity information and commands. As a result, harmful, yet potentially useful, waste products of one enterprise may simply have been discarded into convenient waterways rather than being intercepted and made available as a potentially valuable resource input to another complementary production process, even though the two enterprises might geographically have been located near each other.

Another Soviet academic work has also stressed the importance of valuation problems.[6] It argues that, unless the cost of pollution in the Soviet economy was evaluated, planners would be unable to decide on the proportion between basic production funds and funds for environmental protection.[7]

On the whole, the view that environmental problems could be approached by developing methods for valuing environmental disruption has rendered wide support among Soviet economists.[8] Furthermore a large number of Soviet academics have been engaged with developing a 'Standard

26

Methodology' for the valuation of natural resources initiated by central planners in the mid-1970s.[9] The adoption of rules concerning the use of cost-benefit analysis in central environmental planning[10] further indicates an increased attention of Soviet officials to the problems of valuation.[11]

Other scholars have been more concerned with the problems at the implementation stage, connected with the lack of prices and other incentives at the enterprise level. They indicated that the problems were due to a failure by planners to provide an incentive structure which would have promoted the efficient use of the environment and its natural resources.[12] In particular, they held the view that valuation problems had been complicated by the adherence to the labour theory of value, which was prejudiced against charging for natural resources.[13] Many Soviet as well as Western economists have expressed the opinion that one important factor leading to environmental disruption within the Soviet Union was the low, or in some cases complete absence of, prices for natural resource use. No agent using water and other resources and not having to pay a fee, felt any incentive to use the resource prudently; this was only another example of the irrational Soviet resource-pricing structure in which many resources were treated as free goods.[14] Another problem is that fines for pollution violators were insignificant and usually overturned on appeal.[15] There were no sanctions for increasing the use of natural resource per unit of output. Bonuses and other forms of rewards for decreasing the use of natural resources or reducing pollution were virtually absent.[16] In the early 1960s Soviet economists had suggested that charges for natural resources should be introduced.[17] Such opinions were expressed more openly in later works.[18] Similarly, Thornton, in her evaluation of the Soviet methodology for valuation of natural resources, comes to the conclusion that the methodology would have been more appropriate for pricing (see below) than for valuation at the planning stage, which was the stated goal of the methodology.[19]

Neither Thornton, ZumBrunnen, nor the Soviet scholars have, however, discussed the issue of pricing in the context of the general role of prices in the traditional Soviet economic system. They seem to have ignored the fact that the Soviet system was not primarily intended to react to price signals. The fact that enterprises were only to a very small extent guided by prices implied that the low prices paid for the use of natural resources played a minor role for their actual use, which was instead meant to be determined by planning.

On the other hand, because of the absence of prices for the use of natural resources central planners have lacked an instrument for controlling their use. Valuation in money terms was important from the central point of view as money was the common unit by which the use of resources was measured.[20] Central authorities in particular lacked a mechanism for controlling subordinates who would evaluate and assess performance as regards the use of natural resources. Accordingly what was important for effective control and measurement was not so much the relative prices of resources as that prices were stable.

Problems of valuation might be seen as a breakdown in the information mechanism.[21] The appropriate resource valuation, including the costs of environmental degradation, would not have been available to central decision-makers because of the scale and complexity of the planning procedure. The hierarchical-bureaucratic form of society complicated communication and understanding. The centre would not have known just what had to be done, in disaggregated detail, while enterprise management could not know what society needed unless informed by the centre. Hence, planners may have been unable to design environmental policies in a rational manner even if they had desired to do so. The fact that most economic decisions were made by ministerial and regional authorities and plant managers, none of whom were able to see the total impact of their actions, further aggravated problems of information.

Some of the Western literature on this subject has been concerned with the possible advantages and disadvantages of central planning relative to decentralised decision-making. McIntyre and Thornton argue that the Soviet economy had an important institutional advantage in finding an economically efficient pollution-abatement programme.[22] They further state that centrally planned economies possess an informational advantage over a decentralised economy. As planners would be involved in determining the specific production processes employed by firms, the industrial ministries would have acquired information relevant to calculating abatement costs as a matter of routine. The ministries would also have possessed information about the local circumstances of their enterprises, and thus have been in a position to gather more information when this was required. They also argue that the centralised decision-maker would acquire information about the relative merits of centralised or decentralised abatement strategies. McIntyre and Thornton do not, however, claim that the benefits of these advantages have been fully realised in practice. Their analysis might be taken as a support for the view that these problems could have been successfully addressed by an improved central planning. However, the possible advantage of the centrally planned economy, as put forward by McIntyre and Thornton, is largely irrelevant as problems of implementation are completely disregarded.

Ziegler, on the other hand, has argued that the Soviet planned economic system had no institutional advantage over a capitalist system.[23] He stresses the distortions in the flow of information between Gosplan, ministries and enterprises, and especially how enterprises and ministries may have been inclined to understate the amount of pollutants emitted and the resulting damage to the environment. Ziegler's conclusion is that pluralism would be more efficient than centralism in generating environmental information unless the system of central planning primarily maximised environmental protection. Even though ecologists and scientific groups in the Soviet Union have a certain amount of status, public pressure has been comparatively low. Ziegler might be criticised as he uses the concept 'pluralism' without defining it, and it appears as if he mixes up the aims of central planners with the general functioning of the economic system.

3.1.2 A Conscious Policy of Neglect

In the traditional Soviet system, it was the Communist Party that formulated the basic directions of the national economy, supervised the fulfilment of these plans and ran the government. Its representatives exerted their influence vertically through the economy from the highest levels of the Council of Ministers, down to the local firms. The utilisation of natural resources was planned by the various levels of government, and their exploitation and conservation carried out by agencies and enterprises directly under its governmental supervision. It might therefore be argued that environmental perception of the Soviet Union becomes essentially a question of how the Party viewed the environment and the complexes of natural resources which comprises it.

An important explanation of the environmental disruption in the former Soviet Union which has often been referred to is the possibility that environmental concerns have been consciously discarded as one of the costs of rapid economic growth.[24] The Soviet leadership had, especially since the rise of Stalinism, pursued a relentless policy of rapid industrialisation. Lvovskaya and Ronkin, for example, emphasised that the serious environmental situation was not the result of any particular miscalculation, but rather that it was an inevitable consequence of the command-administrative system which promoted a forced industrialisation of the country.[25] This, in turn, had brought with it gigantic enterprises in heavy industry, and these became the main users of natural resources, and had the highest capacity for polluting the environment.[26] Surrounded by essentially 'hostile' foreign powers, such a policy seems to have been prudent for the Soviet government's political survival. Nevertheless, the priority had long been on increasing production in the short run and not upon such 'non-productive' activities as pollution abatement and nature protection in general. The emphasis on output performance became heavier the more one moved up the hierarchy, towards the major investment decision-maker. Managerial salaries in the Soviet Union were tied to fulfilment of target output, and practically independent of any external damage incurred in the production process. In other words, the costs of environmental disruption were neglected and disinvestment in the environment became a rather typical aspect of Soviet economic development, just as it has characterised economic growth generally in market economies, although the reaction there in many cases came earlier. It may have been that central planners were not concerned with environmental quality until the level of development became such that, in combination with the effect of international demonstration, its presence became pervasive.[27]

The wasteful attitude towards natural resources under Stalin might largely be explained by the heavy emphasis on material production in the presence of a perceived unlimited supply. Natural resources were considered as factors of production, which should be mobilised as quickly as possible. The Stalinist development strategy reflected the opinion that man could master nature and transform it into economic wealth whenever the leaders wanted to. As noted above, the neglect of environmental concerns was further in line with the labour theory of value.

The traditional emphasis on increased material production together with the practice of planning from the achieved level may have further complicated the task of incorporating environmental values and the use of natural resources in the planning process and, in particular, in the plan indicators of agents at the different levels of the economy. This principle, which implied that the plan indicators were derived by means of adding to the relevant *ex post* figures a certain percentage of growth, has generally been used in the planning of production for branches and enterprises as well as in the allocation of inputs to them.[28] The same principle would also have applied to the financial plan, the investment plan, and so forth. The practice of planning from the achieved level tended to conserve existing proportions between planned resource use and planned output.

The failure to adhere to regulations was another problem connected with the general emphasis on material production.[29] While production plans were generally accompanied by the allocation of resources required to fulfil them, laws and regulations were not. This meant that even if enterprises were actually motivated to comply with regulations due to environmental concerns, they might not have been able to. Another important problem concerning the implementation of laws on natural resource conservation was connected with their enforcement. The passing of laws and resolutions did not automatically achieve anything. If, for example, responsibilities of industrial enterprises regulated by law did not have their counterpart in the plan indicators according to which the work of these enterprises was evaluated, this implied that the enterprises would have been committed to breaking the law in order to fulfil the plan, which was the highest law. Such behaviour was further promoted as the enforcement of Soviet environmental laws was often lax. Since the early 1970s the Soviet press had published a chronology of production enterprises being established either without waste treatment facilities being completed or, at least, without the written approval. In addition, while in theory quite stringent, the Soviet maximum permitted concentrations of pollutants, PDKs (*predelno dopustimye kontsentratsii*), were often poorly monitored and enforced.[30]

The traditional investment policy implied that industrial modernisation took place through investment in new plants rather than in existing ones. This meant that most of the gigantic enterprises within heavy industry had

30

obsolete equipment which was intensive in its use of natural resources and a technology which was ecologically aggressive. This provided an opportunity for introducing plants which were beneficial from the environment protectional point of view. The long investment period, which was generally 10–15 years in the Soviet Union,[31] might however have ensured that plants were obsolete before they were taken into use. One effect of the traditional emphasis on quantitative growth was that older plants were maintained in production as long as output plans were fulfilled. If pollution-control equipment was installed it did not fit in well. Moreover, with all the emphasis on production, there was little incentive for the ministry as well as for the enterprise to invest in pollution-control devices, as these would have impeded production activities and thus have threatened the fulfilment of production plans. If enterprises strived to maximise production per rouble of invested capital, non-productive installations could only have reduced output performance.

3.1.3 Different Perspectives of the Soviet Economy

In the preceding subsections two different approaches to explaining environmental disruption in the Soviet Union have been identified. One approach represents the view that problems were connected to an inability of the planned economic system to allocate resources in an 'optimal' way. Lack of information would have caused problems of evaluation, which in turn would explain the 'inoptimal' allocation of resources for environmental purposes.

The other approach views the problems as a consequence of neglect by planners who were simply more concerned with other matters. The perceived abundance of natural resources made a policy of neglect possible, while the 'man-could-master-nature attitude' motivated it. The principle of planning from the achieved level made it difficult to incorporate environmental concerns to the planning process. In addition to this, the lack of incentives and practical possibilities to comply with any regulations in the environmental field made them ineffective. The combined effect of these factors is to indicate that the priority of material production would have been particularly detrimental in the Soviet case.

These two approaches in effect constitute two alternative views as to how the Soviet system actually worked. The first approach saw the system as not working in the way it was intended to. This view assumed that the aim of central planners has been efficiency in resource allocation and balance between supply and demand. Imbalances would have occurred as a result of failures of the system. The alternative view saw imbalances as a consequence of a conscious policy.

Another conclusion is that, although Western and Soviet scholars seemed in some respects to have agreed as regards the main explanations for environmental disruption in the Soviet Union, they differed considerably when it comes to the aim of their work. The general aim of Western academic works seemed to be to specify factors leading to environmental disruption in the Soviet Union. Some of these discussed various institutional shortcomings of the Soviet Union's economic system with respect to environmental quality and resource management.[32] They also focused to some extent on comparing these shortcomings with those of market economies in order to highlight systematic differences between the different economic systems.[33]

Soviet studies, on the other hand, have been more concerned with the task of developing methods for evaluating environmental disruption to be used for determining when measures were needed than investigating the causes of environmental disruption. Some of these also proposed measures which should be undertaken.

3.2   APPROACHES TO THE ANALYSIS OF ENVIRONMENTAL PROBLEMS

3.2.1 *A Divergence from an Ideal Model*

A common feature of both Western and Soviet studies on the environmental problems in the Soviet Union that is related to problems of evaluation was, as we have seen, that they viewed the problems as a result of some kind of divergence from an ideal model of the system. Another common feature was that they seemed to look at it from a Western point of view as they took the reasons for environmental disruption in the West as a point of reference when discussing these problems in the Soviet context. In other words, the discussions concerned divergencies in terms of either the market versus plan perspective or socialism versus capitalism. They indicated that if the gap between reality and the ideal model of how the system should work could have been narrowed, the situation would have been improved.

If the Soviet economy is characterised as a socialist economy, defined as an economy with state ownership, it seems appropriate to focus on differences between socialism and capitalism as regards the ability to combat environmental disruption. One such important difference is that of ownership or property rights, the assignment of rights to use and benefit from scarce resources, and the obligations to bear the costs of them. If one sees environmental problems in the West as caused by the absence of well-defined property rights, then the lack of a clear assignment of property rights to nature in the socialist system appears an obvious explanation of environmental problems there. Just as in capitalist economies, the absence of well-defined property rights over air and water would lead to pollution of these.

The property rights approach indicates that environmental problems could be solved if individuals had the property rights over air, water and other natural resources, that is, the solution lies in approaching an ideal capitalist system. This factor is put forward by Thornton as an important source of pollution problems in the Soviet Union.[34] Under capitalism, property rights belong to private owners, who bear the cost of and reap the benefits from the use of the resources. In the case of resources with a long life span, such as natural resources, the capitalist owner will weigh current and future benefits and will forgo current use if the prospect of future reward is sufficiently high. Thus there is a natural incentive to conserve.[35] In the traditional Soviet system, property rights were assigned to the state or to society as a whole, not to individuals or plant directors. They were rewarded according to short-term performance criteria and no personal benefit was gained from refraining from current use for the sake of future use. The incentive to conserve would therefore have been lacking, unless imposed from above via a change in the existing incentive system. Thornton's approach helps to explain the wasteful use of natural resources and it provides support for the view that the waste of resources would have been greater in the Soviet economy than in a capitalist economy.

If the Soviet economy is characterised as a centrally planned economy, it seems appropriate to focus on the differences between planned economies and market economies. Without the 'appropriate' property rights, environmental disruption in market economies will emerge as an externality caused by structural defects in the pricing system. Agents pay little attention to the environmental concerns as they do not affect profits. Just as the perfect market economy does not exist in the real world, decision-making in the Soviet Union was not perfectly centralised. While conflicts between private resource decision-makers in the market system are attributed to shortcomings in the market mechanism, such conflicts in the planned economy would be explained by imperfect planning. That is, conflicts in the use of natural resources, such as that between hydropower generation and irrigation withdrawals, would be explained by an insufficient planning detail, imperfect plan coordination and inadequate and distorted information.[36] As the Soviet economy was coordinated by 'vertical' flows of information and commands this would have caused real problems.

State officials in the Soviet Union frequently blamed ministries for the environmental problems. The problems would have been caused by ministries' bad morals and 'departmentalism', which is a Soviet term for describing the tendency by ministries to pursue short-term interests to ensure production. Success in the Soviet economy has been determined primarily on the basis of fulfilling short-term output goals. Less easily quantifiable goals such as cost reductions, innovations and environmental quality have not been important in influencing decision-making.

In the Soviet context, externalities might be regarded as those effects which were not integrated in a given unit's performance indicators. The concept of production externalities may hence have included opportunity cost of land and natural resources if these were not included in the plan-indicators that industrial enterprises had to fulfil. If this opportunity cost of land and natural resources was not incorporated into the plan-indicators, their extensive use would have been encouraged. The cutting down of the most easily accessible forests, in the interest of fulfilling short-term plans by over-cutting provides an example of this in some regions. Another example is that state mining and oil enterprises moved their operations from one mine or oil field to the next when they had exhausted the richest and most accessible deposits in a very short period, in order to fulfil the annual plan, rather than continue mining at an old site.

Another relevant distinction is that between democracy and dictatorship. This distinction was used by Ziegler,[37] when he compared the Soviet system with that of Western-type systems with respect to environmental management. He argued that 'pluralism' would be more efficient than centralism in generating information about the environmental situation. Following Alec Nove, one could also make a distinction between 'the Western mentality' and 'the Russian mentality'.[38] While the Western hard-working mentality has evolved from a Lutheran philosophy, 'lazy' Russians have always avoided working more than necessary, as they have been slaves in their own country. Russia has always lagged behind. In the West, man has been inspired to work hard by the prospect of making more money, while in Russia man just tried to avoid punishment.[39]

3.2.2 Part of the General Functioning of the Economy

The alternative approach is to try to characterise the system on the basis of observed features of the actual systems. Rather than considering environmental problems as divergencies from ideal models one could see them as a part of the general functioning of the economy. If one views Western-type economies as mixed economies rather than as pure market economies, it seems appropriate to see environmental problems there not only as a result of market imperfections, but also as being caused by a low political priority. For political reasons environmental policies pursued by Western governments may not have been forceful enough. Seen in such a perspective, as in the case of Soviet-type economies, environmental disruption in Western economies might be explained by the general emphasis on production. The question then becomes partly a matter of how severe the government considers the environmental situation has to get before it takes any action. The fact that Western governments for competitive reasons might find it difficult to do much about the environmental situation unless governments of other countries do so was not relevant in the case of the Soviet Union, which had traditionally been more or less isolated.

In some respects, however, there is a pressure from neighbouring countries to do something about global environmental problems. As the Soviet Union has traditionally been cut off from the Western market economies, it was not subject to this type of pressure. One might perhaps have expected the Soviets to take more drastic, gradual measures as the situation called for them, while in the West, environmental policies would be dealt with more smoothly with time. In particular, it might have been the case that in the Soviet Union measures were not taken until environmental disruption was perceived to obstruct material growth.

If one sees the Soviet economy as an economy that was imperfectly controlled by central planners, then it seems appropriate to see environmental disruption not only as a result of low political priority but also as being caused by the behaviour of agents. Producers would have neglected environmental concerns if these were not reflected in the main performance indicators.

3.3   THE APPROACH OF THE PRESENT STUDY

The two different approaches to economic analysis of the environment that have been discussed in this chapter highlight various aspects which together provide a comprehensive explanation of the environmental disruption in the Soviet Union. In addition, they reflect two different perspectives in respect to the aims of the central leadership. The second approach sees imbalances as a consequence of a conscious policy. It considers political targets to have been traditionally more important than economic considerations. It is this view that will be used as the framework for the subsequent analysis.

In both Western and Soviet literature environmental disruption has been viewed as a result of divergencies in terms of either the market versus plan perspective, socialism versus capitalism, or democracy versus dictatorship. If the gap between reality and the ideal model of how the system should work could be narrowed down the situation would be improved. If, however, political targets were more important than economic efficiency, such an approach to analysis is not relevant. It seems inappropriate to compare performance in efficiency terms if the main objective of the Soviet model has been to serve purposes other than facilitating efficient resource allocation. The dispute over the potentials of the planned economy relative to the market economy is irrelevant as long as problems of implementation are disregarded.

In its further explanation and analysis of these problems, this study applies the view of the Soviet economy as a shortage economy, but adapted to take the low priority of environmental protection into account. This view of the Soviet economy emphasises the role of the producers as well as the importance of central decision-makers' priorities in the explanation of economic phenomena. This approach – to be developed in the next chapter – offers an explanation of the ineffectiveness of environmental programmess as well as of the mismanagement of natural resources. This explanation is compatible with those offered in other studies which indicate the importance of the emphasis on material production. It highlights why the priority of material production appears to have been particularly detrimental in the Soviet economic system. Environmental programmes were more likely to suffer from the general shortage of resources as resources were normally allocated to more 'important' tasks first. In order to provide support for the impact of shortages on the performance of environmental programmes the theoretical analysis is supplemented with empirical data.

Recent works by both Western and Soviet economists have indicated the power of shortage economy processes in the Soviet Union.[40] The shortage economy approach is used to offer a plausible framework not only for analysing problems of inefficient use of resources in the economy as a whole, but also for analysing specific problems such as that of environmental management.

NOTES

1   Gregory and Stuart (1981), p. 393.
2   Ibid.
3   Lvovskaya (1988).
4   Ibid., p. 439.
5   This view has inspired the research into tradable permits (Lvovskaya and Ronkin (1991)).
6   Gusev and Varlamova (1988).
7   Ibid., p. 447.
8   Gofman (1982, 1985a, 1985b); Gofman and Gusev (1981, 1985); Gusev (1985); Gusev and Mustafaev (1983); Kaganovich (1986); Kallaste (1987, 1988, 1989); Kisilev (1985); Kukushkin (1985); Levina (1983); Lvovskaya (1985); Mkrtchyan and Ponomareva (1987); Motkin (1983); Pyazok (1984); Popov (1985); Rabinovich (1985); Sinelshchikov and Ushakov (1985); Ushakov (1983, 1985) all provide theoretical approaches to the valuation of environmental problems and measures.
9   Gofman (1977); *Vremennaya...* (1986); Gofman and Fedorenko (1987).
10 *Pravda*, 23 January 1988.
11 Gofman (1988b); *Doklad...* (1990), pp. 118–60.
12 Bechuk et al.(1991) emphasise the disincentives to engage in environmental-saving technical development (see p. 906).
13 DeBardeleben (1983 and 1985).
14 ZumBrunnen (1987), p. 3.
15 Ibid.
16 Lvovskaya and Ronkin (1990), p. 7.
17 Goldman (1972); Debardeleben (1983).
18 Aganbegyan (1988); Aleksandrov (1986); Gofman and Fedorenko(1987); Kallaste (1987); Kazannik (1985); Kisilev (1983); Monakhova (1988); Rotar and Stavrakova (1988); Shalabin (1987).
19 Thornton (1978b). For a discussion of this 'Handbook', see Chapter 6.

20 Gregory and Stuart (1981), p. 142.
21 Gregory and Stuart (1981), p. 365.
22 McIntyre and Thornton (1978).
23 Ziegler (1980).
24 Gregory and Stuart (1981); p. 392, ZumBrunnen (1987), p. 4. See in particular Goldman (1972), Chapter 2.
25 Lvovskaya and Ronkin (1990), p. 6.
26 Ibid.
27 Gregory and Stuart (1981), p. 392.
28 See Birman (1978).
29 See ZumBrunnen (1987), p. 4.
30 ZumBrunnen (1987), p. 3. According to Lvovskaya and Ronkin (1990), the rights and possibilities of local Soviets as regards environmental management was of a 'declarative nature', as was the normative for PDK (see p. 7).
31 Nove (1982), p. 163.
32 Gerner and Lundgren (1978); Goldman (1972); Gustafson (1980); Kelley (1976); Koutaissoff (1987); Pryde (1972); Sätre Åhlander (1989); Weissenburger (1984), Teil 1; Ziegler (1987); and ZumBrunnen (1987) all contain discussions of problems and policies of the environment. See also Gregory and Stuart (1981), p. 390, footnote 64 for further references to the environmental disruption in the Soviet Union.
33 Goldman (1972); McIntyre and Thornton (1978, 1980); Thornton (1978a); and Ziegler (1980, 1982, 1987).
34 Thornton (1978a).
35 Ibid.
36 ZumBrunnen (1987), p. 3.
37 Ziegler (1980).
38 Nove (1982).
39 Ibid.
40 Davis (1988 and 1989); Åslund (1988); Belkin (1987); Shmelev (1987).

4. A Shortage-Economy Approach

It has already been shown how Western and Soviet studies have identified a number of factors which have contributed to the environmental disruption in the Soviet Union. There is, however, no good theoretical explanation as to why environmental protection has the performance characteristics revealed by the empirical investigations in Chapter 2. One obstacle to analysis is that most existing models do not fully take into account shortage phenomena that are characteristic of socialist economies.[1] Another problem is that there has been insufficient research into 'the formation of priorities' within the socialist economy.[2] It is therefore difficult to evaluate the effects of shortage and priorities on environmental performance. The present study attempts to fill some gaps in the field by applying the view of the Soviet economy as a shortage economy.

Although the model of the shortage economy to be used here has some universal elements, it possesses unique features that are functions of particular arrangements and behavioural patterns in centrally planned economies. What distinguishes this model in particular, is that it assumes centrally planned economies to be characterised by chronic and pervasive shortages.

History reveals that problems with disequilibrium have been recurrent and important in centrally planned economies. As economic plans intentionally established output targets that were 'taut', that is, overambitious relative to available resources, it appears that imbalances or shortages were components of a conscious policy. In the 1980s the Soviet and East European economies have experienced at least occasionally severe domestic and external imbalances, which have adversely affected economic performance indicators and the behaviour of planners, managers, workers and consumers. The study of the shortage model can assist in understanding the actual problems of imbalances and pervasive shortages in these economic systems.

The chapter is organised in the following way. It starts by discussing Soviet and Western approaches to economic analysis of the Soviet-type economy. These are related to the different explanations for environmental disruption discussed in Chapter 3. The model to be used in this study is then elaborated. Finally, some assumptions of the traditional shortage model as developed by Kornai are revised in order to take into account the effects of low priority of environmental protection.

4.1 THE EAST–WEST PERSPECTIVE

In both East and West a lot of effort has been expended on the creation of models of the optimal functioning socialist economy.[3] The optimal planning models deal with the ideal planned economy. Western economists have made important theoretical contributions in this field.[4] In these models resources are allocated to their best uses by means of central planning. With the help of mathematical programming models shadow prices are calculated. The shadow prices express the value of resources in their best alternative use, which should then be used by central planners in their allocation of resources. Just as in models of the perfect market economy scarce resources are allocated to uses whose values exceed these shadow prices, and it is implicitly assumed that the basic function of planning is to balance supply and planned demand. It is assumed that central authorities attempt to do what the market does in the perfect market economy. These models simply apply the fundamental logic of market allocation to central planning.

There is also an extensive list of literature devoted to optimal planning particular to the Soviet Union. Huge models for macroeconomic planning have been developed under the guidance of prominent scholars at CEMI and other economic institutes at the Soviet Academy of Sciences. The aim of such models is generally to work out tools which can be used for improving central planning. Just as in the Western literature on optimal planning, central planning in the Soviet framework is aimed at replacing markets as an instrument for allocating scarce resources and it is assumed that the central leadership wants to attain a balance between supply and demand. In Soviet academic works, however, it is specifically the demand of the Soviet leadership that would balance with supply, although it is assumed that demand is determined on the basis of economic calculations. Economists have been working on such models for several decades. They have worked with the perspective that the aim of central planning is to achieve economic efficiency, given the demand. Yet, these works have received little attention by planners.

Another important area of research in the 1970s, which also used mathematical planning methods, was that of input–output relations.[5] In these models it is assumed that the requirement of proportional development of the economy is a cornerstone of the Soviet economic doctrine. Just as in the optimal planning literature, it assumes equilibrium conditions in the economy.

There is also extensive literature on the Soviet enterprise. Pioneering works in this field are largely institutional in character.[6] The first attempts to apply the fundamental logic of neoclassical modelling to analyse the behaviour of Soviet enterprises were made in the mid-1960s.[7] The Kosygin 'reform' of 1965 gave rise to a considerable amount of literature on the bonus-maximising enterprise. A lot of effort was put into constructing incentive schemes which induced honest reporting and maximisation of planners' objectives. According to this view, decision-making is more decentralised in practice than in theory. It simply ignores the issue of the degrees of freedom available to the managers in executing their plan. In particular, it neglects the fact that the failure of this reform implied that the so-called 'economic incentives' that had been introduced did not work the way they were intended to. One aim of a book on the Soviet enterprise was to show that complex and realistic models, built around a neoclassical model of the firm, made a limited contribution towards understanding and predicting the behaviour of enterprises as they leave out the interaction between the planners and the planned.[8] Just as in the optimal planning models, it seemed natural to assume that central planners, given the demand, aim at balancing supply and government demand and that they attempt to attain economic efficiency in resource allocation.

One problem with neoclassical models is that they do not incorporate the institutional and structural differences between the Soviet economy and that of the industrialised West.[9] Some neoclassical analyses of the Soviet enterprise nevertheless highlight some specific characteristics of the Soviet system, indicating that there is a relation between goal function and general production efficiency. There is a substantial amount of formal literature on Soviet enterprise behaviour which supports the view that emphasis on growth in itself promotes an excessive demand for inputs, and thereby also for natural resource use. However, although effects of shortage in one way or another are analysed in these studies, their causes are not discussed. Soviet microeconomic modelling of enterprises is relatively underdeveloped as compared to the extensive research and literature on macroeconomic models.

A common feature of optimal planning models, neoclassical models and input–output models is that the basic function of planning is assumed to be to balance supply and planned demand. Also, in this literature it seems natural to assume that central planners attempted to attain efficiency in resource allocation. This view of the centrally planned economy is compatible with the approach which focused on problems of valuation in explaining environmental disruption in the Soviet Union, which was discussed in Chapter 3. Accordingly, the system did not work in the way it was intended to and imbalances were the result of failures of the system. The models which were used are similar to the models for explaining imbalances in market economies. If, however, one focuses on the fact that resource allocation was directed by plans instead of markets, and that decision-making was based on administrative rules rather than economic incentives, it appears that many assumptions which were applied are not relevant for centrally planned economies.

The alternative is to assume that central planners ignored economic balance and that chronic disequilibrium in markets and shortages were parts of a conscious policy. With such a perspective, it also seems natural to assume that central planners actively promoted disequilibrium in order to facilitate attainment of certain objectives. In the late 1920s, when the Soviet economic system started to get its present form, Stalin argued that excess demand in markets acted as a stimulus to industry.[10] This view seems to be implicit in the literature of disequilibrium and shortage in centrally planned economies.

The failure to fit centrally planned economies into the logic of Western economic thought inspired research into the modelling and analysis of specific features which are important for explaining the functioning of the centrally planned economy. Even though Soviet-type economies had been afflicted by imbalances and shortages since the very beginning of the Stalinist system, relatively few analyses were made of these phenomena before the mid-1970s. In a pioneering work on the functioning of socialist economies the Hungarian economist Janos Kornai provides an explanatory theory as to the causes and consequences of shortage. In his book *Economics of Shortage*, Kornai makes a special contribution to the understanding of the socialist economy by connecting agent behaviour with conditions of permanent shortage.[11] With the help of a basic shortage model, he aims to explain not only the consequences of shortage phenomena but also their causes. The model of the shortage economy possesses unique features that are functions of particular arrangements and behavioural patterns in centrally planned economies.

An increasing dissatisfaction with explanations of economic performance in Soviet-type economies based on optimal planning models and neoclassical models resulted in research on the nature and implications of priorities in the socialist economy. Although the term 'priority' as such was not new when discussing the Soviet economy it had not been applied as a key concept for explaining behaviour until the late 1980s. It is defined as the degree of commitment of the leadership to ensure that certain objectives are attained irrespective of circumstances in the economy.[12] The concept of the priority-driven command economy was introduced by Ericson.[13] An interesting application of this theory has been made by Oxenstierna, who uses the concept of priority to study labour shortage in the Soviet Union.[14] What distinguishes the model of the priority-driven command economy is the view that non-economic considerations were fundamental in economic decision-making in Soviet-type economies and that central decision-makers were assumed to attribute different priorities to different economic activities. The basic function of the hierarchical and administrative model for resource allocation is that it can guarantee that objectives for high-priority activities are always fulfilled. This view of the Soviet economy emphasises that resource allocation was directed by plans, that economic decision-making was based on political considerations and that the institutional framework facilitated resource allocation in accordance with the priority ranking of the central decision-makers. One problem with the shortage model is that it does not explicitly take into account matters of

41

priority.[15] On the other hand, approaches built on the model of the priority-driven command economy do not consider the effects of shortage phenomena. In this respect, Davis's contribution is particularly interesting as he applies the concept of priority to Kornai's theory of the shortage economy.[16] It is this approach that will be further developed and applied to the problem of environmental disruption and mismanagement of natural resources.

4.2   A VARIANT OF THE SHORTAGE MODEL

4.2.1 Shortage Models

There is an extensive amount of literature on disequilibrium and shortage in centrally planned economies. A few studies in the West were devoted to shortage-related phenomena back in the 1950s,[17] as were some investigations that focused on specific aspects of disequilibrium phenomena.[18]

In the early 1970s, the first Eastern European theoretical analyses were carried out on the causes and consequences of shortages and imbalances in socialist economies.[19] Some modelling of excess demand and the impact of investment cycles, for instance, has been performed in Eastern Europe.[20] In the Soviet Union, however, most analysts either ignored or denied the problem of pervasive shortages. Others followed the Stalinist line which treated excess demand as a beneficial stimulus to industry.

It was not until the second half of the 1970s, when economies in the East were facing a growing instability, that an expansion of research in both East and West into the modelling and analysis of centrally planned economies took place. Following the introduction of the basic model by Kornai there was considerable elaboration of it by him and others. By the mid-1980s there were over thirty Hungarian and fifty English-language studies of shortage models.[21]

Kornai's approach[22] is to examine how the socialist economy actually operates, rather than how it should operate. He argues that shortage is an integral systematic aspect of socialism, and not primarily a consequence of policies pursued by leaders or faulty planning methods. In Kornai's model the behaviour of producing institutions is the primary cause of the initiation and reproduction of shortage phenomena. The emphasis placed on producers is one of the features that distinguishes the shortage model from other models of Soviet-type economies. His analysis is based on the fact that the characteristic of an economic system would be the constraint hit most often by the production of the enterprise. While in capitalist economies this is the demand constraint, Kornai observes that in the traditional socialist economy, it is usually the supply constraint that is binding. This implies that in a socialist economy a lack of inputs will begin to limit production before the demand for the products of the enterprise has been exhausted. This refers to a market situation where buyers are looking for sellers, while the latter rarely experience any difficulty in selling what they can produce. An aspect of this is that, since enterprises have no need to seek and attract customers, they tend to be relatively uninterested in innovation. They would not be interested in innovating new products because it is easy enough to sell the established ones. Neither would they be motivated to innovate new processes because the pressure to cut costs is weak. One of the most important consequences of chronic shortage is, according to Kornai, that the producer feels no economic incentive to introduce new products of better quality. Another consequence is that the enterprise as a buyer is prepared to accept even poor quality of inputs. Hence, in the shortage model the enterprise is assumed to be a poor innovator, to produce mainly traditional goods with outdated technology and to produce output of low quality. Kornai has further developed three hypotheses concerning the input side of the enterprise. These are the existence of chronic shortages of inputs, hoarding of inputs and investment tension, which is a tension between claim and quota, the investment plan is taut and there is a tension between initial demand and the resources actually available.

The very basic difference between the functioning of capitalist and socialist economies is explained as a reliance on the nature of the budget constraint. Kornai's argument runs as follows. In the traditional socialist economy the budget constraint of an enterprise is soft. There is no effective financial restriction on its demand for inputs, that is, the budget constraint works with a loss that does not lead to bankruptcy and the closing of plants. If the socialist enterprise has financial difficulties it receives additional credits or subsidies, its tax is reduced or the selling price of its output is raised. The budget constraint of the socialist enterprise would therefore not constitute an effective behavioural constraint, but exists only as 'an accounting relationship'.[23]

As the central planners generally want the enterprise to produce as much as possible, the production plan of the socialist enterprise is set at the level of the resource constraint. This system of 'taut planning', which implies that the enterprise more frequently hits resource constraints, produces bottlenecks which impede further increases in production. Normal tautness of plans as well as lower and upper 'tolerance limits' would, according to Kornai be historically developed magnitudes fixed by social conventions and practice. The meaning of these concepts is that any departure of the economy from the 'normal value' of some economic variables sets up a behavioural response tending to restore the normal state. This mechanism is called 'control by norms'. Similar mechanisms can be envisaged in which the control process is governed by upper and lower 'tolerance limits' of some economic variable. The 'lower tolerance limit' of plan tautness is the 'acceptance constraint' of the superior authorities determining the plan, while the 'upper tolerance limit' is the 'acceptance constraint' of enterprises. If that were overstepped the situation in the workshop would become unbearable. These norms and tolerance limits would change with the deeper change in society.

A 'normal degree of shortage' is established in the same sense. 'Shortage intensity' is measured by indicators of shortage (that is, queueing, waiting time, forced substitution), which reflect certain definite shortage phenomena. The higher the value of any shortage indicator, the higher the intensity of shortage. Shortage intensity fluctuates around a 'normal value'. If shortage becomes more intense, central authorities are likely to receive more complaints about shortages. Planners can react by allocating additional resources to the activity in question. Sooner or later, central counter-measures will cut back the shortage intensity to an acceptable level and the economy can return to the more routine resource allocation. The meaning of 'control by norms' is that a given normal intensity of shortage could be reproduced over time.

As the enterprise in a shortage economy often encounters difficulties in acquiring all the inputs called for by its production plan, certain input constraints become binding earlier than scheduled. This means that production bottlenecks develop, and the enterprise has to engage in alteration in the composition of output, reduction in the volume or quality of output, and forced substitution of inputs, which means that enterprises use whatever inputs they can obtain to produce output. Enterprises failing to obtain the required combination of goods will acquire more of what is actually produced. All these cases are instances of forced substitution. In a resource-constrained economy forced substitution is a form of instantaneous adjustment to shortage. That is why the shortage model does not formulate discrete functions of demand and supply, and does not attempt to state the degree of shortage on the basis of differences in the two.

So far the motivation of the director in the shortage model seems to be compatible with output-maximising behaviour, or even with bonus maximisation as output performance generally is most important for bonus payments. However, as the director knows that high production in the present period will induce higher production plans in the following period, it seems logical to assume that he aims at fulfilling the plan but not over-fulfilling it. Thus, rather than assuming maximising behaviour, in the shortage model the enterprise is described as if it aimed at fulfilling the plan as exactly as possible.

The chronic and pervasive shortage environment affects the behaviour of all economic institutions in ways that both intensify and reproduce shortage. Due to the unique features of the 'supply-constrained' economic system the primary cause of shortage is the quantity-driven behaviour of economic institutions, which means they consistently strive to increase output on the basis of extensive growth, that is by increasing the use of inputs rather than increasing productivity. Kornai emphasises that the quantity drive, the general input hoarding tendency and shortage are linked together in a mutually amplifying self-generating process. 'Expansion drive' joins quantity drive and hoarding tendency in creating the 'almost insatiable' demand for inputs. Prices play only a secondary role in explaining developments in the shortage economy. Since prices are fixed, agents must respond and adjust to other types of economic signal. Such signals, collectively referred to as 'quantity signals', include information and observations about stocks, orders, queue lengths, waiting times, the availability of substitutes.

Thus, the shortage model of the socialist enterprise rests on three major assumptions. First, the markets for the output of the enterprise are characterised by chronic shortages. Second, the budget constraints of enterprises are assumed to be soft. Third, enterprises have a quantity drive. The behaviour of producing enterprises is the primary cause of the initiation and reproduction of shortage. On the other hand, central authorities are assumed to be actors of secondary importance, to have a paternalistic attitude to subordinates, and to tolerate the quantity drive, investment hunger, and slack budget discipline of enterprises.

4.2.2 Output-Maximising Models and Shortage

Kornai stresses the importance of the motivation of the socialist enterprise director.[24] He argues that the director voluntarily strives to increase production as he aims at fulfilling the expectations of his superiors to win their acknowledgement. As long as physical output is considered to be the most important criteria of success, it will also constitute the critical indicator by which the work of the enterprise director is assessed by his superiors. Kornai's work could be linked to the formal literature which assumes output-maximisation behaviour. He emphasises the importance the behaviour of the socialist enterprise has in generating shortage. In this respect his ideas are not new. The uncertainty of supply and the corresponding tendency to hoard at the enterprise level has been acknowledged by others.

Ames[25] has shown that the output-maximising enterprise will at its best produce at least as much output as the profit-maximising enterprise and that the optimal condition for a profit-constrained output-maximiser occurs where price equals average cost, which falls short of marginal cost. To distinguish between the output-maximiser and the profit-maximiser Ames develops a simple model where the welfare of the enterprise manager is assumed to be a weighted average of output and profits. The result of his analysis shows that, with marginal cost increasing with output, if the welfare of the manager to any extent depends on production as such, this in itself generates a higher output and input demand than does profit maximisation.

Ames's analysis does not contain any constraints, it merely stresses the difference in unconstrained behaviour of an output-maximiser to that of a profit-maximiser. Ames restricts his analysis to the behaviour of the enterprise, but it could just as well be applied to any other institution which has an output plan to fulfil, including the Ministry itself.

The fact that the planning process actually involves at least two stages is often left out in the formal literature. Linz and Martin are an exception.[26] They emphasise that, as the enterprise director does not know the output plans and the input requests of other enterprises, the amount of inputs that he will be allocated as well as the level of the minimum-profit level will at first be uncertain. The actual allocation of inputs may deviate from that which he requested.

Linz and Martin develop a model where this kind of uncertainty is analysed. In the first stage the enterprise manager is assumed to maximise expected utility of output. In the second stage it is assumed that the enterprise maximises constrained output. The analysis shows that the demand for inputs of an enterprise facing uncertainty in the allocation of input plans is greater than input demand under certainty.

Linz and Martin note that others have analysed the effect of tautness in planning without taking into account the enterprise behaviour that leads to the central planners' desire for taut planning. According to them 'tautness' represents the central planning authority's response to observed enterprise behaviour that is due to supply uncertainty, the effects of which they investigate in their model. They do not, however, discuss the causes of supply uncertainty, but merely state that it is a well-documented feature of Soviet economic planning.[27]

Portes[28] analyses the effects on input demand of an output-maximising enterprise under taut planning. By tautness he means the relation between input and output plans.[29] Portes shows that the effectiveness of central planning, or central commands, is higher the higher is the tautness in plans. He observes that the enterprise will normally purchase all of its centrally allocated inputs since quotas are severely limited and the pressure to produce as much as possible is very great, and because experience with breakdowns in the material supply system teaches the enterprise to get as much as it can out of the plan and save any current surplus for future crises. However, he overlooks the fact that the planning process is actually a two-stage procedure. If this is taken into account one could find that the very existence of taut planning in itself causes enterprise managers to overorder inputs.

But tautness in itself also induces another type of uncertainty. While the uncertainty acknowledged by Linz and Martin concerns uncertainty in the input plans allocated to the enterprise, tautness may induce further uncertainty in the input allocation actually received by enterprises. Tautness increases the risk in the enterprise hitting a resource constraint which in turn increases the risk that it will fail to fulfil its output plans, and, hence, its deliveries to other enterprises. The higher the general level of plans, the higher the risk for enterprise failure, and the higher the overall uncertainty in input supply. If the enterprise expects that plans in general are taut it also expects that it will not receive all the inputs that have been allocated in the plans due to failure of other enterprises to fulfil their required deliveries. And, as inputs are scarce within an environment where shortage is a widely existing phenomenon the enterprise cannot count on getting hold of missing inputs elsewhere without difficulties.

To sum up, Ames's analysis indicates that output-maximisation behaviour in itself generates a higher use of inputs than does profit maximisation. Linz and Martin emphasise that as the planning process is actually a two-stage procedure this causes uncertainty in the allocation of inputs. Their analysis shows that the demand for inputs of an enterprise facing uncertainty is greater than under certainty. According to Portes's analysis, tautness in plans is yet another factor which contributes to increased demand for inputs. As the general tautness of plans implies a risk that enterprises are unable to fulfil their obligations, taut planning in itself also incites enterprise managers to overorder inputs. The combined effect of these analyses is to indicate that neoclassical models which assume output-maximising behaviour can assist in explaining the mismanagement of natural resources in the former Soviet Union.

4.2.3 Priority and the Shortage Model

The model of the socialist economy that has been developed by Kornai reflects many aspects of the behaviour and interactions of socialist economic institutions. However, the shortage model has gaps in its coverage and is imprecise in some definitions and specifications of hypotheses.[30] One important criticism of the shortage model to be developed here is that it does not analyse the role of priorities of central authorities in resource allocation.[31] Available evidence suggests that the priorities of decision-makers concerning resource allocation have exerted a major influence on the performance of the different sectors of centrally planned economies.[32] In particular, it appears that the role of central priorities was important during the early years of development of the Soviet economy.[33] If this is taken into account, it seems obvious that central planners played a more active role than postulated in the shortage model.

Priority is an instrument which central planners use to ensure that the most important tasks of an economy can be carried out.[34] The supplies and operating conditions of these tasks are protected from disruptions caused by endogenous problems, exogenous shocks, and plan inconsistencies, in accordance with some ranking by central authorities. This is accomplished through preferential allocation of resources during plan formulation as well as during plan implementation.[35] In an economic system with chronic shortages planners, in particular, have had to be more forceful in priority-linked resource allocations during plan formulation and interventions during the plan implementation period.[36] This implies that the leadership's priorities generate tight supply constraints on less important tasks during plan formulation. Furthermore, the redistribution of resources when plans are implemented causes a tightening of constraints in less important areas and makes the original plans more difficult to fulfil.

In the Soviet Union, the unbalanced growth strategy was established with the adoption of the first Five Year Plan in 1928. This stipulated that growth was to be achieved at an accelerated pace through a drastic increase in capital accumulation, concentration of investment in heavy industry, and expansion of state control in industry and agriculture. Central planners intentionally established output targets that were overambitious relative to available resources and justified them by expecting rapid increases in labour and capital productivity.[37] The period following the adoption of the first Five Year Plan in the Soviet Union was characterised by overambitious plans, emphasis on volume of output rather than quality or efficiency, erratic supplies, and strict discipline.[38] The incentive structure rewarded plan fulfilment in volume terms and inhibited technological innovation; shortages of inputs and bottlenecks in production promoted hoarding of inputs, hiding of reserves from central planners, and an energetic struggle for more investment and other inputs are well-known effects noted by Berliner.[39] Managers in industrial enterprises learned to behave in a manner suitable to their operating conditions at the early stage of the Stalinist system. Thus, the behaviour of directors, which according to Kornai is the primary cause of the shortage economy, is the logical outcome of the rapid industrialisation policy. In effect it was demand as determined by central planners that bred in them a drive to expand the quantity of output and the productive capacity of the enterprise.

Davis has made some original contributions on the interconnections between the traditional shortage model, developed by Kornai, and the central planners' priorities.[40] He uses nine indicators to evaluate the effect of central priorities on performance in the shortage economy. Three of these are modifications of concepts which have been used in the shortage model. Davis assumes that 'hardness of budget constraints', responsiveness to 'tolerance limit violations', and degree of 'shortage intensity' are functions of central priorities. The situation in a low-priority sector would be that the proportionate change in budget allocations would decrease and actual expenditure would be routinely less than planned. In the case of high priority, the opposite conditions would exist. Thus, only the high priority sectors have soft budget constraints. In low-priority sectors, budget constraints are essentially hard. While central authorities would respond immediately when performance of a high-priority sector starts to deteriorate, by allocating additional resources or financial means to that sector, a low-priority sector has no guarantee of such a response. Davis further assumes that while a high-priority sector would have a low shortage intensity, a low-priority sector would be in the inverse situation.

Davis also identifies four indicators which are more directly related to the Soviet-type planning system. These are the fulfilment of plans for output, supplies, and investment, and adequacy of financial norms. In low-priority sectors plans would generally be under-fulfilled and financial norms inadequate, while in high-priority sectors actual plans would be greater than or equal to the planned ones and financial norms adequate to cover the projected supply plan.

In addition, he uses two indicators based on concepts which are used in welfare theory: 'weight in planners' preference functions' and 'relative wage rates'. Davis assumes that if the share of national income of a sector is lower than an international average, the sector would have a low priority, while the inverse relationship would indicate a high priority. Similarly, he assumes that high-priority sectors have generous wages while wages in low-priority sectors would be below the average for the Soviet economy as a whole. He assumes that high priority does not imply that a sector is more efficient, but rather is effective in production because of the priority conditions which allow it to obtain high-quality inputs.

The theoretical arguments concerning the effect of central priorities on performance are supported by empirical studies of the health sector and the defence sector.[41] Davis found that while the former by all criteria had a low-priority ranking in the Soviet Union in the period 1965–85, on the whole, the latter had a high-priority ranking.

Davis also evaluates the validity of the shortage model theoretically and empirically. The theoretical analysis consists of a comparison of ten shortage model hypotheses concerning behaviour with the hypotheses that Davis derives from the concepts of priority. Davis's theoretical analysis indicates that low-priority sectors would be characterised by a high shortage intensity and a relatively hard budget constraint. In contrast, a high-priority sector is minimally afflicted by shortages and has a soft budget constraint. One should therefore not expect to observe both pervasive shortages and a soft budget constraint in the same sector, asserts Davis.[42] He finds that the incorporation of the concept of priority in the shortage model both enriches its description of institutional behaviour in the socialist economy and eliminates certain inconsistencies evident in Kornai's initial formulation.

In the empirical part Davis compares Kornai's hypotheses with actual performance of the Soviet medical sector. He found that most hypotheses were consistent with observable phenomena. There were shortages in output markets, quantity drives, low quality of output, technological problems, forced substitution, production bottlenecks, investment tension and shortages in input markets. One exception was the budget constraint. According to Davis, Soviet medical institutions had relatively hard budget constraints rather than soft ones.

The empirical study of the defence sector shows that the enterprise behaviour was reasonably consistent with shortage-model hypotheses. Despite the various quality control programmes, the output of defence industry enterprises was sometimes of low quality and the technological level was low by international standards. The defence sector was further affected by shortages of intermediate goods and labour, and it had difficulties in obtaining capital equipment. It was also afflicted by production bottlenecks and forced substitution. From the empirical analysis of the defence sector Davis draws the conclusion that high priority was not sufficient to protect this sector from the impacts of shortage-economy processes.

Davis's approach helps to explain differences in performance between various sectors of the Soviet economy. He shows that central priorities have been important for the allocation of resources. Davis also shows, however, that high priority was not enough to protect the military sector from disruption, indicating that developments in production were not completely controlled by central authorities and that priorities were not that important for performance.

Thus, when analysing the role of central priorities it seems appropriate to make a distinction between the importance of priorities for the establishment of a situation and the effect of a change in priorities. Even though priorities were important in the build-up of the Stalinist system, this does not imply that a change in priorities some time after Stalin's death would have had any major effect. Priorities were important in the sense that it would have been difficult to change priority rankings that had been established in the past.

4.2.4 The Effect of Changing Priorities

Davis draws the conclusion that while an increase in priorities to a sector would have minor effects on the performance of that sector, a decrease in priorities might cause an already severe situation to deteriorate substantially.[43] This point needs some further elaboration. Davis's analysis seems to suggest that it would have been very difficult to implement any increase in priorities to a sector in the traditional Soviet system which existed up to the end of 1991. There are, however, two rather different matters at stake here.

One possibility would have been that central planners were really able to implement a change in priorities in the sense that they actually reallocated resources from one activity to another. Davis's approach is suitable for analysing the effect of such a change. If priority increases, the budget constraint becomes softer and shortage intensity decreases. The meaning of a softer budget constraint is that it becomes easier to obtain supplementary finance and real resources if constraints become binding, that central planners would tolerate cost increases, and that there would be a gradual weakening of sanctions for failure. Following Davis's line of thought, this should imply that wages increase and that the fulfilment of production plans, intermediate goods supply plans and investment plans also increases. That is, the reallocation of resources to a sector would increase the effectiveness of that sector, which means that its ability to carry out its tasks will increase.

When it comes to quality of output, high priority was not sufficient to guarantee a high quality of the goods produced. High rejection rates in the high-priority military sector indicated that quality targets were not fulfilled.[44] However, special institutional arrangements to guarantee a high quality of output and the use of several quality control programmes within this sector suggested that central demands on quality were high.[45] An increased priority should, therefore, have ensured that more resources would have been put aside for planning and controlling of quality. However, the incentive to improve quality at the enterprise or at ministerial level would still have been lacking. As long as the seller's market prevailed the director would not have been stimulated to engage in quality-enhancing technological innovation. This implies that high-priority as well as low-priority sectors might have produced goods of low priority, although quality of inputs generally should have been higher in sectors of high priority than in low-priority sectors. Thus, Davis's approach suggests that an increase in priority is not likely to have solved problems of low quality and slow technical change.

If priority targets had to be fulfilled under all circumstances, extra capacity and specialised inputs had to be kept on hand for priority production. Therefore, productivity would have been lower in high-priority sectors than in low-priority sectors.[46] Consequently, an increase in priority would not have solved problems of low productivity. It seems reasonable to assume that if the shortage of a resource was high this should have stimulated resource-saving technical innovations, while if shortage intensity was low, directors would not have felt such an incentive. Thus, if shortage intensity decreased as a consequence of an increased priority, this should have had a negative impact on technical development.

As high-priority sectors are characterised as less productive than low-priority sectors, productivity should decrease as priority increases. If priority decreases the budget constraint becomes harder and shortage intensity increases. However, the deteriorating situation that according to Davis would be the consequence, would partly be offset by an improved productivity. Thus, it is not certain that a lowering of the priority to a sector would have that much of an impact on the performance of that sector.

4.2.5 The Ineffectiveness of Priority Changes

It is also possible that central planners would have been unable to implement a change in priorities because of resistance from the ministerial bureaucracy. It seems reasonable to assume that the large proportion of defence, investment and intermediate goods reflected the priorities of the central leadership in the 1930s.[47] The fact that these proportions were still valid in the early 1990s, might reflect the difficulties of implementing a change in priorities.[48] Similarly, the failure of the seemingly strong efforts to improve the performance of agriculture might suggest that planners were unable to implement a change in priorities.[49]

Davis's approach highlights the difficulties involved in implementing policy changes. As we have seen Davis's analysis of the military sector suggested that high-priority protection mechanisms have not been wholly effective. The fact that the high-priority ranking of the military sector did not have more beneficial effects on performance suggested that central authorities did not completely control development in the Soviet economy, which in turn, reflected the power of shortage-economy processes.

If ministries and enterprises had developed their own objectives they would have resisted changes which were in conflict with their interests. Given supply shortages, ministries would have attempted to develop their own supplies and hoard where necessary. By expanding they could become autarchic and place their own interests above the interests of central planners. As the central power was weakened the effect of new directives would have been weakened as well.

As the 'expansion drive' was stimulated by the uncertainty of supply, it seems reasonable to assume that the incentives to strive for autarchy would have been higher in branches of low priority. Therefore, the effect of changing priorities should have been higher in priority branches than in branches of lower priority.

4.2.6 Conclusions

Kornai might be criticised for not having analysed the effect of priorities. The shortage model is thus incomplete as it does not take priority matters into account. Davis made an important contribution as he added the concept of priority to the shortage model. He showed that priorities were important for the allocation of resources. However, his analysis indicated that high priority was not sufficient to protect a sector from the effects of the shortage economy. This does not imply that priorities were unimportant, but reflects the importance of priorities in the build-up of the Stalinist system and that it was difficult to implement priority changes. It also suggests that if the economic system, which emerged in the 1930s and which remained largely unchanged up to the end of 1991, generated a definite form of institutional behaviour, this behaviour could not have been invalidated by decisions of central planners.

4.3   THE LOW-PRIORITY ENVIRONMENT IN THE SHORTAGE ECONOMY

The shortage-economy approach adjusted to the priority perspective to be used here offers an explanation for the ineffectiveness of environmental programmes as well as for the mismanagement of natural resources. Before the environmental and natural resource implications of the Soviet shortage economy are discussed, the concept of shortage needs to be defined. Kornai does not give an exact definition of shortage. In the shortage model the concept of 'shortage' embraces a large group of phenomena, such as shortages in consumer goods and housing, shortages in producer goods, and it is associated with queuing and waiting in a broad sense of the word. The term 'shortage' is used as if its meaning were self-evident and it is not clear what shortage should be related to. In the present context shortage is defined in relation to the plan. It is defined as the excess of planned demand over supply, where demand, which is determined by central planners is expressed in the form of plan targets.

According to optimal planning models environmental disruption in the Soviet Union would largely have been explained by problems of valuation, problems caused by central planners' mistakes or miscalculations. According to neoclassical approaches environmental disruption would have occurred as it did not affect the bonus of firm managers or ministers, and was not included in the planners' preference functions. The central planners had either failed or simply neglected to create incentives which would have motivated individual producers to take environmental concerns and economise on natural resources. According to the priority approach, environmental disruption would have been explained by the planners' priority of economic growth. The costs of the economic inefficiency of material production were largely borne outside the production sector by the environment. Effectiveness was far more important than efficiency when achieving priority targets. The ineffectiveness of environmental programmes would have been explained by their low priority in the planning and implementation of measures. This approach thus indicates that resources used for environmental conservation would have been used just as productively if there had been greater equity in priority rankings and supply arrangements. Good quality equipment was crucial for the results of measures, but this has not been allocated to low-priority environmental activities in the first place.

According to the shortage model, environmental disruption was a consequence of the soft budget constraint of enterprises, which made pollution charges, fines for environmental violations and charges for the use of natural resources ineffective. Due to the unique features of the resource-constrained economy, environmental disruption was also explained by the quantity-driven behaviour of economic institutions and environmental protection agencies. Environmental programmes were ineffective as they were hit by general shortage phenomena. They would have suffered especially from a low technological level, low quality of environmental equipment and forced substitution.

Davis modifies the shortage approach by arguing that only high-priority sectors have soft budget constraints. Accordingly, because of their low priority, budgets for environmental protection activities should have been quite hard and shortage intensity relatively high. Planners would simply have neglected environmental protection until the environmental situation had become serious enough to affect priority activities and they would not respond to information about shortages of environmental equipment by allocating additional resources for environmental purposes. Similarly, planners would have neglected problems of natural resource use until their depletion started to affect priority sectors. According to Davis's approach, increased priority to environmental conservation would have implied more resources to protect the environment and to reduce the waste of natural resources. However, the increased priority would not have had that much effect on performance because of the power of shortage-economy processes. Even if planners were able to redistribute resources in favour of environmental protection, problems of low quality and slow technical development would have made measures ineffective. When it comes to the use of natural resources, increased priority would have meant that planners would have wanted to achieve an improved productivity. To accomplish this a change in behaviour would have been necessary and efficiency would have had to become more important than effectiveness. A change of behaviour would thus have called for a change of system.

4.4 CONCLUSIONS

In this chapter various approaches to the analyses of centrally planned economies along with the relevance of these approaches for explaining environmental disruption in the Soviet Union have been discussed. A common feature of optimal planning models, neoclassical models and input–output models is that central planners are assumed to attempt to attain efficiency in resource allocation. This view of the centrally planned economy is compatible with the approach which focused on problems of valuation in explaining environmental disruption in the Soviet Union. Accordingly, the system did not work in the way it was intended to and imbalances were the result of failures of the system. However, if one focuses on the fact that resource allocation was directed by plans instead of markets, and that decision-making was based on administrative rules rather than economic incentives, it appears that many assumptions which are applied are not relevant for centrally planned economies. Nevertheless, neoclassical models which assume output-maximising behaviour help to explain how emphasis on output performance, uncertainty and taut planning, which are all specific features of the shortage model, would increase the use of natural resources.

The alternative, which is chosen in this study, is to assume that central planners ignored economic balance and that chronic disequilibrium in markets and shortages were parts of a conscious policy. This assumption is a cornerstone in the priority approach and it is implicit in the shortage-economy approach. Kornai pointed out the influence of shortages on economic behaviour and the emergence of powerful low-level processes in a socialist economy that were imperfectly controlled by the centre. The emphasis placed on producers in the explanation of economic phenomena is one of the features that distinguishes the shortage model. However, Kornai seems to have neglected the fact that the behavioural pattern of socialist enterprises, which he believes to be the primary factor behind the shortage economy, was determined during the early stage of development when industrial managers were under continual pressure from superior authorities to increase output and fulfil over-ambitious plans. The behavioural pattern of the Soviet enterprise was thus determined in the 1930s, when the economic system that largely existed up to 1991 was created. Hence, the shortage model might essentially be derived from past policies.

If this is taken into account, it seems obvious that the demand of central planners played a more active role than postulated in the shortage model. One problem with the shortage-economy approach – as it was originally designed – is thus that it did not take into account matters of priority. Davis has in this respect made an important contribution as he applies the concept of priority to Kornai's theory of the shortage economy. We have chosen to apply his ideas, and view the Soviet economy as a shortage economy, adapted to take the low priority of environmental protection into account.

Davis's approach helps to explain observed differences in performance between different sectors in the Soviet economy. He shows that central priorities were important for the allocation of resources. However, although priorities have been important for the establishment of such differences in performance, this does not imply that a change in priorities would have changed the situation. Davis's empirical investigation of the defence sector suggests that high-priority sectors also produced goods of low quality and had a slow technical development by international standards. This suggests that problems of quality and low technological level of environmental equipment would not have been solved by an increased priority. It also suggests that the effect of new central directives on environmental protection and natural resource use would have been weak. A change in the economic system would thus also have been required to solve the environmental problems in an efficient way.

NOTES

1   See Davis and Charemza (eds) (1989), pp. 17, 22–3.
2   Four recent works on priority in the socialist economy are Ericson (1988), Davis (1988 and 1989) and Oxenstierna (1990).
3   See Ellman (1971); and Sutela (1984).
4   Heal (1973).
5   See Treml, Kostinsky and Gallik (1973); Gallik, Heinemeier, Kostinsky, Treml and Tretyakova (1984); Tretyakova and Birman (1976).
6   Berliner (1957 and 1976); Granick (1960); Feiwel (1965).
7   Ames (1965); Ward (1967).
8   Freris (1984).
9   See Freris (1984), Chapter 3, and Oxenstierna (1990), Chapter 6, for an overview of the major Western works on the Soviet enterprise.
10 Davies (1980), pp. 165, 465 and 478.
11 Kornai (1980).
12 Davis (1989), p. 429; Ericson (1988).
13 Ericson (1988).
14 Oxenstierna (1990).
15 See further below for a discussion of Kornai's model.
16 Davis (1989).
17 Grossman (1953); Bergson (1953); Granick (1954).
18 For instance, Hunter (1961) and Jasnay (1962) focused on problems of disequilibrium in planning, while Berliner (1957) and Kornai (1959) concentrated on disequilibrium problems within industry. For analyses of disequilibrium concerning consumption, see Chapman (1963). In Holzman (1960) disequilibrium problems within the monetary system are investigated.
19 Kornai (1971).
20 See also Davis and Charemza (1989), pp. 11–12 for references.
21 See Hare (1988), Kemme (1988) and Lacko (1988) for detailed, critical surveys of their characteristics and applications.
22 Kornai, who has proven himself elsewhere to be an able mathematician, did not find a mathematical model to be practical in the particular context of explaining resource allocation in the Soviet shortage economy. A non-mathematical approach will be used here as well.
23 Kornai (1980), p. 309.
24 Kornai (1980), p. 63.
25 Ames (1965).
26 Linz and Martin (1982).
27 Linz and Martin (1982), p. 24.
28 Portes (1969).
29 Portes (1969), p. 199.
30 See Davis and Charemza (1989), pp. 22–3 for an overview of criticism of Kornai's ideas.
31 See Davis (1989), p. 429 for an overview of the major work in this field.
32 Gregory and Stuart (1981), pp. 180–81.
33 Carr and Davies (1969); Zaleski (1971).
34 Gregory and Stuart (1981), p. 180.
35 Davis (1989), p. 430.
36 Davis (1988).
37 Davis and Charemza (1989), p. 7. See also Zaleski (1971, 1980).
38 Ellman (1971); Zaleski (1980).
39 Berliner (1957).
40 Davis (1988 and 1989).
41 Ibid.
42 Davis (1989), p. 457.
43 Davis (1988), p. 90.

44   Davis (1988), p. 52.
45   Davis (1988), pp. 50–51.
46   Ericson (1988), p. 31.
47   Gregory and Stuart (1981), p. 128.
48   Oxenstierna (1990), pp. 73–4.
49   See Hedlund (1984 and 1989).

5. Environmental Performance in the Shortage Economy

In this chapter the shortage model developed in the previous chapter is used to analyse environmental disruption. An attempt is made here to evaluate the validity of this approach so as to explain the ineffectiveness of environmental programmes in the Soviet economy. As noted above, Davis modifies three assumptions from the shortage model to take priority into account. These were the assumptions concerning the budget constraint, resource allocation responsiveness to violations of performance norms and degree of shortage intensity. In Sections 5.1–5.3 the hypotheses concerning low-priority sectors that Davis derives from these assumptions are compared with evidence about actual performance and their environmental implications are investigated. Thus, in the first section of this chapter the idea of a soft budget constraint as formulated in the traditional shortage model is revised to take into account the low-priority case, here concerning environmental protection. Priority-linked resource-allocation responsiveness to environmental disruption and its environmental implications are then analysed in Section 5.2. In this context an attempt is made to distinguish a pattern for resource allocation to environmental protection. The effects of the high shortage intensity for environmental equipment are analysed in Section 5.3. One such effect is forced substitution and an investigation is made into environmental implications. In Section 5.4, the effect of changing priorities with respect to environmental protection in the shortage economy is discussed and in the final section, conclusions are drawn regarding the causes of environmental disruption in the Soviet Union.

5.1 THE BUDGET CONSTRAINT

One of Kornai's concepts that has attracted a lot of attention is that of the soft budget constraint.[1] In *Economics of Shortage* Kornai creates the impression that the budget constraints of all institutions producing goods and services in a socialist economy are relatively soft, that is non-binding. He sees this as a general aspect of the Soviet economy and does not discuss whether it is likely to be more prevalent in certain branches of the economy, for certain inputs.

In later works, Kornai develops his ideas of the soft budget constraint. In one article, for example, he argues that the hardness or softness of the budget constraint reflects an attitude of the plant manager.[2] When the enterprise manager submits his production plan to the central planning authority, this includes a request for allocated inputs. According to Kornai's line of thought, this request is affected by the director's expectations of the relative softness of the budget constraint. These expectations would in turn depend upon the director's evaluation of the stochastic properties of recurrent events. The softer the director perceives the budget constraint to be, the less attention he will pay to input prices, and the less relative input prices will affect his choice of inputs. That is, he sees the constraint as an *ex ante* constraint which is related more to the enterprise director's expectations than to the preferences of planners. With such a perspective, however, the representation of hierarchical relations that is assumed in *Economics of Shortage* appears to be oversimplified.

In one of his articles, however, Kornai acknowledges that priority should influence the degree of budget hardness.[3] Kornai further seems to ignore the fact that the financial plan is a two-stage procedure just like the production plan. For conceptual reasons, the planning of budget allocations for the various inputs should be separated from their implementation or vice versa. Budget constraints could be soft or hard at both stages, or they could be soft in the planning stage, while hard in the implementation stage. Budget constraints could be flexible downwards in the sense that they could grow tighter as the authorities respond to inconsistencies in plans and bottlenecks in production by reallocating resources and financial entitlements on the implementation of plans.

The budgets of institutions in the Soviet economy were calculated using centrally determined financial norms that expressed allowable expenditure for a planned quantity of inputs. There was variability across sectors in the adequacy of these norms with respect to actual input prices that reflected relative priorities.[4] Norms were usually more generous for production of high-priority goods, generating initial budgets sufficient to cover the costs of planned acquisitions of inputs. Whereas, for production of low-priority goods the inverse relationship would have existed. Due to stingy financial norms the initial budget of low-priority units might have been inadequate to cover the actual costs of the projected supply plan.

If one derived a hypothesis about the nature of the budget constraint of socialist environmental protection institutions from the experience of state-financed activities in Western countries, then it would postulate a relatively soft budget. However, the situation should be different in the shortage economy because the central authorities give environmental protection a low priority in the resource allocation process and impose on it relatively severe budgetary limits. In fact, the budget constraints of environmental protection activities could grow 'super hard', or be flexible downwards in a shortage economy in the sense that they could grow tighter in the course of the plan period as the authorities responded to inconsistencies in plans and bottlenecks in production by reallocating resources and financial entitlements. In effect this implies that in the case of environmental protection, because of its low priority actual expenditure would be equal to, or even less than planned, while that of high-priority products would be greater than planned.

Directors were usually unable to transfer funds from one item where there was underspending to another where the budget constraint had become binding.[5] This might have created problems for the directors because market conditions and central provision of supplemental funds varied according to input. The enterprise could have had a soft budget constraint for certain factors of production and a hard one for others. The budget constraints for relatively scarce inputs were more likely to be binding than budgets for inputs that were not considered scarce. The perceived abundance of natural resources in the Soviet Union suggests that budget constraints would have been relatively soft for these, if they had existed. Moreover, as it might have been difficult to distinguish to what extent the results of mining branches depended on their work or on natural or geographic advantages, which were external to the individual enterprise, it seems reasonable to assume that it was particularly difficult to apply strictly binding budget constraints in these branches. This suggests that budget constraints for natural resources would have been soft in high-priority sectors as well as in sectors of low priority. Priority could, however, have affected the use of natural resources indirectly. If budget constraints for other inputs were hard, there would have been an incentive at the enterprise or ministerial level to substitute natural resources for other more scarce inputs whenever this was physically possible. The higher the shortage intensity for investment, labour and material resources, the stronger the incentive to substitute these for natural resources. This suggests that the use of natural resources would have been higher in low-priority sectors than in sectors of high priority. On the other hand, the presumed lower degree of efficiency in high-priority sectors would indicate a higher use of resources in high-priority sectors.

Examination of empirical evidence from the Soviet Union during 1970–88 indicates that initial budgets for environmental protection, to the extent that they existed, were rather tight because of their low-priority ranking and to the utilisation of low wage rates and otherwise stingy financial norms in budget calculations. In 1988 about 490 million roubles were budgeted for environmental tasks; including organs for management and control of the environment, corresponding scientific institutions, ecological education and propaganda. The corresponding budget amounted to 470 million roubles in 1985, indicating an increase of 4.25 per cent in three years, which is very low compared to the increase of almost 19 per cent in overall budget expenditure in the same period.[6] The above-mentioned enforcement system consisted of a number of basin inspectorates, which up to January 1988 were subordinated to at least six different state committees or ministries which considered environmental protection to be sideline issues only.

Evidence suggests that their resources were inadequate to perform their tasks. The budgets of even the best-equipped basin inspectorates were small in relation to the wide range of responsibilities they had. In 1976, their budgets seemed barely adequate in high-priority areas for personnel as well as for resources, not to mention all their enforcement and reporting tasks.[7]

The principle of allocating financial budgets at ministerial level adopted up until 1988 implied that funds for environmental protection were not planned for separately as were all the other tasks of ministries. The fact that funds were not allocated to environmental tasks unless other demands had been satisfied strongly suggests that these tasks were the first to be hit by general shortage phenomena.[8] Moreover, as funds for environmental protection were returned to the state unspent unless human and material resources were allocated in the plan,[9] actual expenditure was likely to be less than planned. In the case of air protection, for example, about 80 per cent of budgets went unspent every year between 1981 and 1988.[10] In some cases, as funds were not allocated at the planning stage, there were simply no budget constraints to exceed.

5.1.1 The Role of Prices

As the soft budget constraint implies that demand for inputs is not restricted by cost considerations, the role of money and prices tends to be weak in a socialist economy. Consequently, a change in relative prices of inputs is assumed not to have much influence on the demand for these. Kornai believes that the investment input decision of the traditional socialist enterprise is not responsive to the relative price of inputs. The criterion of cost-minimising is not important when selecting technological alternatives. The interest rate has no influence on the demand for investment, and the enterprise as well as its higher authorities are insensitive to relative factor prices in the choice of technology. Furthermore, methods of mathematical planning play a minor role in the actual selection of investment actions. Even though efficiency calculations made at shadow prices may exert some influence on allocators, this influence is taken to be much weaker than non-price criteria. It is assumed that profitability criteria do not have any influence on investment decisions in the traditional socialist economic system.[11]

The application of selective criteria for investment is, in the shortage model, built on non-price signals. Such signals are embodied partly by numbers and data, and partly by the reactions of those participating in the allocation process, in other words, planners and managers argue, bargain and 'fight' over resources. Subjective factors, such as the prestige of directors, contacts and so on, are also part of the selection of investment as well as lobbies in the form of mutually supporting managers.[12]

If budget constraints are relatively hard as a result of low priority, the effect of changes in relative prices should be stronger than usual. Thus, pollution charges, fines for environmental violations and charges for the use of natural resources should have had a stronger effect on behaviour in low-priority sectors than in branches of higher priority.[13]

5.1.2 Conclusions

One consequence of applying Davis's line of thought is that the assumption of the soft budget constraint as formulated in the original shortage model has to be revised. The situation with respect to environmental protection seems to have been compatible with Davis's ideas. Because of its low priority in the Soviet shortage economy, budget constraints in the case of environmental protection were likely to be rather hard. This implied that the planned increases in budget expenditure on environmental protection were relatively low. The redistribution of resources in the implementation of plans caused a tightening of constraints for environmental tasks and made the original plans more difficult to fulfil. The meaning of the hard budget constraint was not only that budgets could not be exceeded, but also that budgetary means reserved for environmental purposes were confiscated in case the needed environmental equipment was not provided. Up until 1988 it could be said that budget constraints for environmental targets were likely to be tight in low-priority branches. As in the implementation stage in the presence of shortage, there was a risk that if resources were siphoned off from low-priority production to production of high priority, then low-priority branches were not likely to have budgetary resources left for environmental concerns. The fact that budgets for environmental protection have been planned for separately at ministerial level since 1988 might indicate that its priority had increased. It might also indicate that the difference between high-priority and low-priority sectors with respect to budgetary resources for environmental protection had decreased.

When it comes to natural resources, however, the arguments made here were in conflict with Davis's approach. It was argued that the budget constraint was likely to be soft for natural resources, regardless of priority.

5.2   UNRESPONSIVENESS OF RESOURCE ALLOCATION TO TOLERANCE LIMIT VIOLATIONS

In the selection of investment, the principle of 'balanced relationships of the national economy' is thought by Kornai to play an important role. This means a desire for systematic mutual adjustment of future output and input, and resources would be allocated by means of a 'simple rule of thumb' in accordance with permanent proportions. That is, every claimant would in principle be given the same share of the investment quota as he received in previous years.[14] This theory for resource allocation is supported by Soviet practice. In the Soviet Union planning 'from the achieved level' was a well-known expression.[15] The principle of planning 'from the achieved level' was used in the setting of targets for output as well as for allocation of investment and other inputs for all kinds of tasks throughout the economy. The same applied to costs of production, the financial plan and so forth. It simply meant that plan-indicators were derived by adding a few per cent to the figures for the previous period, implying that Soviet planners worked with input–output coefficients which reflected the past.[16]

An important problem with this type of allocation mechanism is that it tends to reinforce established proportions. One important signal that would influence allocation and its deviation from habitual proportion is information about shortage. The more intensive the shortage, the better the chances of the proposal's acceptance, states Kornai. If the claimant of resources could prove that there was a serious shortage of his product, it would improve the chances for approval by the allocator.

In the case of environmental disruption, it was normally the public or some production activity which ended up being afflicted. The public has in recent years shown discontent with the environmental situation in various places within the Soviet Union by demonstrating against the emissions of particular industries.[17]

In the case of a market economy, the lack of price signals as responses to environmental disruption provides an explanation for why investment is not allocated to the environment. In the centrally planned economy investment is not allocated to environmental protection because non-price signals are not strong enough. According to Kornai's ideas, central planners neglected environmental disruption as long as it remained within the 'tolerance limits' (for example, some maximum level of environmental pollution above the official targets or norms), and allocated resources to combat it only when these had been exceeded. The increase in expenditures for environmental programmes at various times and the integration of environmental tasks within the government structure would accordingly indicate such a response. The fact that central authorities have in later years decided to close down some environmentally harmful activities would point to a similar reaction.[18]

Although Kornai suggests that responsiveness to tolerance limit violations is a universal rule, its validity should in reality vary between activities in accordance with their priority.[19] According to Davis, there should be an immediate resource-allocation response to a tolerance limit violation for high-priority goods. But in a low-priority area Davis assumes such a reaction to be less likely. If resource-allocation responsiveness depends on priority rather than on intensity of shortage, then a low priority to environmental protection suggests that the social costs for environmental disruption could remain above 'tolerance limits' for extended periods.

In order to evaluate priority-linked resource-allocation responsiveness to environmental disruption an appropriate social cost indicator needs to be defined. A rather abstract indicator, which obviously is hard to measure, is 'environmental quality'. The corresponding tolerance limit would be the lower limit of an environmental quality index. If this is then defined as the official norms for the maximum permissible concentration of pollutants in the air and water, or some minimum level above these, the serious violations of such norms would suggest that the authorities have been prepared to tolerate high social costs in the environmental area and that the tolerance limit has been violated for a long time without evoking any response by the leadership.[20]

The share of environmental investments of total state investments and its proportionate change are chosen here as rough indicators of the resource-allocation responsiveness of central planners. State capital investment for environmental protection has increased (see Table 5.1).

In order to get an idea of whether central planners have responded to environmental violation, the proportionate change in investment allocations can be compared. An increasing proportionate change from the time the tolerance limit was first violated would indicate high priority.[21] Such a trend is not found in the allocation of investments to environmental protection (see Table 5.1, column 2). An increasing proportionate change in the allocation of environmental investments in the 1980s might indicate that planners were responding to environmental violations when the priority of the activity in question was high enough or when the pollution of this industry was sufficiently high.[22]

The circumstances that environmental investments showed some variability might indicate that central planners have reacted when the environmental situation has become serious enough. The fact that state capital investments for environmental conservation increased by 48 per cent between the ninth and tenth Five Year Plan, while total state investments increased by 27.5 per cent during the same period might then support this hypothesis (compare columns 2 and 4).[23] In particular, increasing shares of total investment devoted to environmental protection despite its low priority suggested that the situation had become an impediment to development in high-priority sectors. If the deteriorating public health had started to affect high-priority activities, this might for example have caused central allocators to react. High pollution levels in the main industrial areas have reportedly caused serious health problems and thereby contributed to labour shortage in high-priority sectors.[24] Empirical data suggest that the serious environmental situation would, together with dietary deficiencies and poor medical services explain why in 1990 less than half of draft-age men were fit for military duty. That is, increasing environmental expenditures might indicate that planners responded when environmental decay had begun to affect the Soviet Union's military strength.[25]

Table 5.1: Allocation of environmental investments as a response to
violations of 'tolerance limits' for environmental disruption

Year	Million Roubles (1)	Proportionate change (2)	Share of total investments (3)	Proportionate change in total inv.
1971–75	1,458		1.30	
1976–80	2,164	+0.48	1.51	+0.28
1981–85	2,224	+0.03	1.32	+0.17
1986–90	2,963	+0.33	1.38	+0.25
of which:				
1981	1,845		1.33	+0.04
1982	1,854	0	1.29	+0.04
1983	1,764	−0.05	1.16	+0.06
1984	2,285	+0.30	1.00	+0.51
1985	2,486	+0.09	1.38	−0.22
1986	2,615	+0.05	1.35	+0.08
1987	2,663	+0.02	1.30	+0.06
1988	3,122	+0.17	1.43	+0.06
1989	3,255	+0.04	1.42	+0.05
1990	3,158	−0.03	1.37	+0.01

Notes: (1) Average per year

(2) $\frac{i(t+1) - i(t)}{i(t)}$, where i is environmental investments.

(3) $\frac{i(t)}{I(t)}$, where I is total state capital investments.

Sources: *Narkhoz* (1982), p. 393; *Narkhoz* (1983), p. 361; *Narkhoz* (1984), pp. 359 and 381; *Narkhoz* (1986), pp. 367 and 387; *Narkhoz* (1989), pp. 252 and 556; *Narkhoz* (1990), pp. 254 and 534; *Narkhoz* (1991), pp. 277 and 551.

If the increases in particular years were consequences of responses to tolerance limits violations, this might indicate that there had been gradual shifts in relative priorities in favour of environmental protection in these years. The increase in expenditures in the late 1980s could also reflect an increase in attention, which may in turn be due to the fact that measures taken had not accomplished the intended results. Notice the relatively large increase in investments that occurred in 1988. They were 17 per cent higher than in the previous year. Together with other measures in 1988 this suggests that environmental protection increased in priority in that particular year.

Table 5.2: Resource allocation responsiveness to tolerance limit violation for environmental disruption

Year	Million Roubles (1)	Proportionate change (2)	Share of Net Material Product Utilised (3)[26]
1981	6,155		1.28
1982	6,146	0	1.20
1983	6,236	+0.01	1.16
1984	6,715	+0.08	1.20
1985	6,644	−0.01	1.17
1986	7,005	+0.05	1.22
1987	7,267	+0.04	1.24
1988	7,988	+0.10	1.29
1989	8,745	+0.09	1.31
1990	9,842	+0.13	1.40

Notes: (1)   Exclusive of investments

       (2) $\dfrac{c(t+1) - c(t)}{c(t)}$, where c is environmental expenditures.

       (3) $\dfrac{c(t)}{G(t)}$, where G is national income.

Sources: *Narkhoz* (1982), p. 393; *Narkhoz* (1983), p. 361; *Narkhoz* (1984), p. 381; *Narkhoz* (1985), p. 404; *Narkhoz* (1986), p. 411; *Narkhoz* (1989), pp. 16 and 252; *Okhrana...* (1989), p. 9; *Narkhoz* (1990), pp. 15 and 254; *Narkhoz* (1991), pp. 13 and 277.

Expenditures for use and maintenance of environmental equipment and installations (exclusive of investments) exhibited a similar development to that of investment outlays (see Table 5.2). A pattern of slightly increasing proportionate changes in expenditures can be deduced (see column 2). In addition, the environmental expenditures percentage of net material product utilised had increased, a development which is more compatible with high priority and a soft budget constraint than low priority and a hard budget (see column 3).

The intervention of central planners might in some cases indicate that they reacted to signals of tolerance limit violations in these particular cases, while on other occasions they did not. Reactions might for instance have depended on whether the polluting activity was considered important, whether its pollution was sufficiently high and whether it was situated in a high-priority area. The closing of a number of paper mills might indicate that the centre reacted when the activity in question was not important enough. The fact that some chemical industries have been closed, thus aggravating an already serious shortage of pharmaceuticals, might for instance reflect the low priority attributed to public health. The seemingly strong efforts to clean up after the Chernobyl disaster might indicate that the accident happened in an area which was considered to be relatively important. It could also have been that actions were taken simply because this was an accident of global interest. That the ecological catastrophe in the Aral Sea region, however, has gone practically unnoticed in terms of counter-measures, might indicate that from the central planners' point of view it was situated in a low-priority area.[27]

To sum up, resource allocation to environmental protection has not been completely consistent with Davis's ideas concerning low-priority sectors. On the contrary, increasing shares of total investment and national income devoted to environmental protection suggest that planners have reacted to the serious violations of norms by allocating more resources for environmental purposes. However, they have responded by allocating resources to the worst-polluting ministries rather than to the most seriously affected regions. This means that they have in effect responded to the violations of norms for permissible emissions rather than to violations of norms for the maximum concentration of pollutants. This pattern for resource allocation to environmental protection suggests that the situation must have been serious and pollution of high-priority sectors high, and/or, high-priority sectors had soft budgets for environmental equipment. Given the low priority to environmental protection, this suggests that the environmental situation had become serious enough to affect high-priority sectors. Problems in recruiting a sufficient number of healthy young men to do their military service supported this hypothesis. The circumstances that planners appear to have been more responsive to problems of air pollution than to water problems further suggest that they perceived the former to be more serious than the latter.

5.3 HIGH SHORTAGE INTENSITY AND FORCED SUBSTITUTION

One implication of the soft budget constraint is that central planners allocate additional resources to a sector when the degree of shortage intensity exceeds its 'normal value'.[28] Davis modifies this assumption by arguing that the normal state of shortage would vary by sector in accordance with priorities.[29] If the budget constraint is hard as a consequence of low priority, this should in effect imply that the sector has been neglected even though it is seriously affected by shortage and that the intensity of shortage is likely to be high. Davis's approach further implies that if the shortage intensity is high as a consequence of low priority, this causes problems of plan fulfilment. One way to adjust to shortages is forced substitution.[30] The aim here is to verify the assumed relationship between a high shortage intensity and forced substitution in the case of environmental protection.

5.3.1 Plan Fulfilment and Quality

One of the primary reasons for the existence of the priority system was to guarantee the fulfilment of the initial output plans of important goods.[31] Given limitations on resources this commitment meant that in low-priority units actual output was often lower than original plan targets. To assess the degree of shortage intensity of environmental conservation on the basis of the fulfilment of output plans is difficult because of ambiguity in the definition and measurement of output, and lack of data.

If the output plan is defined as the established norms for pollution levels, it is clear that most industrial centres in the Soviet Union were unable to fulfil their quotas in the 1980s.[32] Empirical data suggest that health norms for air pollution, pollution of water and waste treatment were not fulfilled in 1985–90 (see Table 5.3). According to official statistics, in 1990 the level of water pollution in the public water supply system complied with health norms in 80 per cent of the investigated samples, when measured by chemical indicators. The corresponding figure for water quality tests by bacteriological indicators was 88 per cent. In the case of waste treatment sanitary norms were down to 53 per cent.[33]

Table 5.3: *Fulfilment of health norms for pollution levels in 1985–90 (in per cent)*[34]

	1985	1988	1990
Air pollution	76	–	82
Water pollution by chemical indicators	74	82	80
Water pollution by bacteriological ind.	88	89	88
Waste treatment	50	53	35

Sources: *Okhrana Okruzhayushchei Sredy i Ratsionalnoe Ispolzovanie Prirodnykh Resursov v SSSR* (1989), pp. 36–7; *Soyuznye Respubliki Osnovnye Ekonomicheskie i Sotsialnye Pokazateli* (1991), pp. 135–6.

Similarly, if output is defined in terms of reduction in pollution levels, then the rise in emissions of waste water in the Soviet Union from 15.1 km³ in 1986, 20.6 km³ in 1987, 28.4 km³ in 1988 and 32.6 km³ in 1989 to 33.6 km³ in 1990 clearly indicates an underachievement.[35] Quite a number of enterprises for instance did not fulfil water protection measures in 1987, which might explain why plans for reduction of waste water were not achieved.[36] In 1981–88, although emissions of air pollutants decreased, plans to reduce air pollutants were consistently not fulfilled.[37]

Output might also be defined in terms of purification of emissions. In 1980–88, according to Soviet official statistics, plans for purification of waste water were generally not fulfilled (see Table 5.4). However, while plan fulfilment in quantity terms increased from 65 per cent in 1980 to 81 per cent in 1988, plan fulfilment in quality terms actually decreased from 71 per cent to 37 per cent in the same period. This suggests that the increased degree of plan fulfilment in the case of water purification has been achieved through quantity-for-quality substitution.

Table 5.4: Plan fulfilment; amount of waste water subject to purification in 1980–88

	1980	1985	1988
Plan (billion m^3)	37.0	38.6	40.3
Actual amount s. t. treatment (billion m^3)	24.0	31.4	32.6
Actual amount as % of plan	64.9	81.3	80.9
of which:			
unsatisfactorily purified (billion m^3)	7.0	9.0	20.5
in %	29.2	28.7	62.9
satisfactorily purified (billion m^3)	17.0	22.4	12.1
in %	70.8	71.3	37.1

Source: Okhrana Okruzhayushchei Sredy i Ratsionalnoe Ispolzovanie Prirodnykh Resursov v SSSR (1989), p. 62.

According to official Soviet statistics, in 1989 about 40 per cent of the investigated samples of waste water subject to treatment were inadequately purified. The reasons given were that either the load of waste water exceeded the capacity of treatment facilities or equipment suffered from technological shortcomings.[38] The quality of purification appeared to be lower in sectors of low priority than in high-priority sectors. In the medical industry, which belonged to the low-priority public health sector, only seven per cent of the treated waste water was adequately purified to comply with quality targets.[39] Within heavy industry, plan fulfilment with respect to quality of water purification ranged between 48 and 74 per cent in the same year, while in light industry, targets were fulfilled to just 29 per cent.[40] The lower degree of plan fulfilment with respect to quality in low-priority sectors might suggest that the quality targets they faced were higher and/or that their performance was relatively bad. One exception was the coal industry, which, although belonging to the high-priority heavy industry and being the heaviest water polluter in industry, nevertheless fulfilled quality targets to only eleven per cent.[41] This might reflect the general inefficiency of high-priority production.[42]

The distinction between output and input is not always apparent. Output might for instance be defined as the amount of treated water, while installations for purifying water would be an input. One way to estimate roughly the output of environmental conservation is to use indicators based on inputs. Increased expenditures for state capital investments and equipment for environmental protection might have increased environmental conservation. If, however, the upward trends in quantities of inputs have not been matched by similar advances in quality, there might well have been a substitution of quantity for quality. The low priority of environmental protection suggests that the increases in investments that have taken place have been in equipment of low quality.

The use of indicators based on inputs to estimate output of environmental conservation might thus prove to be misleading. As has been shown, purification facilities have not been working properly.[43] In the case of the purification of emissions into the air, for instance, a comparison between developments of output and input suggests that purification devices have been ineffective. Even though purification devices were installed, they sometimes did not work at all. This is where enforcement problems came in. While central authorities double-checked on output performance by means of 'control by the rouble',[44] it would have been more difficult to control environmental performance.

5.3.2 Non-Fulfilment of Plans for Investment and Supply

Another major function of priorities was to protect the initially planned supplies of intermediate goods and investment destined for production of important goods from disruptions caused by endogenous and exogenous factors.[45] This meant that the planners wanted to ensure that the actual allocation of inputs to high-priority units was not less than the quantities originally planned. Conversely, a low-priority unit would not have been so well protected and would therefore have experienced chronic shortages of inputs. As non-fulfilment of output plans implied a shortage of inputs and investment resources, it seems plausible that the shortage of resources for environmental protection was relatively high. The high shortage intensity might further have implied that an input of inferior quality would have been substituted for a planned one.

Despite their modest nature and although plan fulfilment increased in the second half of the 1980s, in 1981–90 investment plans for environmental protection throughout the Soviet Union were generally not fulfilled.[46] In 1990, investment plans were fulfilled to 81 per cent for the Soviet Union as a whole. Investment plans for air protection and water protection were fulfilled to 78 per cent.[47] Throughout the 1980s, many enterprises and ministries did not fulfil their plans for installations of water purification systems and air protection facilities.[48]

In 1988 investment plans for environmental protection were not fulfilled in any of the 15 republics.[49] The plan for the construction of waste water control facilities throughout the USSR was fulfilled to only 59 per cent; the Ministry for Chemical Industry completed only 13 per cent of its norm, the Ministry of Atomic Energy, 27 per cent, while Georgia satisfied only 12 per cent of its norm, Azerbaidzhan two per cent and Kazakhstan one per cent.[50] In some industries no parts of the plans were realised in practice.[51]

Available evidence does generally suggest that in the 1980s, the record of investment plan fulfilment in environmental protection was worse than the mean for the economy as a whole.[52] If the modest nature of investment plans for environmental protection is taken into account, it indicates that the shortage intensity has been higher than average.

5.3.3 Problems in Recruiting Labour

Hypothesising that environmental conservation was of low priority and that the budget constraint was hard makes one assume that there were also problems of labour recruitment for environmental institutions and that the labour shortage was relatively high. There are two aspects to this problem. First, one might at the planning stage assume that the allocated wage fund would have been rather stingy. Second, with wage rates and other benefits being below average, it would have been difficult to attract the necessary labour, especially in an environment where labour shortage was a widely recognised phenomenon.[53] People working in environmental inspectorates should preferably be relatively highly qualified. However, people with the required qualifications were presumably able to find more attractive jobs. The Moscow–Oka Inspectorate has had difficulty in attracting qualified personnel. In 1976, most of the inspectors working there, including the chief inspector and his chief engineer, were retired military officers, and many of the everyday functions of the basin inspectorates were carried out by volunteers.[54]

Employees at environmental inspectorates would on the other hand have had good opportunities to earn a lot of money from bribes. Bribing was an important ingredient of the Soviet economy, and making money from bribes was considered to be more acceptable than earning money in other ways. Since money income had a limited role in the Soviet economy, working conditions often played a more important role in attracting potential employees than did wages and bonuses.

5.3.4 A Quantity Drive at the Expense of Quality

Plan fulfilment must not be mixed up with the tendency of administrators of institutions to strive for continuous increases in the quantity of output. The non-fulfilment of plans for environmental conservation does not mean that there has not been a 'quantity drive' in the performance of these tasks.[55] On the contrary, judging by Soviet statistics, there has been a considerable quantity drive. The quantity drive further appears to be most significant in sectors of high priority.[56]

The quantity drive of environmental protection is illustrated in Table 5.5. It shows that, while outputs did not generally increase by more than 35 per cent in 1980–90, if there was any increase at all,[57] the increases in inputs were 50 per cent or more.

Table 5.5: The quantity drive of environmental protection in 1980–90

Indicator of output	1980	1985	1990	1990 as a % of 1980
Water subject to purification (billion m³)	37.4	38.6	43.5	118
Emissions of air pollutants subject to purification (million tons)	194.4	209.3	199.4	103
Forest planting (million hectares)	1,083.0	983.0	983.2	91
Forest protection (1,000 hectares)	749.0	1,000.0	1,003.0	134
Land improvement (1,000 hectares)	18.0	153.0	159.0	135
Protection of land:				
National Parks	7.0	13.0	23.0	329
Nature Reserves	135.0	150.0	172.0	127
Indicator of input (million roubles)				
Total expenditures	7,400	9,130	13,100	177
Capital investment, of which in	1,845*	2,486	3,158	171
water protection	1,362*	1,683	2,056	151
protection of air	141*	234	409	290

Note: * The figures refer to 1981.

Sources: *Narkhoz* (1982), p. 303; *Narkhoz* (1986), p. 387; *Narkhoz* (1989): p. 252; *Okhrana Okruzhayushchei Sredy i Ratsionalnoe Ispolzovanie Prirodnykh Resursov v SSSR* (1989), pp. 9, 62, 83, 98, 113, 116 and 118; *Narkhoz* (1991), pp. 264, 267–8, 271 and 273.

This might imply that increases in quantity have not taken place as a result of improved technology, but rather at the expense of improved technology and that the increase in quantities of output and inputs was not matched by similar improvements in the quality of environmental facilities. In the case of air protection the fact that the heavy increases in investment outlays have not been matched by corresponding increases in the purification of pollutants supports this hypothesis. While capital investments in the cases of air protection increased by 190 per cent, purification of emissions increased by only three per cent. The fact that, despite a considerable expansion of water treatment facilities, the emissions of polluted water actually increased, suggests that the expansion in quantity of equipment might have taken place at the expense of quality.[58] While the quantity of water subject to treatment in 1980–90 has increased by 18 per cent, the amount that has been properly purified has decreased by 40 per cent in the same period (see Table 5.5). Accordingly, if requirements on quality had not become considerably stricter, there would have been a decrease in the quality of purification. This means that the actual quality of environmental protection would often have fallen below planned values or international standards.

5.3.5 A Sacrifice of By-Products

Developments in the West in the fields of technology and techniques have generated production processes which make use of by-products from their primary production activities. Managers of Western industries are especially encouraged to use by-products if this enables them to increase net revenues. The shortage model implies that the producing enterprise in a resource-constrained economy will exhibit a contrasting behavioural pattern and sacrifice the production of by-products. In their drive to expand the quantity of production, which is measured in terms of tons of output, production and delivery of by-products is excluded. The manager can be rewarded whether or not he carries out contractual obligations in respect of the product mix. Managers thus feel no incentive to produce by-products if this does not increase chances of promotion and other benefits.

In the case of the extraction industries, managers have not been subject to an incentive to make use of by-products from their own extraction processes. They faced plan targets in terms of tons of their primary product, and the waste of natural resources was promoted if this facilitated plan fulfilment. Similarly, in the timber procurement industry, managers would have been obliged only to take care of the trunks, leaving the rest to rot. The quantity drive further explains why the technology for making use of by-products has not been available. As by-products had no value either to the manager or the Ministry, the development of such technology was not promoted. As a consequence, natural resources were likely to be wasted.

5.3.6 Conclusions

The shortage intensity in the case of environmental protection appeared to be consistent with Davis's ideas. Shortage intensity was reflected in the non-fulfilment of plans for environmental protection as well as in plans for capital investments in environmental protection. Empirical evidence suggests that the increased purification of water took place at the expense of quality of purification. While plan fulfilment with respect to the amount of water that was subject to purification has increased, plan fulfilment with respect to quality decreased. While the quantity of water subject to purification increased, its quality appears to have decreased. The fact that environmental protection exhibited a quantity drive despite the high shortage intensity suggests that there has been a quantity-for-quality substitution.

5.4 THE EFFECT OF CHANGING PRIORITIES

One way to gain insight into the relative value of environmental conservation by central decision-makers would be to compare the share of national income utilised for this with an international standard.[59] The data, indicating that in 1988 expenditure for environmental conservation amounted to 1.3 per cent of the national product in the Soviet Union while it amounted to two per cent in the USA, show that in that particular year the relative priority of environmental conservation was lower in the Soviet Union than in the USA.[60] Comparisons of the environmental share of Soviet national income with Western standards also suggest a low though slightly increasing priority.

An idea of whether the priority of environmental protection has changed with time can be formed by comparing the expenditure or investments for environmental protection with the national product. A comparison of the share of environmental expenditures of the national income according to output or expenditure over a given period gives a slight indication of an increased relative priority of environmental conservation in the Soviet economy. While expenditures for environmental conservation, including capital investments, have, according to official Soviet statistics, increased by more than 62 per cent between 1980 and 1989, the national product has increased by 49 per cent, national income by 42 per cent, and utilised national income by 44 per cent during the same period.[61] As the calculation of the Soviet national income is not an undisputable task,[62] it might be more appropriate to compare the share of total state investments devoted to environmental conservation. If the share of national income or total state investments devoted to environmental conservation in the Soviet Union was less than an international standard this would indicate that its priority was low. Similarly, if the share increased with time, this would indicate that its priority had increased.

The use of this indicator and Soviet official statistics indicates that the priority of environmental protection increased slightly during the period 1981–90. However, it also suggests that priority was at approximately the same level in 1988 as in the early 1970s, when environmental programmes were first funded. Up until then, the Soviet Union had hardly any environmental programme worthy of the name. In 1973, annual investment for water quality abruptly rose fivefold, from 300 to 1,500 million roubles.[63] After having increased in the 1970s, the share decreased again (Table 5.1).

Another factor which might indicate that the priority to environmental protection has increased is that the increase in inputs has been substantial even in relative terms in the case of material equipment for environmental protection. The expenditure of basic funds by industries for environmental conservation between 1980 and 1986 has increased by 56 per cent, while basic funds for all expenditures by industry during the same period increased by only 46 per cent.[64] From the early 1970s and up until 1989, state capital investments concerning environmental protection have increased by 123 per cent, of which air protection alone has increased by 179 per cent, while total state capital investments in the Soviet economy increased by 102 per cent during the same period.[65]

A slight indication of a relative increase in the priority of air protection was noticeable. The share of investments in air protection for the whole of the Soviet Union of the total investments in environmental conservation increased from eight per cent in the tenth Five Year Plan to 12.4 per cent in 1989, while water conservation decreased from 77 per cent to 67 per cent during the same period. In the RSFSR and Kazakhstan this share has increased slightly since the early 1970s. On the other hand since the mid-1970s the relative share has changed in favour of water protection in the Ukraine, Latvia and Estonia.[66] In 1988 in Uzbekistan and Kazakhstan capital investments in air protection were 19 and 15.9 per cent of total state investments in environmental protection in these republics respectively, thus indicating a relatively high priority for air protection compared with the Soviet Union as a whole. On the other hand water protection seems to have been attributed a higher priority relative to the Soviet standard in the Baltic republics, Turkmenia and Belorussia, where their share exceeded 80 per cent.[67] In Latvia and Lithuania the shares were as high as 97.5 and 91.7 per cent, respectively.

In official statements from the mid-1970s it was clearly specified that environmental protection was not to interfere with the fulfilment of high-priority production targets or with local employment.[68] The adoption of a special decree on *perestroika* within the sphere of environmental conservation (see Chapter 6), in January 1988 might have indicated a change in the preferences of central planners in favour of environmental conservation.[69] The creation of Goskompriroda in the same year, with its corresponding state organs at republican and local levels and the preparations for an all-Union law for environmental protection in 1991, are other signs of an increasing attention to the environmental problems in recent time. As noted above, up until 1988 environmental conservation had been no more than a side-line occupation spread among various ministries and state committees.[70] One might thus suspect that environmental protection had a relatively low priority within each of these sectors. With the establishment of Goskompriroda environmental conservation became the main objective of at least one responsible state organ at ministerial level. The fact that higher education has been set up for specialists in various fields within the sphere of environmental conservation might possibly be taken as an indication of an increased priority.[71] Another factor is the increased control of pollution levels.[72] In 1988, for instance, air pollution was measured regularly in twice as many cities as in 1970.[73] Further, if central planners reacted to alarm reports by allocating more resources to environmental protection, this might indicate an increased priority attributed to this activity. The abrupt increase in expenditures in the early 1970s suggests that environmental issues increased in priority at that time.

5.4.1 Relative Wages and Job Status for Environmental Protection Activities

In a centrally planned economy, wage rates are determined by the planners rather than by market forces. Although factors of labour quality and market conditions influence wage setting, the priority of sectors are of considerable importance.[74] As a general rule, units of high priority have higher wage rates whereas wage rates of low-priority units are below average.[75] Similar differentials were likely to exist with respect to bonuses and non-pecuniary benefits of employment such as holidays, housing, and so on. The priority should also be reflected in the status of jobs, such that the status of a job in a high-priority sector is higher than that of a low-priority sector. Increasing relative wages for employees at environmental organisations and inspectorates might be taken as an indication of an increased relative priority to environmental tasks.

In 1988 the average monthly wage for a state employee of either Goskompriroda, the State Committee for Hydrometeorology and Environmental Control, Gidromet, or other agencies for environmental protection was 235.4 roubles.[76] This was slightly below the all-economy rate of 240.4 roubles, and 21 per cent lower than the 301 roubles of industrial office workers. The relative increase between 1970 and 1988 was about the same as that of industrial office workers, 89 versus 87 per cent, but it had decreased somewhat when compared with the national average which had increased by 97 per cent. Available data suggest that employees at environmental inspectorates have had relatively low wages and small opportunities to obtain bonuses, an indication of their low priority. For instance, inspectors at the Moscow and Oka Basin Inspectorate earned 130 roubles a month in 1976.[77] This was below the national average in 1975 of 145.8 roubles, and substantially lower than that of office workers within industry in the same year which was 183.6 roubles.[78] In the 1970s, the status of the job would still have been low. In 1976 for instance, in the Moscow–Oka Inspectorate, most of the scientists and technicians employed in the inspectorate's laboratories were women, which in Soviet terms is a sign of low status.[79] However, according to a state official at Goskompriroda, the status of the job as well as relative wages of the employees at the environmental organs had increased over the last couple of years.[80] In 1991, wages were comparable to the average wages in the civil service. An increased share of the total wage fund had been allocated to environmental tasks as, with the establishment of Goskompriroda and its subordinates, the number of employees within this sector increased. This supports the impression that priorities with respect to environmental protection had increased.

5.4.2 A Low But Increasing Relative Priority?

In the preceding chapter it was argued that the shortage economy emerged as a logical result of the forced industrialisation policy. Similarly, it might be said that the low priority of environmental protection and the wasteful use of natural resources was a logical consequence of this policy of rapid development. The emphasis on ever-expanding industrial and agricultural production, given in the first Five Year Plan, led to the evolution of a managerial incentive system in which plan fulfilment irrespective of environmental effects yielded benefits. During the early stages of the Stalinist system, managers in industrial enterprises learned to behave in a manner which suited their position. Not only were environmental concerns neglected during this process, but the environment was also to be transformed in accordance with the 'needs of society'.

The evaluation of the performance of environmental programmes in the Soviet Union on the basis of the data presented above indicates that planners' priorities and associated resource-allocation rules exert external influences on environmental performance. It demonstrates that environmental protection was given a low, although slightly increasing priority in the Soviet economy during the period 1970–90. The increased priority to environmental protection seemed to have implied that more resources were allocated to heavy polluters within high-priority sectors, while the worst-polluting activities within low-priority sectors were shut down. Further, there was a tendency towards an increased degree of plan fulfilment in quantity terms. However, the signs of an increasing priority were not matched by similar improvements in quality. On the contrary, evidence indicates that in the case of water purification, quality deteriorated. A decreasing degree of plan fulfilment in quality terms might also have suggested that regulations on quality had become stricter.

It seems reasonable to assume that in the West stricter regulations and a more rigorous environmental legislation have stimulated improvements in the quality of equipment. Directors of polluting enterprises in the West would improve the quality of environmental equipment rather than increase its quantity, if this would enable them to minimise costs. Similarly, forest owners in the West have presumably been stimulated to respond to the negative effects of large cutting areas on the possibility of regenerating forests by reducing such areas.

However, empirical evidence suggests that in the Soviet economy stricter regulations in the environmental area might have stimulated institutions to sacrifice quality in order to expand the quantity of environmental equipment. Rather than improving quality, the quantity which was subject to treatment was increased. A greater capacity for purification was installed and more equipment was mobilised rather than improving those plants already in existence.

This suggests that an increased priority to environmental protection should have had a greater effect on high-priority sectors. These would have had stronger incentives to follow central directives as they were more dependent on central allocation. Moreover, they had better opportunities to adjust to new directives as they received the better-quality equipment. As we have seen, forced substitution of quantity for quality appeared to have been higher in low-priority branches than in branches of high priority.

5.5 CONCLUSIONS

The application of the view of the Soviet economy as a shortage economy, adapted to take low priority into account, suggests that the budget constraint is rather hard. According to this approach, resource-allocation responsiveness depends on priority rather than on intensity of shortage. The meaning of the hard budget constraint is that planners are prepared to tolerate high social costs for environmental disruption for extended periods without taking counter-measures. The fact that measures have been taken despite low priority indicates that the environmental situation must have been rather serious and/or that priority to environmental protection had increased. The hard budget constraint also means that pollution charges and charges for the use of natural resources should have had a stronger effect on behaviour in low-priority sectors than in branches of higher priority. If they could not reduce pollution, they were put out of business.

The low priority further implied that the shortage intensity in the case of environmental protection was generally likely to be relatively high. This should have been the case particularly in low-priority branches since the high-quality environmental equipment that was available was allocated to sectors of higher priority. This was reflected in the problems of plan fulfilment in the case of environmental protection as well as in the non-fulfilment of investment plans. Further, high general shortage intensity in low-priority branches might have been particularly detrimental to the use of natural resources, as these might have been substituted for other more scarce inputs when this was possible.

Evidence indicates that there has been a considerable quantity drive despite a hard budget constraint and high shortage intensity. This suggests that achievements in environmental protection were not accomplished by increases in productivity, but through an expansion of inputs. Empirical data further indicates that this quantity drive had taken place at the expense of the quality of environmental equipment, new technology and an effective supply and use of by-products.

This explanation is a complement to those emphasising problems of valuation and priority of material production, which were discussed in Chapter 3. It offers a rationale for the problems of low-quality technology as well as for the ineffectiveness of laws and regulations. This approach also provides an explanation as to why high-priority sectors as well as low-priority sectors might well have been important contributors to pollution. As environmental equipment has been allocated primarily to high-priority sectors, low-priority activities were not able to do much about their pollution. However, as high-priority sectors would have been less efficient, even though they received the required equipment, it was of little use if it was not used competently. Our explanation further stresses the ineffectiveness of 'economic incentives' in high-priority sectors. In contrast to the original shortage model it suggests that pollution charges, fines for environmental violations and charges for the use of natural resources might have affected behaviour in low-priority branches.

One difference compared to Davis, however, was that budget constraints for natural resources would have been soft for high-priority as well as for low-priority branches. In contrast to Davis, we argue that extracting branches were likely to have had relatively soft budgets, not because they were of high priority, but for geographical or physical reasons. The perceived abundance of natural resources contributed to the increasing softness of budget constraints, as did the fact that their use was difficult to control. There were no physical constraints that limited their use in the same way as for investment, material resources and labour.

Although the official view on the environment had, to some extent, been revised when compared to the environmental programmes since 1970, it is doubtful whether the situation could have been improved. Even if the policy had changed, problems of low-quality and slow technical development with respect to environmental protection were not likely to have been solved. Nevertheless, an increase in priority might have improved the environmental situation in some places inasmuch as it led to the closing of polluting industries.

NOTES

1   For a critical evaluation of this concept, see Hare (1988) and Gomulka (1985).
2   Kornai (1986).
3   Kornai (1982a), p. 508. See also Davis (1989), pp. 437–8 and 448–9, and (1988), pp. 52–6. Davis finds that the budget constraint of the medical system was relatively hard, while that of the defence sector was relatively soft.
4   See Davis (1989), pp. 435–6.
5   Davis (1989), p. 438.
6   *Okhrana...* (1989), pp. 3 and 9; *Narkhoz* (1989), p. 625. In 1990, about 500 million roubles were budgeted for environmental protection, indicating an increase of only two per cent in two years, personal interview with Sergei Kutukov, Goskompriroda, Moscow, 15 March 1991.
7   See Gustafson (1980), pp. 133–4.
8   '*O korrenoi Perestroike dela Okhrany Prirody v Sstrane*', postonovlenie ot 7 yanvaria 1988 g. No. 32, Tsentralnyi Komitet KPSS I Soviet Ministrov SSSR, Moskva, Kreml.
9   Gustafson (1980), p. 131. Confirmed by Professor Gofman, in an interview with him, December 1988.
10 Peterson (1990b), p. 7.
11 Kornai (1980), Chapter 14.
12 Kornai (1980), Chapter 9.
13 This issue will be discussed further in Chapter 6 when the effect of changes in environmental policy under Gorbachev are investigated.
14 Kornai (1980), Chapter 10.
15 'Po dostignutomu urovnyu'. In the West this expression has become known through Igor Birman (1978), 'From the achieved level'.
16 See Nove (1982), p. 39; Birman (1978), p. 160.
17 Protests against separate plants have, for instance, taken place in 1987 in Erevan and Ufa, in 1988 in Kirishi and Volgograd, at various places in the Baltic states, and in 1990 in Moscow (*Sotsialisticheskaya Industriya*, 19 July 1987; *Izvestiya*, 11 November 1987; *Literaturnaya Gazeta*, 9 December 1987; *Radio Liberty Research RL* 421/87, 30 December). There have also been many public protests against the building of a new nuclear power plant near Minsk (*Sotsialisticheskaya Industriya*, 8 April 1988). According to Yablokov (1990), during 1988 various ecology-related demonstrations, rallies and strikes involved at least as many people as the national question (p. 12). According to an opinion poll conducted in the Soviet Union at the end of 1988, 47 per cent of the persons interviewed thought that environmental pollution was an urgent problem in society. 87 per cent held the view that pollution was an urgent problem which should be dealt with immediately. In the Moscow area, 19 per cent of the interviewees gave priority to problems of environmental pollution (pp.12–13).
18 For instance, decisions were made to close down two reactors of the nuclear power plant in Erevan in 1989 (*SSSR i Soyuznye Respubliki...* (1989), p. 425; *Izvestiya*, 22 March 1988). Other examples of closures are the paper plants at Baikal and in Priozersk, and a few chemical industries. In 1989, scores of enterprises were closed or had their production scaled back (see also Peterson (1990d), pp. 10–11, for examples of closures).
19 See Davis (1989), pp. 433–4.
20 Soviet norms for a number of air pollutants in 1988 are given in *Okhrana...* (1989), p. 32. See also Feshbach and Friendly (1992), Appendix, Tables 10a–10d for a more detailed account. However, it might be appropriate to understand the norms as goals; they are sometimes referred to as desirable goals, unobtainable in the near future. This interpretation also supports the impression that the leadership has accepted high social costs from environmental pollution as environmental concerns were of low priority.
21 Davis (1989), p. 434.
22 *Okhrana...* (1989), p. 148.
23 *Narkhoz* (1988), pp. 577 and 295.
24 See also Oxenstierna (1990), Chapter 8.

25 See Feshbach and Friendly (1992), p. 3, for the effects of environmental disruption on the Soviet military sector.

26 The national income utilised is equal to the value added of the productive sector, that is, exclusive of services, net of depreciation and the balance of external trade.

27 The ecological catastrophe in the Aral Sea region has been described as comparable to a nuclear power accident although it has happened gradually. 'Aralskaya katastrofa' (1989).

28 Kornai (1980).

29 Davis (1989), p. 440.

30 Kornai (1980), Chapter 2.

31 Davis (1989), p. 436; Ericson (1988).

32 *Vestnik Statistiki*, No. 11, 1991, p. 65; *Narkhoz* (1989), p. 251; *Okhrana...* (1989), pp. 36–7 and 80; Morgun (1989), p. 62. For details about specific places on this issue, see *Literaturnaya Gazeta*, 29 April 1987; *Pravda*, 5 June 1987; *Izvestiya*, 10 October 1987; *Pravda*, 20 January 1988; *Sotsialisticheskaya Industriya*, 2 February 1988; *Pravda*, 18 April 1988; *Pravda*, 2 July 1988; *Sovetskaya Rossiya*, 7 August 1988; *Izvestiya*, 6 February 1989; *Sotsialisticheskaya Industriya*, 18 February 1989; *Sotsialisticheskaya Industriya*, 21 March 1989.

34 *Okhrana...* (1989), pp. 36–7.

33 See also p. 9 of this study.

35 *Narkhoz* (1987), p. 613; *Narkhoz* (1988), p. 569; *Narkhoz* (1989), p. 247; *Narkhoz* (1990), p. 248; *Soyuznye respubliki osnovnye ekonomicheskie...* (1991), p. 131.

36 *SSSR i Soyuznye Respubliki v 1987 gody* (1988), pp. 46, 76–7.

37 *Vestnik Statistiki*, No. 11, 1991, p. 65, Peterson (1990b), p. 7.

38 *Narkhoz* (1990), p. 249.

39 Ibid.

40 Ibid. According to Serge Kutukov, Goskompriroda, the environmental equipment that was available was usually allocated to sectors of high priority, personal interview, Moscow, 15 March 1991.

41 *Narkhoz* (1990), p. 249.

42 Ericson (1988).

43 See Chapter 2.

44 Gregory and Stuart (1981), p. 142; (also see Chapter 7 of this study).

45 See Gregory and Stuart (1981), p. 180.

46 *Okhrana Okruzhayushchei Sredy i Ratsionalnoe Ispolzovanie Prirodnykh Resursov v SSSR* (1989), p. 3; *Soyuznye Respubliki Osnovnye Ekonomicheskie...* (1991), p. 131. In 1987, for example, the Ministries of Energy and Gas Production fulfilled 56 and 34 per cent of their plans, respectively.

47 *Soyuznye Respubliki Osnovnye Ekonomicheskie...* (1991), p. 131.

48 Morgun (1989), pp. 59–60; *Sotsialisticheskaya Industriya*, 21 July 1988. For further details concerning the different republics in various years, see *SSSR i Soyuznye Respubliki v 1982 gody* (1983), p. 22; *SSSR i Soyuznye Respubliki v 1983 gody* (1984), p. 44; *SSSR i Soyuznye Respubliki v 1985 gody* (1986), pp. 24 and 45; *SSSR i Soyuznye Respubliki v 1986 gody* (1987), p. 36; *SSSR i Soyuznye Respubliki v 1987 gody* (1988), pp. 222, 302, 369, 403, 461, 527 and 556; *SSSR i Soyuznye Respubliki v 1988 gody* (1989), pp. 53, 202, 242, 276, 309–10 and 396.

49 *SSSR i Soyuznye Respubliki v 1988 gody* (1989), pp. 18, 53, 115, 143, 205, 242, 276 and 309.

50 Yablokov (1990), p. 3; *SSSR i Soyuznye...* (1989), pp. 18, 115, 203, 276, 308, 342, 368, 396, 453 and 489.

51 For examples, see *SSSR i Soyuznye Respubliki v 1987 gody* (1988), pp. 396–7, 455 and 484; *Pravda*, 18 April 1988.

52 See various editions of *SSSR i Soyuznye Respubliki* for plan fulfilment in the Soviet economy.

53 See Oxenstierna (1990), Chapter 1.

54 Gustafson (1980), p. 133.

55 Davis (1989).

56 The quantity drive with respect to environmental investments, for example, was highest in the fuel-energy complex, in which investments in 1986–88 were 49 per cent higher than in 1981–85 (*Okhrana...* (1989), p. 148).

57 That is if we disregard the increase of 229 per cent in national parks.

58 Dumnov and Pospelov (1991), p. 65. The emissions of polluted water were more than twice as high in 1990 as in 1986. See *Narkhoz* (1991) for the expansion of various treatment facilities in 1976–90.

59 See footnote 26.

60 *Okhrana...* (1989), p. 10. See also Feshbach and Friendly (1992), p. 258.

61 *Okhrana...* (1989), p. 9; *Narkhoz* (1990), pp. 6 and 15. Expenditures, exclusive of capital investments, increased by 61 per cent in the period 1981–90 (see Table 5.2, column 1).

62 See Åslund (1988) and Harrison (1993).

63 Gustafson (1980), p. 129.

64 *Narkhoz* (1987), pp. 101 and 619.

65 *Narkhoz* (1986), p. 387; *Narkhoz* (1988), pp. 295 and 577; *Narkhoz* (1990), pp. 254 and 535. It should perhaps be noted that the increases in total investments have been rather stable, while those in measures for environmental conservation have not. For instance, they increased by 48 per cent between the ninth and the tenth Five Year Plans but only by three per cent between the tenth and the eleventh Five Year Plans.

66 *Narkhoz RSFSR za 70 let*, p. 432; *Narkhoz Estonskoi SSR v 1986 g.*, p. 302; *Narkhoz Latviiskoi SSR v 1986 g.*, p. 208; *Narkhoz Kazakhstana v 1985 g.*, p. 172; *Narkhoz Ukrainskoi SSR v 1986 g.*, p. 394.

67 *Okhrana...* (1989), pp. 148 and 150.

68 See Gustafson (1980).

69 '*O korrenoi perestroike...*' (1988). Gorbachev had also started to mention the ecological problems in his speeches (*Pravda*, 30 July 1988).

70 The responsibility for making and implementing environmental policy in the Soviet Union had formerly been undertaken by nine state committees and seven ministries (*Pravda*, 20 April 1987).

71 See also *Okhrana...* (1989), p. 10 for number of graduates from the various disciplines of environmental protection in 1986–88.

72 See *Okhrana...* (1989), pp. 32–3.

73 Ibid.

74 See also Oxenstierna (1990), Chapter 5 for wage-setting principles in the Soviet Union.

75 Davis shows that in the past wages were higher in the high-priority defence sector, while wage differentials have declined in later years. See also Davis (1988), pp. 43–7.

76 *Narkhoz* (1989), pp. 77–8; *Narkhoz* (1990), pp. 76–7.

77 Gustafson (1980), p. 133.

78 *Narkhoz* (1984), p. 393, *Trud v SSSR* (1988), p. 189. Office workers, or white-collar workers, generally gained more than blue-collar workers in every industrial sector. The average monthly wage of inspectors at the above-mentioned inspectorate in 1976 was at approximately the same level as that of office workers in the clothing industry in 1975, which had the lowest average wages in industry (pp. 189–95).

79 Gustafson (1980), p. 133.

80 Sergei Kutukov, Goskompriroda, personal interview, Moscow, 15 March 1991.

6.   The Effect of Changes in Environmental Policy Under Gorbachev

One conclusion from the preceding chapter is that an increased priority given to environmental protection would have only minor effects on the environment in a shortage economy. In Chapters 2–5 the causes of the serious environmental situation in the Soviet Union have been analysed, along with the possibility of curing the crisis with measures taken within the framework of the Stalinist model. It was found that even with a radical change in priorities, any major changes in the environmental situation were not likely because of problems of low quality and inferior technology. The purpose of this chapter is to discuss changes in environmental policy in the *perestroika* programmes up to 1991 and their potential effects on the environment in the Soviet Union.[1]

In the first section of this chapter there is a brief account of the administrative and legal changes with respect to environmental protection and use of natural resources from the early 1970s up to 1991. Then, in Sections 6.2 to 6.4 three items which were directly connected with the increased role of economic tools and economic incentives under Gorbachev are discussed. The effectiveness of these is investigated in Section 6.5, and Section 6.6 then concludes the chapter.

6.1 OFFICIAL RECOGNITION

After a long period of neglect, environmental issues suddenly caught the attention of the central planners in the early 1970s. The immediate cause was an impending crisis in public health.[2] Cholera had for instance broken out around the southern river basins. At the same time, a demand for clean water in the South was rapidly increasing due to the spread of irrigated agriculture.

Accordingly a heavily funded environmental programme chiefly aimed at preserving clean water was established. Annual investment for water quality and waste treatment was increased abruptly, and in 1970–73, detailed water legislation for each of the Union republics came into effect. In the eleventh Five Year Plan (1976–80) a section on nature and environmental protection was incorporated into the national economic plan, and a special division for the environment, with subdivisions for air and water quality was established within Gosplan, the State Planning Committee. In short, attempts were made to incorporate the environment into most parts of the government structure.

In addition to the primary aim of preventing immediate threats to public health, the environmental programme was aimed at protecting natural resources for future economic uses to facilitate further economic growth. A water charge for the industrial use of water was introduced in 1982.[3]

Gidromet, the State Committee for Hydrometeorology and Environmental Control, was established in 1978. Special environmental subdivisions were also created within the State Committee for Science and Technology and Goskomstat, the Statistical Administration. The Commission for Environmental Protection and Rational Use of Natural Resources under the Presidium of the USSR Council of Ministers was set up in 1981. At the beginning of 1988, the increasing alarm that marked the ecological debate led to the creation of one central authority, Goskompriroda, the State Committee for Environmental Protection.[4] As noted above, this implied that, from having been sideline occupations for various ministries and state committees, environmental conservation now became the main objective of at least one responsible state organ. Thus, the responsibility for the use and protection of water resources was transferred from Minvodkhoz, the Ministry for Melioration and Water Resources, to Goskompriroda. In the spring of 1991 Goskompriroda was elevated into a ministry.[5]

The increased official attention to environmental problems in the early 1970s was also reflected in a number of resolutions in the period 1972–78.[6] The Soviet Union further enacted a comprehensive set of laws and regulations which set air quality standards, required approved filters before factories were permitted to operate and prohibited various damaging practices.[7] By 1987, norms for the maximum permitted emission of air pollutants had been established for 15,000 enterprises.[8] Apart from the law on protection of the atmosphere (1980), the Soviet Union also adopted national laws for public health (1970), a subsoil legislation (1975), and legislation on forest utilisation (1977) and protection of wildlife (1980). In 1978 and 1985, several all-Union laws were enacted for protecting the environment, as well as rulings on protecting many specific natural sites, like Lake Baikal, the Volga, the Urals, the Black and Azov Seas, and so on.[9]

Waste-treatment and water-recycling programmes as well as targets for the provision of pollution-control equipment have been assigned to ministries along with material resources for their fulfilment. The authorities have also attempted to control the ministerial preference for concentrating investment in heavily populated, long-established industrial areas. There was, for instance, a list of 34 towns in the Russian republic where construction of new or expansion of existing enterprises was forbidden.[10] In 1988, the level of air pollution was checked in 537 cities by the Ministry of Health and

Gidromet.[11] In 1990, a new type of organisation was set up.[12] The 'environmental business organisation' had the right to deal with foreign companies, and to represent other Soviet enterprises who wanted to do so. In the early 1990s Soviet enterprises would have exported natural resources, waste and in some cases even technology and with the hard currency they bought environmental equipment.[13]

In January 1988 a resolution on *perestroika* of the environmental protection in the Soviet Union was adopted.[14] The programme was an important cornerstone of the official environmental policy for the period 1991–2005, at least for Russia. It is not clear how relevant it was for the other republics.[15] Three items which were directly connected with the increased role of economic tools, economic incentives and the enterprise law can be identified.[16]

1. The use of cost-benefit analysis in environmental decision-making.

2. The introduction of pollution charges and payments for the use of natural resources.

3. The adoption of self-financing systems for environmental protection measures on the national and regional levels.

The general principles for using cost-benefit analysis in environmental decision-making were worked out by Gosplan, together with the Academy of Sciences and the State Committee for Construction in the form of a Handbook (*Vremennaya Tipovaya Metodika*) for valuation of environmental measures.[17] This focused on how natural resource evaluations could be used to provide a basis for choosing environmental protection measures and determined the order in which measures should be carried out. It also provided a method for valuation of damage from environmental pollution.

Proposals for the other two items were worked on in a new version of the Handbook which was released by the Central Economic Mathematical Institute (CEMI) in 1987. These reflected the changes in Soviet economic policies concerning the governing of the enterprise towards more independence and more reliance on economic incentives. The Draft Handbook from 1987[18] also contained suggestions on how these proposals could be implemented such as premia for fulfilment of environmental protection measures. Another proposal was that enterprises pay money into special environmental funds at different levels of the economy to finance environmental protection measures. In the autumn of 1989 a resolution stating that ecological experts must be consulted before any decisions on large-scale production are made was adopted.[19]

We thus see considerable administrative and legal changes. But laws and resolutions did not automatically achieve anything. While production plans generally were accompanied by the allocation of resources required to accomplish them, regulations were not. If the necessary inputs and technical equipment were not provided, even enterprises actually motivated to comply might not have been able to do so.

6.2 COST-BENEFIT ANALYSIS IN DECISION-MAKING

A special decree on the use of cost-benefit analysis in environmental decision-making was adopted in 1983[20] and revised to be better coordinated with *perestroika*.[21] But the principles and foundations of cost-benefit analysis developed in the document were not subject to any major changes.[22] The Handbook stated that certain measures were needed to satisfy basic quality requirements of the environment. These were expressed as norms in physical units and were determined to protect health and conserve nature.[23]

The Handbook emphasised that all the social revenues and costs of measures were to be taken into account. A measure was defined as socially efficient if its social gain exceeded its social cost.[24] According to the Handbook the central planner was to choose the measure which maximised the social net revenue per year, provided that the given norm was achieved. In the Soviet context, however, measures may have been considered for political reasons even if they were socially unprofitable. This was evident from a statement taken from the Handbook that if costs exceeded benefits, these were to be chosen so that the loss was minimised.

The practice of using cost-benefit analysis for environmental problems in the Soviet Union differed from that of conventional theory in a number of ways. One basic difference concerned the estimation of benefits. The principle of evaluating benefits of environmental improvements in accordance with the marginal willingness to pay, which is used in conventional theory, was rejected on the grounds that it gives too much imprecision and subjectivity to evaluation.[25]

Instead, such evaluations were based on estimations of only those economic consequences which could be measured 'objectively'. Benefits from reducing health risks would, for instance, have been estimated from the saved costs for medical care and the evaluation of the additional labour from those who did not become ill. It was emphasised that such evaluations would only have included one part of the benefit of measures, but that they corresponded to conventional methods of estimation of GNP, productivity and other economic parameters that are used in most countries.[26] Moreover, cost-benefit analysis was mainly seen as an instrument for fixing the minimum level of national expenditures on environmental protection.

It was also emphasised that the method of evaluation would differ depending on the aim. The method outlined above would be used for decisions on lower levels. It would, for instance, be used to evaluate the effect of sewage facilities at a certain plant. But it would not be used when it was important to evaluate the total social effects of a large-scale health project. In such a case the desired level of health security would have become the aim of the project and the problem was how to achieve this aim with minimum costs.

In the Soviet methodological framework, the marginal cost of environmental pollution was estimated differently, depending on how measures to prevent it were financed. The social gain from reduced pollution which was generated by the introduction of new technology, financed by the state budget, in other words by either central, regional or local funds, was evaluated according to the shadow price used in long-term planning.

But, said the Handbook, if the social gain arose from measures financed by the enterprise itself or by money that it had borrowed from the bank, then the marginal cost was defined as the normative cost of reducing pollution.[27] This was substantially lower than the corresponding long-term shadow price, which was used in perspective planning.[28]

One change in environmental policy in the *perestroika* programmes was thus that cost-benefit analysis was to be used in decision-making. It would have served as an analytical basis for determining the gravest ecological threats and for helping new decision-makers choose which ones to address first. The use of cost-benefit analysis in environmental decision-making might have helped to motivate the ambitious environmental programme undertaken by Goskompriroda.[29] However, according to the approach used in this study, more resources to environmental protection would not have had that much of an impact on the enterprise and their compliance with the rules concerning environmental protection. Moreover, it would have been difficult to implement the programme as Goskompriroda did not acquire the power to inspect, modify or overrule development plans of other state agencies.[30] In effect, the Goskompriroda design for environmental recovery in the Soviet Union amounted to a list of goals. It did not, for instance, provide any concrete proposals as to how to stimulate technical development.[31] Nevertheless, the use of cost-benefit analysis in environmental decision-making implied a new way of thinking which might be fruitful in the longer perspective.

6.3 PAYMENTS FOR NATURAL RESOURCES AND POLLUTION CHARGES

The Handbook further stated that prices should be set so as to make it profitable for the enterprise to take measures which were socially beneficial. The enterprise itself decided when measures were to be included, although it obtained directives from superior authorities by way of norms for the maximum emission of pollutants. To make it profitable for the enterprise to fulfil its norm, the Handbook suggested that it obtained premiums that were added to profits.

The financial revenue (*khozraschetnyi rezultat*) of an enterprise taking a certain measure was equal to the increase or decrease in revenue. Costs for capital investments would not be included since these did not generally affect the enterprise. In effect this meant that the state would have paid for investment in water purification, filters, and so on, while the enterprise paid for running costs. Compliance with norms was secured if the premiums for compliance plus the pollution charges avoided exceeded operating costs.

Shadow prices were to be used for activities which were financed by the state budget. If, however, the enterprise was governed by the principle of self-accountability, matters became different, as the enterprise did not face shadow prices, but prices which were set on the basis of normative costs of production.[32]

Payments for utilisation of natural resources such as land, water, forests and minerals were introduced in the Russian republic in 1991.[33] The stated functions of such payments were:[34]

1. To secure complete self-accountability.

2. To provide an economic incentive for the efficient use and protection of natural resources.

3. To provide an instrument for controlling the market price of products of extracting industries.

4. To provide financial revenue for budgets at various levels of the economy.

5. To remove differences in production costs in extracting industries due to differences in natural conditions.

The idea was that these charges would undergo two stages.[35] First they would be calculated administratively. Later on when the market economy had started to operate the charges would have become flexible and determined by the market. Apart from payments for the use of natural resources, pollution charges were to be introduced in 1991 in all branches of the Soviet economy.[36] In 1989 and 1990, Goskompriroda carried out experiments with pollution charges and payments for the use of natural resources.[37] In about 50 cities in the RSFSR, the Ukraine and in Tadzhikistan, the method worked out by Gofman and his colleagues was used.[38] Goskompriroda also mandated stiff penalties for infringing environmental rules on an experimental basis in 50 cities and regions in 1989 and in 64 in 1990.[39]

Pollution charges were to be established for all principal pollutants emitted into the air and water and also for solid waste. One rate was to be levied on ordinary, permissible emissions. Another on pollution in excess of the norm.[40] Pollution charges were to be set in the Five Year Plan and would include calculations of annual reductions in emissions. The size of the charge to be paid would be calculated taking three factors into account: physical quantity, toxicity and geographical dispersion. The charge would be paid out of profits except for emissions above the norm or accidental emissions which would be paid from the income of the workers (*khozraschetnyi dokhod kollektiva*).[41]

Listing 210 different harmful substances, the Russian republic Goskompriroda fixed average pollution charges of 3.3 roubles for each ton of atmospheric emissions within set yearly norms and for each ton in excess of the norm the charge was 15.8 roubles.[42] Average charges for emissions of water pollutants, which were established for 129 substances, ran from 443.5 roubles per allowable ton to 2,346 for each ton in excess of the norm.[43]

In the experiments carried out in 1990 in Moscow, the charge on pollution in excess of the norm was five times higher than the charge on permissible emissions. However, if the enterprise had not bothered to apply for a permit to pollute, which it could obtain free of charge at the Moscow Committee for Environmental Protection, Moskompriroda, it was liable to pay twice the charge.[44] The more severe the violation, the higher the charge would be.[45] The charges that were actually imposed in the capital in 1991 were higher than those in the Russian republic as a whole.[46]

The pollution charge was not levied on the actual amount of pollution. It was equal to the quantity regulated by the pollution norm. This norm would be determined on the basis of knowledge about the technology used at the plant and by statistics on previous emissions from the plant. This implied that the polluter had to prove that the actual amount of discharge was lower than the norm in order to decrease the charge to be paid. He would, for instance, have had to improve environmental equipment at the plant and install systems for measuring pollution.[47]

6.4 REGIONAL ENVIRONMENTAL FUNDS

In order to ensure that means for environmental protection would be available, special funds were created at the regional or national level.[48] The assets of these funds would mainly be derived from enterprises in the form of pollution charges, payments for the use of natural resources, penalties for breaking environmental laws and payments for the use of environmental funds.[49] The point here was that payments would not go into the state budget as before, but would be paid mainly into regional funds from which regional environmental programmes would be financed.[50] Of the proceeds from the penalties that were introduced on an experimental basis in 1989–90, by Goskompriroda, for example, 85 per cent were to go to local budgets, 10 per cent to regional budgets and five per cent to the central, all-Union fund.[51] In the Russian republic however, all funds collected would go to local authorities, none for national environmental protection work.[52] In the Moscow fund in 1990, ten per cent were to go into the republican fund of the RSFSR, two per cent to an insurance fund for accidents and emergencies and five per cent to a fund for premia to enterprises and environmental inspectors.[53] The intention was also that environmental protection activities were to be financially accountable, just like any other industrial activity.

The regional environmental funds were to be used to cover the difference between the industrial enterprise's own assets for financing environmental measures and current costs. As a first step, the funds would be used to subsidise the above-mentioned activities at individual plants.[54]

Gofman proposed that these environmental funds be transformed into environmental banks in the future. The bank would be used to finance measures of environmental conservation and have the same sources of income (charges and so on) as the funds as well as having the right to issue special environmental bonds. By adjusting the price ratio between payments for the use of natural resources and payments for conserving them, the bank would dispose of an economic device for controlling the use of natural resources. This would be a major policy instrument for development.

The idea of creating regional funds for financing environmental measures was not new.[55] In the 1970s, however, it received little response from state officials. By 1988, Estonia was the only republic where such a fund had been set up.[56] In Latvia, Kazakhstan and Georgia, environmental funds were created shortly afterwards by the republican Goskomprirodas. By 1990, regional funds had been created in every economic region in the Soviet Union. The intention was that the republics themselves were to decide on the use of the funds.[57]

The internalisation of all activities under a single administrative head in each region was a precondition for more effective monitoring and exercise of ownership rights over resources. Accordingly, it mattered less whether it came from pollution charges or from the budget. This was, however, provided that regional bodies had power to enforce their right over resources and that they could obtain physical resources required to carry out their programmes.

6.4.1 Environmental Funds at the Enterprise

Another type of fund proposed would be specific for each enterprise. In this case, the enterprise itself would finance its own environmental measures out of its own profits, assets or by means of credits.[58] The Handbook suggested that environmental funds be created at enterprises which are heavy polluters. The fund would have worked like a bank account in a special 'bank' for environmental preservation and would have been used to finance environmental measures taken by the enterprise.[59]

The advantage of specific funds was that the money stayed within the enterprise although its use was restricted. Furthermore, if the fund were not enough to cover the necessary expenditures, the Handbook suggested that means could be borrowed from the 'environmental bank' up to a certain limit. Moreover, if this limit was reached, the enterprise would have been obliged to use its 'Material Incentive Fund', which had an incentive effect since it was used as a form of bonus payment.

Moreover, it was proposed that funds which had not been used during the year be saved for later years. This was not generally the case for the funds for 'economic incentives' that existed at a Soviet enterprise. These funds were confiscated if they had not been used within the prescribed period.[60]

6.5 THE EFFECTIVENESS OF ECONOMIC INCENTIVES

In the traditional Soviet system, an official ambition to reduce environmental pollution would have led to the introduction of a plan-indicator or a norm for reduction of emissions. The problem was that the fulfilment of such plans would, at least in the short run, have implied a reduction of production. This is presumably why there has not been any sign of such a change in major plan-indicators. The traditional emphasis on plan-indicators expressed in output terms reflected the long-established priority to material production.

As noted above, the Handbook stated that it should be profitable for the enterprise to take measures which were socially beneficial. Thus the first requirement was that enterprises showed an interest in increasing profits. The law on state enterprises from 1988 did indeed set the stage for such a change.[61] The intention was that the enterprise become more independent of its 'superiors' and to a great extent be guided by economic incentives. This would at least require that net profits were left in the enterprise for the benefit of its staff and not, as in the Soviet Union, confiscated by the state.

6.5.1 The Incentive Effect of Charges

The introduction of charges for the use of water and other resources was an important change from the earlier ideological 'principle of free use of natural resources'. Soviet resource economists long persisted in the view that charges were compatible with Marxist theory if they were based on the labour expenditure necessary to restore a particular resource to its original state.[62] They argued that the charge be equal to the differential rent, without discussing the consequences on resource use and it was not clear what incentive enterprises would have had to maximise the differential rent if the money was then confiscated.

The Handbook's proposal implied that the enterprise would have paid two kinds of payments for pollution. The pollution charge would have been paid to the regional fund while payments in the form of deductions from profits would have been made to the enterprise fund. As noted above, one aim of the payments was that the enterprise itself financed all its production costs. In the light of the law on state enterprises it was natural that there be payments for the use of natural resources and pollution. In the Moscow region, however, the charges were not allowed to constitute more than seven per cent of enterprise profits, which implied that the principle of 'complete self-accountability' was valid only if profits were high enough.[63]

The effectiveness of a charge further depended on whether it was paid for in money that had an alternative use to the company. Most payments for the use of natural resources that existed in the Soviet Union were paid from the profits of the enterprise. They were, however, paid from the 70 per cent of the profits which went to taxes without affecting the fixed 30 per cent share of profits left in the enterprise. The payment ought to come from profits which the establishment otherwise could dispose of.

6.5.2 The Nature of Budget Constraints

One intention behind the enterprise law from 1988 was to increase the dependence of enterprises on economic incentives. In Kornai's terminology this meant a general attempt to change from 'soft' to 'hard' budget constraints. No budget constraints would, however, have had any incentive effect unless the enterprises were able to obtain the technical equipment and other physical resources needed for reducing emissions.[64] Profits did not provide an incentive as the enterprise needed materials that had not been allocated by the central authorities in the first place and were not available due to general shortage. The possibility of solving technical problems by importing the appropriate equipment was severely limited by a shortage of 'hard currency'. In this respect, the availability of environmental funds was worthless as these were in roubles.[65]

The creation of environmental funds at the enterprise was thus not likely to have much effect in itself. The effectiveness of regional environmental funds might further be questioned, for the same reasons. This is reflected by the circumstances that such regional funds have generally been used for purposes of ecological education, such as for exhibitions, conferences and personal training.[66]

The effectiveness of economic policy devices was dubious as by 1991 only a fraction of the industrial enterprises had begun to shift from dependence of plan targets of gross output to a measure of self-financing. The introduction of charges appears to have been just another attempt to administer a change in environmental behaviour. To the extent that charges were actually implemented, this simply indicated that the environment was integrated in the administrative price system. According to one investigation carried out in 1991 at 65 large enterprises, 80 per cent of the investigated sample did pay charges.[67] However, the effect of charges was small. Although about ten per cent of the investigated enterprises made losses because of the charges, they were not adversely affected, as non-binding budget constraints weakened the effect of charges and other economic incentives. In Moscow according to the experiments conducted by Moskompriroda in 1990, 90 per cent of enterprises – mainly the big enterprises – paid no charges at all.[68] The high-priority energy production, for instance, although it was the worst polluter, did not pay any charges. Nevertheless, pollution charges which were paid for from the income of workers might possibly have provided these with an incentive to prevent pollution.

6.6 CONCLUDING REMARKS

Reform in the Soviet context has been a rather difficult concept. Although the leadership legislated on far-reaching reforms, there were often no apparent changes. Two examples of this are Khrushchev's attempts at reform after Stalin's death in the late 1950s, and the so-called Kosygin reform which was started in 1965. The Gorbachevian reforms seem also to have been hit by a similar fate. It has been shown here that measures of environmental protection taken under the Gorbachevian regime were not likely to have had any major effects on the environmental situation in the Soviet Union.

Now that the Soviet Union has ceased to exist, the prospects for the environment will have to be analysed for each former republic separately. The political and economic policies to be followed up in the new countries are still an open issue but a number of points appear to be at least slightly promising in this otherwise rather bleak picture. More resources to institutions for environmental protection have presumably resulted in improved control and measurement. Better information on the state of the environment has at least upgraded statistics on which decisions about measures can be based in the future. Similarly, improved methods of evaluating damages to the environment help towards the allocation of resources to where they are most needed. Such achievements can possibly be of advantage for the former Soviet republics. Much of the institutional framework at the all-Union level has been taken over by Russia. Goskompriroda has, for instance, been turned into the Russian Ministry for Ecology and Health. The system for pollution charges that was projected for an all-Union implementation in mid-1991, was at least implemented in the Russian republic. Even though the rates of charges would have to be corrected for inflation to be effective, they could essentially be used in

Russia if the ongoing reforms there are successfully implemented. Although the funds for the financing of environmental protection that were created during the Gorbachev period have become worthless because of inflation, they can be useful in future if payments into these funds continue, provided that reforms continue and charges are corrected.

The tendency for increased investment resources allocated for environmental purposes was another step towards an improved environmental situation. However, even if enterprises were allocated financial funds during the Gorbachevian era, this did not necessarily mean that they actually got the required material equipment, especially if the activity was of low priority.

The so-called 'economic incentives' that have been introduced were not likely to be effective as the whole economy was not built on the basis of economic incentives. Nevertheless, the experiments conducted by Moskompriroda suggest that if budget constraints were relatively hard in branches of low priority, it is possible that pollution charges and payments for natural resources could have affected their behaviour.

NOTES

1   For environmental policies in the former Soviet Union, see also Sätre Åhlander (1994).
2   See also Gustafson (1980), p. 130.
3   DeBardeleben (1983), p. 38.
4   Trehub (1988) describes the tasks of this committee.
5   Feshbach and Friendly (1992), p. 245.
6   *Doklad...* (1990), p. 119.
7   Many decrees on environmental protection have been adopted in the 1980s in which ministries have been blamed for not following instructions from above, and for not having implemented measures. Such decrees have been published in *Pravda*, 10 June 1987; *Pravda*, 15 July 1987; *Izvestiya*, 21 July 1987; *Izvestiya*, 25 September 1987; *Izvestiya*, 7 October 1987; *Pravda*, 17 January 1988; *Pravda*, 27 January 1988; *Sotsialisticheskaya Industriya*, 23 September 1988; *Pravda*, 30 September 1988; *Izvestiya*, 3 December 1988; *Izvestiya*, 14 March 1989; *Izvestiya*, 1 May 1989. Not one government resolution on basins and rivers has been fulfilled (*Sotsialisticheskaya Industriya*, 6 August 1988).
8   *Pravda*, 7 September 1987.
9   See also Jancar (1987).
10   Dyker (1983), p. 48.
11   *Okhrana...* (1989), p. 32. These are cities where the population is 100,000 or more.
12   Sergei, Yu. Kutukov, Goskompriroda, personal interview, Moscow, 15 March 1991.
13   Ibid.
14   'O Korrenoi Perestroike Dela Okhrany Prirody v Strane', postonovlenie ot 7 yanvaria 1988 g. No. 32, Tsentralnyi Komitet KPSS I Sovet Ministrov SSSR, Moskva, Kreml. The text of the resolution was published in *Pravda*, 17 January 1988.
15   *Doklad...* (1990), pp. 118–60.
16   Gofman (1988b). See also *Doklad...* (1990), p. 127.
17   *Vremennaya...* (1986).
18   Gofman and Fedorenko (1987).
19   'O neotlozhnykh merakh ekologicheskogo ozdorovleniya strany', *Byullentin...* (1990), p. 16.
20   *Vremennaya...* (1986).
21   Gofman and Fedorenko (1987).

22 Gofman (1988b), p. 3.
23 *Vremennaya...* (1986), p. 4; Gofman and Fedorenko (1987), p. 9.
24 This might be compared with the social cost-benefit criteria of traditional microeconomic theory, according to which a measure is socially beneficial if the total maximum willingness to pay exceeds the total costs.
25 Gofman (1988b), p. 3.
26 Gofman (1988b), p. 4.
27 The normative cost of reducing pollution was defined as the average cost, over a five-year period, for purifying emissions for the country as a whole.
28 No figures for this are given in the Handbook. However, for the twelfth Five Year Plan the normative cost per unit of air pollution was 20 roubles, while the corresponding shadow price was 100 roubles. The figures for water pollution were 130 roubles and 300 roubles, respectively. See Gofman and Fedorenko (1987), p. 23.
29 This programme amounted to doubling the proportion of Soviet GNP spent on environmental protection (Feshbach and Friendly (1992), p. 256).
30 Some ministries simply resisted the transfer of resources to Goskompriroda (*Sotsialisticheskaya Industriya*, 27 March 1989).
31 Bechuk et al. (1991), p. 903.
32 See footnote 26.
33 Such payments were planned to be introduced on a nationwide scale in 1991, *Doklad...* (1990), p. 129. They were, however, only partially implemented, Feshbach and Friendly (1992); *Vestnik Statistiki*, No. 5, 1992, pp. 37-8.
34 '*O Korrenoi Perestroike...*' (1988), p. 12; Gofman (1988b), p. 6.
35 Rabinovich (1991), p. 102.
36 '*O Korrenoi Perestroike...*' (1988), p. 12; *Doklad...* (1990), p. 128.
37 *Doklad...* (1990), p. 129; personal interview, Goskompriroda, Moscow, 15 March 1991; *Byullentin...* (1990), p. 17.
38 In 1989, experiments with charges were conducted in Zaporozhe, Kemerovo, Krasnoyarsk, Donetsk and Sumsk (Morgun (1989), p. 62).
39 Feshbach and Friendly (1992), p. 246.
40 '*O Korrenoi Perestroike...*' (1988), p. 12; Gofman (1988b), p. 7; *Doklad...* (1990), pp. 127-8.
41 '*O Korrenoi Perestroike ...*' (1988), p. 12; *Doklad...* (1990), p. 128.
42 Feshbach and Friendly (1992), p. 247.
43 These were only average charges. The charge for emitting one ton of a form of leaded tetraethylene into the air, for example, ran to 333,333 roubles. For ten water pollutants, including DDT and hexachlorophene, the fine was set at 20,000 roubles per ton (Feshbach and Friendly (1992), p. 247).
44 Aleksander Yatskov, senior specialist, Moskompriroda, personal interview, Moscow, 11 March 1991.
45 Ibid.
46 Feshbach and Friendly (1992), p. 247. Inside the city of Moscow a ton of heavy metal salts put into the water system, within fixed margins, would cost 29,000 roubles and every ton above the norm, 70,000 roubles.
47 Aleksander Yatskov, Moskompriroda, Moscow, 11 March 1991.
48 *Doklad...* (1990), p. 129; Morgun (1989), p. 62; *Vestnik Statistiki*, No. 5, 1992, p. 37.
49 Gofman and Fedorenko (1987), p. 63; *Doklad...* (1990), p. 129.
50 Gofman and Vitt (1990), pp. 25-7; *Doklad...* (1990), p. 129.
51 Feshbach and Friendly (1992), p. 246.
52 Feshbach and Friendly (1992), p. 247.
53 *Reshenie, 14 Aprelya 1990 g...* (1990), Appendix, p. 2.
54 Gofman (1988b), p. 9.
55 See Gofman (1977), pp. 61-7.
56 Norak (1986). The main income of this fund in 1984-85 was obtained from fines paid by a factory that produced consumer goods, a cellulose-producing factory and a *sovkhoz* for the

pollution of rivers in Estonia. In the same period the fund was used mainly for improving the environment around Tallinn and for developing non-polluting technology.

57   G.I. Ozipov, personal interview, Goskompriroda, Moscow, 5 December 1988.

58   '*O Korrenoi Perestroike...*' (1988), p. 12.

59   Gofman and Vitt (1990), p. 27.

60   Gofman and Fedorenko (1987), p. 71.

61   See Chapter 9.

62   See DeBardeleben (1985), Chapter 8.

63   'O provedenii ekonomicheskogo eksperimenta po sovershenstvovaniyu khozyaistvennogo mekhanizma prirodopolzovaniya v g. Moskve', *Reshenie,* 14 Aprelya 1990 g., No. 840, Moskovskii Gorodskoi Soviet Narodnykh Deputatov Ispolnitelnyi Komitet, p. 1.

64   One example might be taken from Volgograd where the director of a silica processing factory had been trying to find an electrostatic filter since 1987. In 1988, the manufacturer accepted the factory as a customer, in 1989 it got a plan for it, the equipment was to be received in 1991, ready for operation in 1993. Nevertheless, the factory was charged 22,000 roubles for its emissions (this was after negotiation; the initial charge was twice as high) and then a penalty of 50 roubles for every ton of discharge above the set norm This was in 1990 when the experiment with pollution charges began in Volgograd (Feshbach and Friendly (1992), p. 246).

65   Aleksander Yatskov, Moskompriroda, personal interview, 11 March 1991.

66   Sergei Kutukov, personal interview, Goskompriroda, Moscow, 15 March 1991.

67   *Vestnik Statistiki,* No. 5, pp. 37–9. The average sum expended on environmental investments, pollution charges and so on in the investigated enterprises in the first nine months of 1991, was equal to 1.7 per cent of the aggregated production costs, of which pollution charges alone amounted to 0.2 per cent.

68   Personal interview with Aleksander Yatskov, Moskompriroda, Moscow, 11 March 1991.

A Case Study on the Use of Forestry Resources

7. Central Forestry Policy

Chapters 2–6 analysed the effect of the shortage economy on the environment, stating that low priority in the shortage economy might, because of its negative impact on environmental technology and quality of environmental equipment, provide one explanation for the serious environmental situation in the Soviet Union. To get further insight into the impact of the shortage economy on the management of natural resources, this study will now focus on a case study of the use of forestry resources. In this chapter, an investigation will be made into how the interests of timber production came to dominate those of regeneration activities. In order to investigate the possible effect of the shortage economy on the use of forestry resources, the behaviour of the timber industry is outlined empirically in the next chapter. Changes which were in tune with Gorbachev's *perestroika* will be analysed in Chapter 9, to evaluate the possible effect these have had on the use of forestry resources.

This chapter is organised as follows. The forestry sector is described in Section 7.1. This information is important for analysing the functioning of the timber industry and for discussing the relevance of our hypotheses about the use of forestry resources in a shortage economy. Section 7.2 will discuss how central policy promoted a forced expansion of timber procurement, and how this policy led to the neglect of forestry interests. Section 7.3 then deals with the policy for forestry development pursued in the traditional Soviet economic system.

7.1 THE FORESTRY SECTOR

As the main focus of interest here will be on the utilisation of forests, the forestry sector is defined as the institutions which are directly related to the use of this resource. As forest materials are used in a wide range of different production processes, a comprehensive definition of the forestry sector would be complicated. Within the forest product industries alone there are losses in timber production, various wood-working processes, and in the production of pulp and paper. Evidence shows that losses of raw materials are substantial at all the different stages of the various production processes.[1] If we look at the demand for forest products a number of minor competing forest users can be identified. Forests are required for recreational purposes. Forests would help protect fields from soil and wind erosion, as well as from being flooded. For analytical convenience we abstract from other uses of forest land than that of which timber production is the principal activity.

7.1.1 The Forest Fund

The forests of the USSR formed a single state forest fund. This consisted of state forests and collective farm forests. While 94.5 per cent of the state forest fund came under the direct control of the centralised forestry system, 1.8 per cent were under the control of collective farms and the remaining 3.7 per cent were attached to other ministries. The forest fund included roughly one-third of the total land mass of the Soviet Union and covered forest land or land planned for forestry needs. Since 1943 all forests have been officially separated into three groups depending on their location or special function, and according to the degree to which each would be economically exploited or protected for particular purposes.

Group one comprised forests where felling was allowed for maintenance purposes only, in other words, industrial felling was forbidden and the only felling allowed was in connection with forestry maintenance. According to a 1973 survey these forests covered 16 per cent of the total forest area of the state forest fund, one-third of which is located in the European part of the Soviet Union and the rest in Asia.

Group two constituted 6.5 per cent of the forest fund and comprised forests mainly located in the European part of the USSR, where forest resources were limited. These were areas such as central European Russia and the region around the southern Urals where the forests had been over-exploited in the past. Industrial felling was allowed on a limited scale in these forests. Since many forests in group one and all those in group two were situated in the European part of the country they suffered badly during the Second World War when some 20 million hectares were felled or damaged.[2]

By far the largest is group three which covered 80.2 per cent of the state forest fund. These forests were situated in areas rich in timber such as Siberia and the Far East where the timber-processing industry was mainly to be found. The main subdivisions of group three were those to be exploited for logging, and those to be kept as reserve forests, which were forests which were not yet ready to be logged, usually due to their remoteness or the lack of a proper transport network.

7.1.2 The Organisation of Forestry

The State Committee for Forests of the USSR Council of Ministers, Goskomles, the Union organ for the management of state forest land, was created in 1988. It replaced the earlier State Committee for Forestry of the USSR Council of Ministers, Gosleskhoz. Corresponding committees or ministries were set up in the eight Union republics richest in forests. While forestry associations operated at regional level, the forestry enterprises were the main forestry organisations working at local level.

In the Union republics, a tree-felling fund (*lesorubochnyi fond*) was set up by the republican Council of Ministers; at regional level it was established by the regional Executive Committee. The relevant documents stating the right to procure timber were issued by forestry bodies. The tree-felling ticket (*lesorubochnyi bilet*) was the only document allowing the cutting and transportation of timber.

Those forests belonging to group two or group three produced timber. Proceeding according to the national needs for timber, the Council of Ministers of the USSR would annually approve the volume of timber to be transferred to all-Union ministries and the Councils of Ministers of the Union republics. The Ministry of Timber and Wood-Processing Industries of the USSR, Minlesprom, was responsible for the felling of forests as well as for operations planned to ensure their regeneration.

Although the main responsibility for ensuring the regeneration and improvement of forests lay with Goskomles it was also clearly stated in laws as it was in other official documents that these tasks were also the responsibility of Minlesprom.[3]

7.1.3 *The Organisation of Timber Production*

The annual plan for a timber enterprise for a given year was based on certain general indicators which were settled in the Five Year Plan. The indicators referred to the level of production, employment, payment to manpower, costs of production, profitability, and the main elements of finances for the enterprise. The task of the Ministry was to coordinate all individual plans, to put them together into basic aggregates such as total production, total labour requirements, labour productivity and so on, and send them to Gosplan. Gosplan then adjusted the plans to see that these were consistent with plans of other ministries. When the Supreme Soviet had verified the plans, they were submitted downwards through the hierarchy, via Minlesprom to the timber enterprises. Ideally, the figures that the enterprise received did not differ much from those submitted the first time round.[4]

The twelfth Five Year Plan of the timber enterprise was divided into eleven sections: the basic plan indicators, the plan of production and sales, including the supply plan, the plan for raising production efficiency, the plan for norms and normatives, the investment plan, the labour and wages plans, the plan for costs, the plan for profit, profitability and size of economic incentive funds, the financial plan, the plan for social development and the plan for environmental protection and use of natural resources.[5]

The first section of the plan contained the performance indicators to be fulfilled during the year.[6] The production and sales plan for a timber enterprise was divided into 25 sections broken down on a quarterly basis. For forest cutting most elements of the plan were worked out in physical units. All indicators related to the activities of felling and transporting were described in physical units. The supply plan detailed the amount of the various supplies, payments, details of delivery conditions and so on. The State Supply Agency, Gossnab, dealt with both the distribution of these inputs to the forest industry and most of the final distribution of timber.

The enterprise's financial plan expressed in value terms the contents of the general economic and production plans where these were formulated in physical terms. It tied productive concern into the financial system. Every physical transaction was affected through bank deposits and therefore was reflected on their financial flows. Hence fulfilment of the financial plan should have reflected that of the physical plan. Every physical transaction should have had a counterpart in the financial flows. This allowed a greater degree of overall control, as it was exercised in two ways. One line of control coming from Gosplan via Minlesprom was concerned mainly with production, while the other came via the State Bank, Gosbank, and the financial plan. This was the 'control by the rouble', whereby authorisation to effect or receive payments via bank accounts were cross-referred by Gosbank.[7]

7.2 THE STALINIST DEVELOPMENT STRATEGY AND THE LOW PRIORITY TO FOREST CONSERVATION[8]

This section provides a historical background to the forestry policy and the behaviour of timber enterprises in the Soviet Union. The aim here is to highlight the interconnection between the traditional priority system and the shortage model as we believe this body of thought is relevant for explaining the waste of natural resources. It is argued that the Soviet strategy for development and the priority system that it implied directed managers to emhasise timber production and thereby promoted a forced expansion of timber production at the expense of the protection and rational use of forests.

7.2.1 A Forced Expansion of Timber Procurement

Timber had a broad range of uses in the industrialisation of the Soviet economy.[9] The central policy for development is reflected in the rapid expansion of timber procurement during the years of the first three Five Year Plans. Over the period 1928–40, production on the whole rose fourfold.[10] Although timber procurement increased by approximately 2.5

times during the years of the first Five Year Plan, in 1932 plans were not fulfilled indicating that they were overambitious.[11]

During the first Five Year Plan timber procurement was increased in both the timber surplus and timber deficit regions.[12] The gradual shift towards the exploitation of Siberian forests started here, reflecting the political priorities for the development of Siberia. The sheer volume of the Siberian forest resources made them a target for the central leadership. As decision-making was based on political priorities, cost considerations did not constrain development. The distances incurred by the transport of timber from its place of procurement to its market of sale or final use increased. The average distance per ton of timber rail freight rose from 688 kilometres in 1933 to 1,055 kilometres in 1937 and bears witness to the development of more remote areas by the late 1930s.[13] The central preference for the development of Siberia was an important goal in the drive towards industrialisation, and reflected the view that man could master the environment. The second Five Year Plan favoured a substantial decline in the proportion of timber produced in the forests of the European regions of the Soviet Union, while operations in Siberian forests increased.[14]

In order to ensure the supply of timber for export and the domestic market the centre needed to control timber procurement. Just as in the case of agriculture, when control was needed to facilitate the extraction of food and materials,[15] control over timber procurement was needed to support the rapid industrialisation drive. Thus, timber production increased rapidly in the pre-war period. The central planners' high ambitions concerning the development of timber production were a logical result of the Soviet strategy for development which was settled in the first Five Year Plan.

7.2.2 Labour – the Binding Resource Constraint

The high goals for timber procurement accelerated the exhaustion of forestry resources in the most densely populated areas where labour was most easily mobilised. The need to increase the supply of timber rapidly made it rational to pursue a short-run forestry policy where the most easily accessible resources were harvested first. As resources became exhausted timber procurement had to move to more distant forests, and recruitment problems became of even greater significance. When workers could no longer be mobilised on a free basis, compulsory methods were introduced in the early 1930s in order to get the required timber.[16] Legislative enactments at the time enforced a degree of compulsion on the peasantry and in reality obliged peasants to enter work in timber procurement. An increased degree of compulsion was also used amongst workers in order to mobilise labour for timber production. This in turn caused a fall in labour productivity, which led to an even greater need for manpower. Forced and convict labour was also used in the production of timber.[17] The high level of mobility of forced and convict labour was of strategic importance for timber procurement. Forced labour could be used in areas with extensive forest resources but severe climatic conditions, such as the northern regions, eastern Siberia and the Far East where other forms of manpower were relatively unobtainable.[18] As more coercion was used, labour productivity dropped even further and the system created a vicious circle where marginal productivity of labour fell and labour shortage remained. Productivity amongst timber camp workers in particular, was lower than in other spheres. Forced labour had little motivation and low nutritional level, and the death-rate among prisoners in Soviet timber camps was high.[19] Hence labour continued to put a constraint on the expansion of timber procurement and hindered the planned production increase. Thus, the high targets for timber production led to a mobilisation of labour, and the urgent need for labour also demanded that this was mobilised by force.

7.2.3 A Centrally Imposed Technical Development

Before the introduction of the first Five Year Plan in 1928, little attention had been paid to technical development in the timber procurement industry. In the 1920s production was of a seasonal character, felling work was conducted almost exclusively by hand and horses constituted the major power source in hauling. The high targets for timber production established in the first Five Year Plan placed heavy demands on technical development.[20] As labour shortage delayed growth, it became important to mechanise production in order to increase timber procurement and to develop remote forest tracts. The centrally chosen strategy for industrialisation required that technical development should be planned from above, and hence research institutes for development of technological equipment and the training of workers in the timber procurement industry were established. In addition to a central institute for mechanisation of the timber industry, set up in 1931, and responsible for many technical achievements in timber procurement during the 1930s, a number of research organisations were established to conduct research in specific areas of timber production.[21]

Despite the technical developments which took place during this period, the timber procurement industry was a long way from realising the targets for technical developments set by the second Five Year Plan.[22] The planned level of mechanisation in timber haul by rail or tractor was fulfilled to about 47 per cent, the targets for skidding by mechanised means were fulfilled to just about 9 per cent while the level of mechanised felling was negligible even in 1940 compared to the planned level of 65 per cent by the end of the second Five Year Plan in 1937.[23] Thus, we can see that the rapid increase in timber production together with problems of labour recruitment necessitated the adoption of ambitious plans for mechanisation of production, in other words technical development was planned from above.

7.2.4 Central Investment Policy

In the rapid industrialisation drive the high targets for timber production were accompanied by heavy increases in capital investments. In the timber procurement industry investments were raised from 13 million roubles in 1928/1929 to 57.6 million roubles in 1929/1930. This meant investments quadrupled in one year in the beginning of the first Five Year Plan. Investments continued to rise sharply in the following years of the first Five Year Plan, and between the first and the second Five Year Plans they were to increase by 87 per cent.[24] During the first Five Year Plan capital investment was directed towards the northern regions, Karelia, the Urals, Siberia and the Far East, an indication of the central preference for development of remote forests at this time. The fact that in the first Five Year Plan more than half of the investment was allocated to the mechanisation of timber transportation, while less than two per cent was directed to the mechanisation of felling, strengthens this view.

Of the capital investment allocated to the timber industry as a whole in each of the first three Five Year Plans, approximately one-third was directed to timber procurement, indicating that the priority of timber procurement remained unchanged compared to the rest of the timber industry. However, a comparison with total capital investment in industry as well as with investments in the national economy as a whole indicate a declining priority to timber procurement.[25] The rapid expansion of capital investments reflected the emphasis on output performance and a neglect of costs.

7.2.5 The Priority of Timber Production over Forest Conservation

There was an evident contradiction in terms between the wish for forest preservation and the aim of the Soviet government to maximise timber production in the short run in order to satisfy both domestic requirements and the export trade.[26] By focusing on short-term planning little attention was paid to the use of forest resources. Central policy in particular implied that the forest resource was treated as a mine rather than as a crop as neither the means nor the incentives for regeneration activities were provided.[27]

The extractionist policy drawn up in the first Five Year Plan and the need to control production in the case of timber procurement was reflected in the institutional framework that was set up to administer this activity. In 1929 the administration of forestry and timber production at local level was united into one large-scale organisation, an indication of the low priority of forestry conservation in the first Five Year Plan.[28] Glavlesprom was established in the same year for the overall administration of *lespromkhozy*, and in the following year Soyuzlesprom, an all-Union organ, was made responsible for timber production. Its administration was not centralised and forests were not put into the hands of the industrial commissariat for exploitation by the timber industry until 1930. The centralisation drive culminated in 1932 when a specific People's Commissariat for the Timber Industry, Narkomles, was established.[29] This was made responsible for the elaboration and supervision of reafforestation projects, control over all branches of the timber, wood-processing and paper industries and for conducting scientific research.

The central maximisation policy for timber procurement implied that, although in official documents attention was given to forest conservation, this meant little in practice. The state organs created to administer forests of importance for the environment – Glavleskhoz in 1931, replaced by Glavlesookhran in 1936 – seemed virtually powerless if forests in protected areas were found suitable for industrial exploitation.[30] The hard pressure on timber procurement from the centre implied that the forestry law on water protection adopted in 1936[31] was frequently ignored. In the water protection zone within which the law prohibited felling, timber procurement was practically the same in 1938 as before the law was introduced (see Table 7.1).

Table 7.1:   Timber haul by region 1928/29–1940 (Million cubic metres)

	1928/29	1932	1934	1936	1938	1940
Water protection zone	39.4	70.6	69.2	71.5	73.7	75.7
North, Northwest and Urals	36.6	70.8	86.4	102.4	90.4	93.4
Other regions of European USSR	1.1	2.4	2.3	3.0	4.3	4.0
Asiatic USSR	8.2	20.9	23.4	35.9	44.2	51.6
Total timber haul	85.3	164.7	181.3	212.8	212.6	224.7

Source: G.M. Beneson (1947), *Drevesina v narodnom khozyaistve SSSR*, Moscow, pp. 146–7.
        Cf. Ilic (1986), p. 22.

The priority of timber production over forest conservation was further reflected in research and education. During the first Five Year Plan, the development of labour-saving techniques was promoted in order to save on labour. The separation of felling from hauling allowed a greater division of labour, and as production was mechanised the need for labour diminished. However, this is where priorities become important. Although the first Five Year Plan prescribed a wider use of mechanised equipment not only in the timber procurement industry which was labour intensive, but also in forestry which was also labour intensive, as both activities were put in the hands of the same state organ, the high targets for timber production forced it to concentrate on the former task.

7.2.6 Conclusions

It has been seen here how the central policy for expansion of timber production ensured that the use of forestry resources was maximised rather than optimised. It has also been shown that the priority system which was introduced in the first Five Year Plan directed managers to emphasise output performance over other plan targets and how this generated a behaviour which, according to Kornai, is the primary cause of the shortage economy. The empirical evidence from the forestry sector suggests that the shortage model can essentially be derived from past policies. It also implies that the low priority to forestry was a logical result of the rapid industrialisation drive. It has been seen here how the mobilisation of inputs to achieve timber targets led to the overcutting of forests and a neglect of forestry concerns.

7.3   THE CENTRAL POLICY FOR FORESTRY DEVELOPMENT

The previous section showed how the forced expansion of timber production guaranteed that the easiest accessible resources were exploited. This had some undesirable consequences: forestry resources were depleted and wasted; large clear areas were created in easily accessible locations, such as along rivers, roads and railways, and even around cities and towns in the heavily forested areas of Siberia.[32] Another consequence of the pursued policy was a regional imbalance. This section discusses the changes in forestry policy that these problems implied, up to about 1988 before Gorbachev's reform measures were implemented.

There seems to have been a change in the overriding forestry policy in the period following Stalin's death. Since the early 1960s Soviet officials have repeatedly stressed the need for implementing strategies to increase the amount of usable timber supplied to the domestic economy without an increased over-cutting of forests already being harvested.[33] Rather than extending the raw material base by increasing the area worked, policies in the post-Stalin period emphasised the more efficient utilisation of accessible timber resources and the reduction of waste at both harvesting and processing levels.[34] One important aspect was the intensification of reforestation activities in harvested areas. The eleventh Five Year Plan called for a fuller use of the forest resources in the European part of the country.[35] Minlesprom has been blamed for 'departmentalism' and bad morals.[36] In official documents it was directed to see that its enterprises worked harder, in order to improve efficiency. Party officials frequently blamed Minlesprom for not having carried out instructions from above.[37] Compliance was not promoted, however, as instructions were frequently changed.[38]

The absolute decline in timber production from the European-Uralian forest during the period 1960 to 1988 reflected the decreased supply of forests in these regions.[39] Extensive clear felling seems to have been used throughout the European-Uralian RSFSR without proportionate investment in regeneration.[40] This had produced a regeneration backlog and a serious disproportion in the age and species composition of accessible stands.[41] In Siberia, active reforestation measures had hardly been carried out at all.[42] Natural reforestation ensured that conifers were replaced by broad-leaved trees. The industrial distribution had further contributed to the overcutting of forests in the central European part of the Soviet Union, as well as in southern Siberia, while large areas in northern and eastern Siberia were as yet untouched.[43] Thus, logging operations moved north and east.

The relocation of logging activities to Asian forests created problems as most of the demand for Soviet timber was concentrated in forest-deficient European regions and beyond the western borders of the Soviet Union.[44] The Soviet Union met this demand to some extent through shipments from the northern parts of Russia and from Siberia, but paid for it with rapid cost increases.[45] Some steps to move the demand for timber to the supply were also taken. However, in some respects these investments failed.[46]

As forest activities moved east and north, exploitation costs increased.[47] The development of forests in the northern and eastern regions placed heavy demands on investment.[48] Competing demand for capital was one of the reasons for the relatively slow development of northern and eastern forests. Another reason was the shortage of manpower in these regions.[49] The prevailing climatic and transportation conditions, and problems in harvesting and processing technologies also appeared as constraints on the further expansion of raw material supply.[50]

Thus, a further expansion of logging activities in the eastern parts of the country would have led to serious short-term repercussions. First, unless an extensive capacity of timber-using production was initiated in the eastern parts of the country, transport distances would be greater. Second, the productivity of labour in logging operations would have been reduced, but the wages that would have had to be paid, and therefore costs, would have increased continually.[51] In some cases logging towns would have had to be built with all the costs associated with that. The sometimes harsh working conditions also reduced the appeal of a career in forestry when compared to other industries, making it more difficult to recruit and keep the workforce. It would have been especially difficult to recruit specialists,[52] who already had good jobs in the western part of the Soviet Union.

This suggests that the development of forests in the northern and eastern parts of the Soviet Union was quite simply neither a realistic, nor even possible, short-term alternative.[53] The further development of forestry in Siberia placed heavy demands on investments in social infrastructure. On the other hand, not only were Siberia's forestry resources abundant, but energy was cheaper and water resources were richer.[54] The supply of energy and water were factors which were particularly advantageous to the production of cellulose. Another factor which made development of the Siberian forests advantageous from a national point of view was the supply of land. Although the west and south offered the greatest potential for regeneration of forests, they also had the greatest demands for agricultural land and land for urban and industrial growth.

While Voevoda[55] suggested that the timber procurement industry should be relocated to eastern regions, other exercises[56] in deriving optimal values for regional utilisation of timber were unable to provide unequivocal evidence that the development of Siberian forests would benefit the Soviet economy more than the development of the western forests. Thus, the forestry policy would have placed heavy demands on investment if it was to be continued, regardless of whether felling was concentrated in Siberia or in the European Soviet. It was just a question of the types of investments.

7.4 CONCLUSIONS

This chapter provides an example of how the low priority to environmental concerns emerged as the logical result of the rapid industrialisation policy drawn up by Stalin in the first Five Year Plan. As over-ambitious plans and the focus of the annual plan implied a short-term policy, there was no room for forestry concerns. It has also been seen how the Stalinist strategy for development created a managerial system which permitted and even promoted the waste and destruction of natural resources.

This chapter also provides an example of how the strategy for growth, which was built on continuous mobilisation of resources rather than on increases in productivity, was established. Although the procurement of timber rapidly increased, the use of inputs expanded even more and forestry resources where exhausted in densely populated areas where labour was most easily mobilised. Such a policy placed heavy demands on investment regardless of whether development was concentrated in Siberia or the European Soviet.

NOTES

1   Barr and Braden (1988); Blandon (1983); Morozov (1986), p. 68; *EkonomicheskayaGazeta*, No. 19, 1986; *Ekonomicheskaya Gazeta*, No 27, 1988.
2   Although some attempts have been made to replant those forests, these have not beensuccessful (Barr and Braden (1988)).
3   *Lesnoi Kodeks RSFSR* (1986).
4   However, as we shall see, this was not likely to be the case. The rational director was likely to understate his production possibilities and overstate his requirements of inputs.
5   Morozov (1986), pp. 89–90. The plan for environmental protection and use of natural resources was new in the twelfth Five Year Plan.

6   According to Blandon (1983, see p. 185), there were usually 31 such plan-indicators.
7   Gregory and Stuart (1981), p. 185.
8   The arguments made in this section are based primarily on data presented in Barr and Braden (1988); Blandon (1983); and Ilic (1986).
9   Medvedev (1970), p. 11.
10   Ilic (1986), Appendix, Table 1.
11   Ilic (1986), Appendix, Table 2.
12   Ilic (1986), Chapter 1.
13   Ilic (1986), p. 24, Table 2.
14   Ilic (1986), Appendix, Table 1.
15   Davies (1980).
16   Blandon (1983), pp. 158–62.
17   Dallin and Nikolaevsky (1948); Swianiewicz (1965).
18   Ilic (1986), p. 95.
19   Ilic (1986), pp. 100–101. Blandon (1983), p. 162.
20   However, it was not until after the Second World War that significant efforts were made to equip the timber industry with modern technology (Blandon (1983), pp. 92–4 and Barr and Braden (1988), p. 65).
21   See also Ilic (1986), Chapter 10.
22   Ilic (1986), p. 117. See Blandon (1983), Chapter 4, for the history of mechanisation in logging.
23   The actual level of mechanisation of timber haul was 26.3 per cent as against the planned level of 56 per cent, In the case of skidding the corresponding figures was 5.6 per cent as against 65 per cent, *'Konferentsii po rekonstruktsii lesnoi promyshlennosti vo vtorom pyatiiletii 1933–37'* Trudy I p. 59, Moscow, 1932; Lobov (1932), p. 12; *'Lesnaya promyshlennost' SSSR: statisticheskii sbornik'*, Moscow–Leningrad, 1957, p. 105. Cf. Ilic (1986), pp. 134–5, 138, 140–41 and 183.
24   In the second Five Year Plan capital investments were assessed at 721 million roubles. Volkov (1959), p. 27. Cf. Ilic (1986), p. 158.
25   See Barr and Braden (1988), p. 65.
26   The export of timber during this period was an important source of hard currency needed for buying foreign machinery and technical equipment. In 1930–31 timber was the Soviet Union's third most important export commodity after grain and oil, accounting for 15–20 per cent of the total Soviet export trade.
27   Barr and Braden (1988), Chapter 3.
28   The *lespromkhoz* (*lesopromyshlennoe khozyaistvo*) replaced the *lesozagotvitelnaya kontora*, which was responsible for timber procurement, and the *lesnichestvo*, which was responsible for regeneration and other forestry conservation activities.
29   Mallin and Korobov (1957), Tom 1, pp. 15–17 and 62–77; Popov (1957); p. 20, Medvedev (1970), p. 12; cf. Ilic (1986), pp. 12–13 and 35.
30   Bowles (1958), p. 80; cf. Ilic (1986), p. 14.
31   According to this law, over 70 million hectares of forests along many rivers of the central and western regions were designated a 'water protection zone' in which felling was prohibited.
32   Koutaissoff (1987).
33   Blandon (1983), Chapter 2.
34   Ibid.
35   See Blandon (1983), p. 31. This meant an increase in the use of smaller, younger timber and an increase in the output of timber from thinning operations.
36   *Pravda*, 23 September 1984; *Pravda*, 12 August 1986.
37   Such documents have been published in *Izvestiya*, 6 January 1985; *Sovietskaya Rossiya*, 1 November 1986; *Izvestiya*, 7 October 1987; *Pravda*, 22 June 1987; *Pravda*, 7 September 1987; *Izvestiya*, 26 January 1987; *Sotsialisticheskaya Industriya*, 10 January 1988. The RSFSR Deputy Minister of Forestry Industry, Bobrov, was to be removed from his post. Zverev, the Chairman of Gosleskhoz and Prileipo, RSFSR Minister of Forestry Industry,

would be made strictly answerable if they failed to take exhaustive measures to improve the ecological situation in the forests in the Lake Baikal region (*Pravda*, 16 May 1987).

38 The norms for permissible emissions at the Baikalsk cellulose combine had, for instance, been changed six times in twenty years (*Pravda*, 11 March 1987).

39 *Narodnoe Khozyaistvo RSFSR v 1988 godu* (1989), pp. 378–83.

40 Barr and Braden (1988), Chapter 3.

41 Ibid., p. 47.

42 Personal interview, Akademgorodok, 22 November 1988; Barr and Braden (1988), p. 73.

43 Barr and Braden (1988), Chapter 3.

44 Barr and Braden (1988), Chapter 5.

45 See Barr (1983), pp. 419ff; *Lesnaya Promyshlennost*, No. 8, 1986, p. 3.

46 One example was the huge forestry combine erected with foreign assistance in Ust-Ilimsk. About 60 per cent of the equipment used there was foreign, but the combine has not been running well due to problems of obtaining spare parts. The construction of the pulp combine was finished before the wood-working factory. This was important since, according to the contract, pulp was to be delivered to the foreign partner. However, the most valuable timber, which should have been used in wood-working, was used in the production of pulp instead. The forest resources around the complex were exploited much more quickly than was planned, and there was already a shortage of high quality timber even before the wood-working factory had been put into operation. According to Babenko, Doctor of Forestry Economics, the forest resource was planned to last for about 100 years, but in 1988 half of it had been already exploited (personal interview, Akademgorodok, November 1988).

47 Turkevich (1977), p. 25. Between 1970 and 1980, for example, production costs per unit increased by 77 per cent, and by 118 per cent between 1970 and 1985 (Chapter 8, footnote 63 in this study). Cost increases varied considerably between enterprises: Morozov (1986), Chapter 9; Voevoda and Petrov (1987), Chapter 7, *Lesnaya Promyshlennost*, No. 1, 1987, p. 12; *Lesnaya Promyshlennost*, No. 2, 1987, p. 4.

48 Voevoda (1980).

49 The role of forced labour in the Soviet economy declined after Stalin's death (Blandon (1983), p. 162).

50 Blandon (1983), Chapter 3.

51 According to Professor Ivan Voevoda wages in Siberia were in 1988 on the average 50–100 per cent higher than in the western part of the Soviet Union, personal interview, Akademgorodok, 22 November 1988. See also Morozov (1986), pp. 169–70 and Chapter 8 of this study.

52 Blandon (1983), p. 144.

53 See also Barr and Braden (1988), Chapter 4 and Blandon (1983).

54 Voevoda (1980).

55 Voevoda (1980); Voevoda and Petrov (1987).

56 See, for instance, Blam (1983).

8. The Timber Procurement Industry in the Soviet Shortage Economy

The preceding chapter discussed how the behavioural pattern was determined at an early stage of development when directors were under constant pressure from their superiors to increase output and fulfil over-ambitious plans. But low priority of environmental concerns at the central level did not fully determine the institutional behaviour which led to environmental disruption. One hypothesis to be investigated in this chapter is that the functioning of the Soviet economic system in itself incited ministries and their subordinates to adopt a wasteful attitude towards the use of natural resources. Hypotheses concerning the input behaviour of Minlesprom and the timber-producing enterprises in the Soviet Union are empirically evaluated. Hence, attention is shifted from the central level to the sectoral and enterprise levels. In this chapter a study is made of the behaviour of the timber enterprise in the shortage economy. First, the supply and demand for timber is discussed. Section 8.2 deals with the timber industry's quantity drive. In Section 8.3, the nature of budget constraints in the timber industry is investigated. The behaviour of Minlesprom is discussed in Section 8.4.

8.1 A SHORTAGE OF TIMBER

In the shortage model the demand for an enterprise's output consistently exceeds supply. This means that the enterprise as a seller would face an almost insatiable demand. On the other hand, buyers would face chronic shortages and 'suction' in the market for the products of selling enterprises. In the shortage model the existence of 'sellers' markets' is important for enterprise behaviour. This section analyses the factors behind timber shortage in the Soviet Union.[1] It will be argued that the Soviet policy for the development of timber production within Minlesprom had created a situation which in the long run would have made it very difficult to increase production unless production efficiency was improved.

There were three different markets for timber. Timber was sold on the world market. In 1970 four per cent of the total timber production in the Soviet Union was exported, and in 1988 it had increased to 5.3 per cent.[2] Most important, timber was an input in the production of forestry products within Minlesprom. In addition to this, timber was also used by *kolkhozes* and households. The quantity of timber sold to households and agriculture increased steadily in the period 1970–88, and by 1988 it amounted to 1.7 per cent of the total timber produced.[3]

There was no doubt a potential for selling more on the foreign market. A number of foreign enterprises were waiting for the opportunity to trade with the Soviet timber industry. They were willing to buy timber, which was one of the few Soviet goods tradable in the West.[4] The Soviets should have had every incentive to increase the export of timber in order to obtain foreign currency.[5]

The most obvious explanation as to why the Soviet export of timber was not higher was the domestic shortage of timber. As in Kornai's framework the definition of demand is complicated by forced substitution effects;[6] the shortage of timber would have to be evaluated in an indirect way, by studying indicators of shortage-related phenomena, such as the time spent waiting for forestry products.

Because of a shortage of timber, the forestry products industry was not able to fulfil its plans. Evidence shows that there was a shortfall of most forestry products. Even though consumption of paper per capita was only about ten per cent of that in the United States or Sweden, eight per cent of the total paper used in the Soviet Union was imported.[7] The long, early morning queues at the newspaper kiosks were an indication of the shortage. Moreover, the central authorities had declared that the production of newspapers was to be reduced because of the paper deficit. The shortage of furniture was another example. An ordinary family might have had to wait a couple of years to get the new furniture they had ordered. In 1987, 11.4 per cent of all furniture in the Soviet Union was imported.[8]

There appears therefore to have been a shortage of timber in accordance with Kornai's theory. But shortage could also be defined in conventional terms. In an international perspective, demand for Soviet timber exceeded supply at existing world market prices.

8.2 THE QUANTITY DRIVE OF THE TIMBER INDUSTRY

This section discusses the meaning of the quantity drive and its consequences in the timber industry. In the shortage model the 'quantity drive' describes the tendency by enterprise directors to strive for continual increases in the quantity of output.[9] The meaning of the term, which is one of Kornai's key concepts, is that increases in output are achieved through 'extensive development', which means that the proportional growth in the quantity of inputs is at least as great as that of outputs.[10] In other words, increases in the quantity of output would characteristically be achieved by expanding inputs rather than improving productivity.

An investigation of Soviet data indicates that the quantity drive played a major role in the development of production within Minlesprom. The increase in capital investments, for instance in the timber and wood-working industries of 16 per cent,[11] between the ninth and the eleventh Five Year Plans, was not matched by a corresponding increase in production.[12] The production of timber did not increase in the period 1970–88 – indeed, in 1975 it even exceeded that of 1988. However, after the decline between 1975 and 1980 there was a further increase (see Table 8.1).[13]

Table 8.1: *Timber production in the Soviet Union in 1970–88 (millions of*
            m^3)

Year	1970	1975	1980	1985	1988
Timber	385.0	395.1	356.6	368.0	386.4

Source: Narkhoz (1989), p. 401.

Regardless of which years we compare, the comparison indicates that the growth in material input was greater than that in output. Between 1970 and 1987 the basic industrial production funds in the timber industry increased by 114 per cent and for the whole of the forestry products industry they increased by 177 per cent.[14] As the structure of the fund did not change much over the years[15] one might deduce that there was a balanced growth in the various components of the fund. However, the rate at which facilities were brought into service exceeded that at which they were taken out of service (compare Tables 8.2 and 8.3).

Table 8.2: *The capacity brought into service in the forestry products*
            industry (expressed as a percentage of overall funds at the end
            of the period under review)

Year	1971–75	1976–80	1981–85	1986–88
Per cent	40	37	33	19

Sources: Narkhoz (1986), p. 123; and *Narkhoz* (1989), p. 357.

In the shortage model, one implication of the quantity drive is the sacrifice of production of by-products. Applied to the present context, the timber manager would not have been motivated to make use of waste products in the production of timber. The expression of output in terms of physical units meant that those trees most easily accessible would be those actually chosen for processing.[16] As it was easier to fulfil the plan if the output was in the form of coniferous species, the lumberjacks used to fell, extract and process the coniferous timber and leave the broad-leaved trees.[17] Thus, the fact that the Soviet timber industry did not make use of by-products from forest cutting appears to be consistent with Kornai's ideas. There was no development in technology to make use of by-products in the Soviet timber industry.[18] Neither the incentives nor the means to promote such progress in technology were available. In an economy of shortage, the supplier is powerful. He can insist on his own terms, knowing that he can cause great inconvenience; the customer, generally, has no choice, as he is tied by the plan to a particular supplier. He simply can not go elsewhere. In the timber industry, the plan-indicator that had to be fulfilled before all the others was timber production in physical units.[19] Therefore, the production and delivery of by-products dropped out of the incentive system and management was rewarded whether or not it carried out the contractual obligations in respect of the product mix.

Table 8.3: *The capacity taken out of service in the forestry products industry (expressed as a percentage of overall funds at the beginning of the period indicated)*

Year	1971–75	1976–80	1981–85	1986–88
Per cent	22	18	15	10.8

Sources: *Narkhoz* (1986), p. 123, and *Narkhoz* (1989), p. 359.

Developments in the quality of plantings also seem to conform to the hypotheses derived from Kornai's theories. Evidence suggests that in order to expand the quantity of forest plantings forest managers in the Soviet Union have instead sacrificed the quality.[20] In the western areas where planting measures were undertaken on a regular basis, the common practice seems to have been to expand planted areas rather than to keep up plantings from earlier years.

8.2.1 Bonuses and the Quantity Drive

As the plan for timber production was confirmed by the higher authorities, enterprise performance was evaluated by them rather than by their customers. But as the fulfilment of some plan-indicators might have made it impossible to fulfil others, there was always some room for individual interpretation of the plan.[21] As only some of the plan-indicators were important for chances of promotion and the determination of wages and bonuses,[22] the fulfilment of these plan-indicators in the annual plan was more important than others.

Even though payments are attributed a minor role in the shortage model, it is assumed that a bonus attached to the quantity of production would further encourage the director to fulfil the expectations of his superiors.[23] An investigation into the incentive scheme in the timber industry strengthens the hypothesis that there was a connection between enterprise behaviour and the quantity drive within this industry. The shortage of inputs would have promoted hoarding of inputs in the planning stage in order to secure plan fulfilment. If bonus payments were important for enterprise behaviour, the prospect of earning a bonus would have strengthened the tendency for production increases to take place by means of resource mobilisation rather than through improvements in production efficiency.

The fund-forming indicators in the timber industry were the 'value' of timber sold, the production of 'useful' timber in terms of volume (excluding brush), labour productivity and profitability.[24] As the rewards received by directors and workers depended on the fulfilment of the plan, there was an incentive for them to submit a plan that was easy to fulfil. This also applied to the fund-forming plan-indicators. It is important to note that these were planned administratively just as the plans in physical units. The three incentive funds available to the enterprise – the Material Incentives Fund, the Development of Production Fund, and the Socio-Cultural and Housing Fund – were set up mainly to cope with this problem.[25]

The major source of the incentive funds for the timber enterprise was the Material Incentives Fund, MIF. The actual size of the fund available to the enterprise was based on its planned size and on whether the enterprise offered any counter-plans. In the timber industry, it was expressed as a percentage of the wage fund.[26] The Socio-Cultural and Housing Fund, although formed from profits, was expressed as a percentage of the Material Incentives Fund.[27] It therefore increased or decreased according to the degree of plan fulfilment as reflected by payments into the Material Incentives Fund. This fund was used for living accommodation for the workers at the timber enterprises, day-care centres for the workers' children and for holiday camps.[28]

The norm in the case of the Development of Production Fund was a percentage of the planned value of basic capital.[29] This fund was meant to constitute an additional source to centralised financing of new technology in the enterprise, and the mechanisation, renovation and modernisation of existing equipment and processes. It was formed mainly from a deduction from profit and the depreciation funds set aside by the Ministry. The total sums set aside could be increased or decreased depending on whether the planned profit and planned depreciation funds turned out to be larger or smaller than the actual, realised ones.[30]

The Material Incentives Fund was formed from the enterprise's profits on condition that the most important plan-indicators were fulfilled.[31] Management bonuses were financed from this fund. Most of the bonuses paid to workers formed part of the wages fund, but they also shared in the Material Incentives Fund. Management as well as workers should thus have been interested in performance which leads to an expansion of this fund.

The fund further acted as some incentive to reduce labour turnover as bonuses were paid only to those workers who were still at the timber enterprise at the end of the year.[32]

The initial planned level of the Material Incentives Fund was determined in the Five Year Plan.[33] However, the value of this fund could be manipulated by the timber enterprise. One problem recognised by the Soviet planners was that the plans which were formulated were not 'taut'. Therefore, in order to promote taut plans in the timber enterprise, the planned size of the Material Incentives Fund was increased if the enterprise offered counter-plans which were higher than the figures set in the Five Year Plan. An increase in the fund-forming indicators in the counter-plan over the figures for the relevant year in the Five Year Plan would have increased the payments into both the Material Incentives Fund and the Socio-Cultural and Housing Fund, if the plan was fulfilled. A one per cent increase in these in the counter-plan, for example, would have increased the funds of the timber enterprise by 2, 0.5, 0.3 and 0.2 per cent (see Table 8.4).

Table 8.4: The fund-forming indicators

Indicator	Change in the funds for a 1 per cent increase in the figures in the Five Year Plan	Increase for every extra 1 per cent achieved over the suggested plan	Penalties for under-fulfilment
Value of sales	2.0	1.40	2.60
Production of useful timber	0.5	0.35	0.65
Productivity of labour	0.3	0.21	0.39
Profitability	0.2	0.14	0.26

Source: Blandon (1983), p. 194.

Extra benefits were incorporated with over-fulfilment. These were 0.7 times the norms. The intention was that the enterprise thus found it better to express the full potential of the cutting in the suggested plan, than to override the original plan. Penalties for not fulfilling the plan were 1.3 times the basic norms to ensure realistic plans.

The sales indicator was the most important factor when checking how much was contributed to the Material Incentives Fund. As the value of this indicator was not improved if costs of production were reduced it did not provide the timber enterprise with any incentive to save on inputs. On the contrary, as it was a monetary aggregate and included the value of inputs, it stimulated a quantity-driven behaviour. It might even be argued that it caused management to waste rather than economise on inputs.[34] The same applied to the indicator of gross output, which was the second most important element for payments into the Material Incentives Fund. One advantage with the sales indicator compared to the indicator of gross output was that it excluded unsold production. Thus if production could not be counted unless it was paid for, the timber enterprise should have been motivated to make sure that valuable timber was not left in the woods or the production of low-quality timber, unsuitable for use, was avoided. This was provided that payment did not occur unless delivery had actually taken place, a requirement which was seldom fulfilled.

However, the material-technical supply plan was not incorporated into the plan-indicators or the incentive schemes on which payments into the incentive funds were dependent. Although there were financial penalties for not keeping to the supply plan, such as fines for non-delivery and delays, the success of the operation of the enterprise was not judged on the basis of whether it operated strictly within its supply plan. The enterprise was answerable primarily to its subordinates, not to the enterprises it was supposed to deliver to. Moreover, there was practically no reward for abiding by the input plan. Since the enterprise could not legally obtain inputs other than those allocated in the plan, breaches of the input plan either remained concealed or were authorised by planners.

The third fund-forming indicator, the labour productivity indicator, might have provided the enterprise with an incentive to save on the use of manpower. However, the quantity drive and the hoarding of inputs should have ensured that the incentive effect of this indicator was to increase supply of output rather than to decrease demand for manpower, especially as saved wages would have decreased payments into the Material Incentives Fund.[35]

Similarly, the incentive effect of the profitability indicator on the use of inputs should have been weak. In the context of the Soviet timber enterprise profitability was defined as:[36]

$$\text{profitability} = \text{profit/capital}$$

In the shortage model it is assumed that the profitability indicator is of little importance for the behaviour of the socialist enterprises.[37] 'The budget constraint is merely an accounting relationship', asserts Kornai.[38] If this is correct, the effect of the circumstance whereby the enterprise operated on *khozraschet*, which literally stands for profit-and-loss accounting[39] (meaning that the enterprise was to cover its own expenses out of income), was limited. The fact that in the timber industry the cost indicator appeared to have stimulated reductions in the quality of output rather than to cost reductions strengthens this shortage-model hypothesis.[40] The aim of *khozraschet*, which was to encourage the enterprise to carry out instructions with due attention to efficiency, would consequently not have been realised in practice in the timber industry.

The fact that the various costs of production, payments into incentive funds, the profit or loss, labour productivity and so on, were all planned administratively, strengthens the view that the effect of *khozraschet* on enterprise behaviour was weak. The actual level of the planned magnitudes was quite simply of minor importance to the enterprise. For instance, as the profit remainder was paid into the state budget and did not remain at the disposal of the enterprise, the prospect of making a profit did not in itself constitute an incentive for the enterprise.[41] In principle, the enterprise did not have to care whether it was geared to make a profit or loss.

The enterprise was not directly affected by changes in prices on inputs or outputs. Such price changes would only have led to increases or decreases in the planned level of profits. Similarly, if the enterprise substituted an expensive input for a cheaper one, it would only have led to an increase in the planned level of profits. It was only in relation to their planned values that increases in revenues or decreases in costs influenced the plan-indicators which were used to evaluate enterprise performance.

If price changes did not affect enterprise behaviour, as is postulated in the shortage model, then capital charges and rental payments would consequently not have induced the enterprise to save on the use of production factors. This would not even have been the case for the actual, relative to their planned, values, as such savings would not have contributed to the payments into the Material Incentives Fund. An increase in either of these would just have reduced the profit remainder which was paid to the state budget. It does not make any difference to the enterprise if its payments to the budget are called capital charge or profit remainder.

Although profit was planned administratively, it might have affected enterprise behaviour through its effects on the indicators of profitability. The higher the planned profits, the higher the planned profitability. It is not clear whether the fund-forming profitability indicator used in the timber industry was gross or net profitability. This is crucial to whether the reduced capital charges would have had any effect on the payments into the Material Incentives Fund. If profitability was defined as gross profitability (*balansovaya rentabelnost*) deductions from profits for capital charges, rental payments and interest charges on loans and credits had not been made. In calculating net profitability (*raschetnaya rentabelnost*) all these payments and charges had been deducted from profits.[42]

However, as argued above, the rational enterprise director had strong incentives to maximise rather than minimise costs of production, as performance was rewarded in relation to the figures which had been settled in the plan. If the planned level of profits was high, the planned value of the profitability would be set high as well, and the risk that the enterprise would be unable to fulfil its quota increased.

As the director was deprived of all bonuses if a fund-forming plan indicator was not completely fulfilled, the incentive to strive for modest plan-indicators in the planning stage was strong. This incentive was further strengthened by the fact that the enterprise operated in an environment with permanent shortage.

As the Soviet system depended on administrative orders and as producing enterprises were told what to do, the role of money, prices and profits was weak. The plan had to be fulfilled whatever the effect on profits. The prospect of making profits did not constitute an incentive in any way to the enterprise, as what was left after paying the capital charge, the forest charge and transferring sums to the incentive funds went to the state budget.[43]

The incentive effect of bonuses was weakened by the fact that the Soviet system was dependent on administrative orders. The Soviet director had to obey many orders which had no effect on his bonus, and in some circumstances even reduced it, because his chances of promotion and avoidance of demotion depended on his reputation for discipline and carrying out orders. He had to avoid any trouble which could arise from him annoying influential customers, the regional party secretary, or anyone on whom he depended for supplies. This is to say that he was dependent on the established contacts as there might have been no-one else to turn to. Each one of them was a monopolist. The kind of behaviour which earned a medal or a commendation might or might not have earned a bonus.[44] Thus, payments into the incentive funds which threatened the fulfilment of quantitative targets were likely to be ineffective.

8.2.2 A Strive Towards Modest Plans[45]

The aim of this section is to investigate how the various components of the Soviet incentive system might have contributed to the quantity-driven behaviour of the timber enterprise. In order to do this an investigation is made into how these components have stimulated the Soviet enterprise in general to adopt modest plans for production. A major difficulty from the standpoint of management arose from the fact that there was a danger that different elements of the plan failed to cohere and that when the current plan was amended this was not done systematically. The enterprise had to take into account the fact that the output plan could be changed by superior authorities without analogous changes in the supply, finance and wages plans.[46] Uncertainty of supply had many consequences: enterprises stockpiled goods as a hedge against possible shortages and overapplied for supplies in the plan in the hope of obtaining what was needed. The rational director also aimed towards a modest plan to insure himself against a breakdown in the flow of inputs. Shortage also caused work stoppages when this breakdown had occurred, irregularity and rush periods if supplies arrived late. The combination of supply delays and the need to fulfil a plan by a given date caused the phenomenon known as 'storming'.[47]

The final yield was really the joint product of many enterprises. If all of them were rewarded and praised for fulfilling or over-fulfilling an output plan, and if in addition this output was expected to increase year after year, then this was a direct incitement to waste,[48] an observation consistent with the general ideas of the shortage model. This was because a change in the intermediate commodity good provided threatened the plan-fulfilment of the enterprise providing the input if it caused a reduction in its measurable quantity.[49]

As noted above, the responsibility of supplying enterprises was left primarily to superiors, not to the enterprise. It is important to bear in mind that the overall target figures had priority for the director and the Ministry alike.[50] As the enterprise was judged by plan-fulfilment, and penalised for not reaching the prescribed target, it became important that the plan was modest enough to be safely within reach.[51] This was especially so because the director could not be sure that supplies would arrive, and there was a risk that the higher authority would alter the plan. The strive towards a modest plan was further motivated as the director had every reason to believe that the higher authority assumed that the enterprise would not tell the whole truth.

Similarly, the rational enterprise director would have been deterred from over-fulfilling the plan by too wide a margin, as the authorities might have then decided on an impossibly ambitious goal for the next plan-period.[52] Stimuli for the adoption of insufficiently taut plans were therefore likely to exceed the additional reward of aiming high and adopting taut plans.[53] The fact that the director was wholly deprived of bonuses if planned fund-forming indicators were just not fulfilled strengthened the incentives for avoiding taut plans. Non-fulfilment also injured his standing and chances of promotion. The higher the planned norms of utilisation, the easier they were to fulfil, to show a saving and to get bonuses.

As the Ministry wanted to be able to report that its enterprises fulfilled their quotas,[54] it might have increased the plans and the financial burdens of the successful enterprise. In particular, there was a risk that the Ministry would level off observed inequalities between enterprises through discretionary redistribution.[55] This could be done physically or financially. Such anti-stimuli encouraged concealment of reserves rather than their mobilisation. The evaluation of the production unit and its manager was often based on plan-fulfilment regardless of the tautness of plans.

The non-stability of norms represented another reason for not aiming too high.[56] The advantages of doing better were thus removed by a change in the plan or by an amendment of the rules governing the payments into the incentive funds and therefore of the bonus entitlements, in a downwards direction. As the Ministry was given limits in the form of maximum sums for incentive funds, the rights of enterprises to allocate money into these funds could be cut back.

8.2.3 Conclusions

The development of the timber industry appears to have been consistent with Kornai's ideas. It has been shown how the quantity drive has played an important role in the production of timber. As a consequence of this quantity drive, the production of by-products in the timber industry was sacrificed and quality of plantings was low. It has also been shown that to the extent that bonuses affected behaviour in the timber industry they strengthened the quantity drive and stimulated hoarding of inputs. While the fund-forming indicators used in the timber industry stimulated the fulfilment of output plans, they did not encourage the realisation of input plans.

We have also seen how various components of the Soviet incentive system might have contributed in making the timber enterprises as well as the Soviet enterprise in general strive for modest plans. The emphasis on output performance, uncertainty of supply, non-stability of norms and the risk that output targets were ratcheted upwards made it advantageous to strive for modest production plans and avoid taut planning. Thus, the incentive structure facing the Soviet enterprise in general might have contributed to the generation of quantity-driven behaviour in the timber industry.

8.3 VARYING 'HARDNESS' OF BUDGET CONSTRAINTS

The hoarding tendency of the socialist enterprise is selective, according to Kornai.[57] The enterprise is expected to accumulate as much of the materials that are difficult to get hold of as possible. On the other hand, it would be content with smaller stocks of easily substitutable or easily available materials.[58] Empirical evidence suggests that the tendency of enterprises to increase inputs was selective, depending on the 'hardness' of resource constraints. Some resource constraints would have become binding before others. The fact that basic industrial production funds within the timber-cutting industry increased by 114 per cent between 1970 and 1987, while the wage cost increased by just 43 per cent during the same period might indicate that the resource constraint on labour was harder than that for capital.[59] The enterprise probably saw the resource constraints on investment resources, labour and material resources as relatively harder than any resource constraint on the use of forests. Directors were usually unable to transfer funds from one article where there was lack of spending to another where the resource constraint had become binding.[60] This created difficulties because market conditions and central provision of funds varied according to input.[61] In the case of forest use, the enterprise could simply violate the relevant restrictions and laws if it found it necessary in order to fulfil its production quota for timber. There was no physical constraint on forest use as there was for other resources. If the enterprise hit the physical resource constraint for any other input this caused disruption in production. As the quota might have been hard to fulfil the rational enterprise director would have been induced to substitute forest raw materials for other inputs. For instance, just using the most valuable timber stocks, while leaving less valuable timber at the forest site, and then moving on to another location, saved labour.[62]

Soft budget constraints in the planning stage might manifest themselves through increasing yearly budget allocations. In the timber industry total production costs increased by 73 per cent between 1970 and 1984. As this was considerably less than the increase in production costs for industry as a whole,[63] it might indicate that budgets were harder than average in the timber industry. On the other hand, the fact that the cost per rouble of timber output was allowed to increase by 4.6 per cent in 1980–84, while that of industry as a whole during the same period decreased by 0.7 per cent, indicates that the planners tolerated relatively soft budgets in the production of timber.[64]

In the timber industry, the budgets for labour appeared to be binding in the sense that wages were not raised enough to attract sufficient manpower to go and work in the less accessible forests of Siberia. On the other hand, budgets for the timber resources should have been relatively soft as they were considered to be abundant. The vast subsidies for replanting trees strengthened this impression. Soviet official statistics supported the hypothesis that the softness of budget constraint was different for different inputs within the timber industry. Between 1970 and 1984, the largest increases in the timber industry were the budgets for energy and raw materials. These budgets increased by 184 per cent and 178 per cent respectively.[65] During the same period wage costs increased by 33 per cent.[66] The budget for labour increased less than the budgets for all the other production factors.[67]

Reference could also be made to other pieces of evidence suggesting that budget constraints at the planning stage were relatively soft in the forestry sector in 1970–87. The average monthly wage in the forestry products industry increased from 135.3 roubles in 1970 to 230.8 roubles in 1987, an increase of 71 per cent.[68] As the number of workers within the sector did not decrease by more than five per cent during the same period, this implies that the central planners had allowed for gradual increases in the wages fund allocated to Minlesprom. This might in turn be taken as an indication of a soft budget constraint in the planning of labour. In the timber industry, the average monthly wage increased from 147.5 roubles in 1970 to 250.2 roubles in 1987, an increase of 70 per cent.[69] But as the number of workers decreased by 16 per cent[70] during the same period, total wage costs increased less in the timber industry than in the forestry products industry as a whole.[71] The increase in monthly wages in the period 1970–87 was a little higher in the timber industry and within the whole of Minlesprom, than it was in industry as a unit, where the increase in average wages was equal to 66 per cent.[72] In 1987 the wage rate within Minlesprom was four per cent higher, and that of the timber industry alone 13 per cent higher than the average wage for industry workers in general.

Some softness in the budget constraint in the planning of capital investments in the forestry products industry can also be seen. There was a gradual increase in capital budgets allocated by central planners to the timber and wood-working industries. The level of capital investments in 1981–85 was seven per cent higher than in 1976–80, and 16 per cent higher than in 1971–75.[73] In 1987 the amount of capital investments within Minlesprom as a unit was 28 per cent higher than the annual average of the ninth Five Year Plan, spanning the years 1971–75.[74] In the timber industry alone capital investments were seven per cent higher in 1976–80 than in 1971–75.[75] Although enterprises paid charges for the use of state capital investments it has been implied that the payments of capital charges would have increased as well. The increase in basic industrial production funds of 114 per cent within the timber industry between 1970 and 1987 is another indication of soft budgets for capital investments.[76]

An additional indication of softness in budget allocations at the planning stage is that budgets for circulating capital increased by 31 per cent in 1980–87.[77] This is the aggregated expenditure for raw materials, intermediary inputs, energy and so on for the forestry products industry as a whole.

It is difficult to generalise about the hardness or softness of budget constraints of the timber enterprise. As noted above, it is possible that the budget constraint grew tighter or became looser in the implementation stage. A soft budget at this stage would have meant that actual expenditure was routinely greater than planned.[78] In contrast, in the case of hard budgets, actual expenditure would have been equal to or less than planned. Empirical evidence suggests that in 1979 the actual cost per rouble of output and actual production costs generally exceeded planned costs at six *lespromkhozy*.[79]

8.3.1 Varying Shortage Intensity of Inputs

Kornai emphasises that the quantity drive, the general input hoarding tendency and shortage are linked together in a mutually amplifying self-generating process. It is the 'expansion drive' that joins quantity drive and hoarding, and this is said to explain the prevalence of investment hunger at all levels of the administrative hierarchy. Whereas in the traditional socialist economy investment goods are allocated free of charge, its demand would be limited only by tactical self-restraints. Kornai argues that the budget constraint for capital investments tends to be softer than for other inputs.[80]

According to the shortage model, the 'investment hunger' and the paternalism of central authorities result in unrealistically ambitious investment plans. During plan implementation it emerges that costs of approved programmes have been underestimated, new capital projects are added and actual supplies of capital goods turn out to be less than projected. This causes 'investment tension' throughout the economy and chronic shortages in capital markets.[81] Consequently, the enterprise as a buyer experiences difficulties in obtaining machinery and equipment. Hence, the investment plan of the individual enterprise tends not to be fulfilled.

In the case of an expansion drive and urge to invest, the enterprise director wants to increase capacity and capabilities in order to satisfy demand. As the timber enterprise experienced problems in obtaining the required labour resources, its urge to invest should thus have been oriented towards labour-saving investments. Similarly, the director would have been motivated to try to obtain investment allocations which would have made it possible to save on the use of scarce material resources. The risk-averse director should have engaged in activities in order to avoid difficulties in the implementation of plans. It would have been worth his while reducing the risk of having resources reallocated from the timber enterprise to areas of higher priority. Moreover, he would have wanted to avoid disruptions and shortages in intermediate goods caused by suppliers not fulfilling agreed delivery plans. On the other hand, if he considered available forest resources to be almost infinite he would not have been interested in resource-saving investments. Thus the investment tension for most other investment resources would have corresponded to a restrained demand for investment which promoted a decreased use of forest raw material per cubic metre of timber output.

The very old machinery and equipment in the forestry products industry indicated that there was a need for investment.[82] The declining share of investments allocated to this industry should therefore be taken as an indication of decreasing priority,[83] implying that the timber enterprise was facing greater difficulties in obtaining approval for projects, investment funding, and allocation of rationed capital goods during the planning of investments.[84] In the presence of such a development a selective urge for investments as outlined above was even more probable.

With investment tension throughout the economy there was a risk that the authorities would either initiate or tolerate a siphoning of capital goods away from the timber industry to areas of higher priority. This would have amplified investment tension in the timber industry and caused it not to fulfil investment plans thereby delaying the completion of capital projects.

8.3.2 Slow Technical Development

One of the most adverse effects of chronic shortage on economic performance is the inhibition of the producer's incentive to engage in technological innovation.[85] As regards the timber industry operating in a shortage environment, one would hypothesise that the technological level was relatively low and that technological innovation was slow. Kornai emphasises primarily the negative effect of shortage on the incentives of enterprise directors to promote quality-enhancing technological innovations. The existence of the seller's market, which suggests that the producer can sell almost anything regardless of the quality, would make producers uninterested in promoting qualitative improvements of output. Quality improvements are seldom rewarded simply because they are difficult to measure.[86]

Quality is typically very difficult to incorporate effectively into quantitative indicators.[87] However, in the case of timber production quality could be expressed in quantity terms as it depended on the size of stocks.[88] The production of timber thus did not face the traditional problems of low quality, as is the case for most other raw materials. Therefore, when we speak of technological improvements within the timber industry we have in mind resource-saving innovations that increase output per unit of input. However, the general problem of low quality of output in the Soviet economic system indirectly affected the timber industry through its use of other industries' output as inputs.[89] This was particularly true of the low quality within the machine-building industry, which affected the timber industry and all other production where its equipment was used.[90]

Moreover, the non-priority to the timber procurement industry meant that it was not favoured in the allocation of capital investments and technical equipment, and hence technological development would have lagged behind that of priority sectors.[91] Non-priority further meant that technical development was not promoted by the centre, and capital investments in timber procurement meant an increase of inputs in quantitative terms, while quality was the same as before.[92]

The state of technology and its development had both a demand side and a supply side. In the case of demand, potential timber users do not seem to have had any impact on technological innovation. Although the use of inputs had increased considerably, production in 1988 was at about the same level as in 1960. As the shortage of timber impeded production within Minlesprom itself, the Ministry should have been interested in technological improvements which increased production of timber. However, the shortage of timber did not seem to have made Minlesprom promote such investments.[93] On the contrary, the proportion of basic industrial production funds allocated to the timber industry within Minlesprom declined, relative to the allocations to the wood-working, and the pulp and paper industries.[94] Moreover, the fact that in 1978–88, according to official

Soviet statistics, the plan for timber cutting was generally under-fulfilled might indicate that the Ministry was unable to promote increases in timber production.[95] Not being able to fulfil plans for putting capacity into service is another indication of the inability of Minlesprom to implement technological progress in the timber industry in order to secure an increased supply of timber for its own production.[96]

The evidence of deficiencies in technological levels in the Soviet timber industry was consistent with the related hypothesis in the shortage model. Empirical data indicate that technological development was impeded on the supply side by deficiencies in domestic distribution and the technology of domestically produced equipment.[97] The industry was also unable to solve its problems of obtaining adequate technology through foreign trade.[98] Much of the machinery was obsolete because of low replacement rates, which in turn were a result of the miserly budget norms mentioned above.[99] In addition, maintenance of existing technology was made difficult by shortages of engineering staff and spare parts.[100]

It seemed likely that incentives to engage in technological innovations varied depending on what was achieved. In the presence of shortage of inputs, the enterprise director should have been interested in technological developments if they reduced the need for scarce inputs. The scarcer the input the more interested the enterprise director should have been in promoting increases in this particular input. The director should have been especially interested in technolgical improvements which would have saved on the use of inputs at the implementation stage. If he could manage with fewer inputs than he was entitled to at least according to the plan, the enterprise might have been able to fulfil output plans even if deliveries were delayed or did not arrive at all. Technical innovations which would have saved inputs at the planning stage, on the other hand, were risky as they might have led to a reduced allocation of the particular input.

Between 1970 and 1987, labour productivity in timber cutting increased by 52 per cent.[101] However, the increase in labour productivity was less in timber cutting than in the forestry products industry as a whole, and it was substantially lower than the industrial average.[102] This might indicate that technical development in the timber-cutting industry was slower than that of the other industries within Minlesprom and in particular slower than the industrial average.[103] Since gross output in terms of timber production did not increase by more than 0.3 per cent when comparing 1988 with 1970 (as noted above, production fell between 1970 and 1989), the increase in labour productivity can hardly be explained by increased production. From 1970 to 1987 the number of workers in the timber-cutting industry decreased by 16 per cent.[104] It is difficult to know if the labour productivity indicator contributed to the reductions in the use of labour. The falling number of workers employed in the timber-cutting industry might just as well be due to problems of recruitment of manpower. The fact that wages in timber cutting were substantially higher than the industrial average might indicate that market forces played a role when it came to the allocation of labour to this sector. High wages might have been necessary to attract manpower, and if central planners were not willing to increase the allocated wage fund to allow for this, then the timber-cutting industry might have been forced to decrease its manpower to compensate for the necessary increases in wages. Thus, if the timber enterprise faced difficulties because of problems of labour shortage, then it should have been interested in innovations which could have increased labour productivity.

Similarly, the shortage of capital and other material inputs should have made the enterprise interested in technological improvements. As argued above, it is not likely that the labour productivity indicator stimulated the timber enterprise to technological innovations, which reduced its need for labour. It seems even less likely that the indicator of profitability stimulated the enterprise to technical development. If one disregards 1982, profitability in the timber industry declined between 1970 and 1983, in 1980 and 1981 it was even negative (see Table 8.5).

Table 8.5: Profitability in the timber industry 1970–83 (in per cent)

Year	1970	1975	1980	1981	1982	1983
Per cent	16.4	6.3	−2.6	−3.6	9.3	7.5

Source: Narkhoz (1984), p. 539.

Basic industrial production funds within the timber industry increased over the years.[105] This provided one explanation for the declining profitability rate. The declining profit rate within the industry provides a second explanation for the negative development of the indicator of profitability. Profits and profitability developed in much the same way over the period considered (compare Tables 8.5 and 8.6). The downward trend is the logical result of the fact that production costs were steadily increasing, while the price of timber was fixed at the same level. The loss in 1981 of 376 million roubles was turned into a profit of 1,026 million roubles in 1982. This is probably explained by the general price revision which took place in the Soviet Union in 1982, at which the price of timber was raised by 40 per cent.[106]

Table 8.6: Profits in the timber industry 1970–83 (million roubles)

Year	1970	1975	1980	1981	1982	1983
Million roubles	901	512	−258	−376	1,026	865

Source: Narkhoz (1984), p. 538.

In the shortage model, it is assumed that investment decisions are made on the basis of quantitative signals, while profitability criteria would not influence decisions.[107] The statistics of the development of profits support this hypothesis and do not suggest that the indicator of profitability would have had any effect on technology. However, the decreasing profitability rate in the 1970s within the forestry products industry as a whole might have made central administrators reluctant to invest in this branch. The proportional decline in basic industrial production funds allocated to this sector suggested that such a negative impact of the declining profitability on central decisions could not be excluded.[108] Similarly, one cannot exclude the possibility that the low profitability of the timber-felling industry relative to the wood-working and pulp and paper industries, has influenced Minlesprom to reallocate investment resources in favour of the latter.[109]

Profits do not seem to have had any stimulative effect on the timber enterprise. There again the development of profits seems to have been outside the control of the enterprise. Given that environmental conditions varied geographically, and that enterprises differed with respect to technology and skills of manpower, then obviously costs would have varied between enterprises. Empirical evidence indicates that profitability may have varied considerably between enterprises.[110]

As the combination of the output plan and price of output might have been unfavourable for individual enterprises, it might have been necessary to make them adhere to given plans in order to avoid imbalances in the central plan. What we have here is a basic conflict between the Ministry's interest in plan fulfilment and the interests of the enterprise. It appears as though the formal penalty/reward system could have solved this conflict. However, the enterprise had very little chance to react to such stimuli. In particular, in the presence of a perceived abundance of forest resources, the timber enterprise had little incentive to promote technological innovations which would save on the use of forest resources per unit of timber output.

The technological development also depended on such things as the supply of equipment and machines. This, in turn, depended on the quality of production within the machine-building industry, domestic distribution, foreign trade, and so on. The quality of domestically produced equipment and machines should further have depended on the priority of their production.[111] That is, technological developments which were of low priority, if there were any such developments, were more likely to suffer from low quality than technological improvements which were of relatively higher priority.[112] For instance, if labour shortage was an important national problem, the central planners should have given priority to labour-saving technologies.

In the wake of an abundance of forest resources, the central authority should therefore have had little interest in promoting technological developments which saved the use of forest resources. Moreover, it should not have been willing to spend scarce hard currency to obtain such resource-saving technology from abroad. The timber enterprise was therefore more likely to be able to buy labour-saving technology than technology which saved on the use of forestry resources.

As the timber industry was not one of the high-priority industries, it was not likely to receive the most advanced technology. This was particularly likely to be the case for technology which improves the quality of forest plantings and saves the use of forest raw materials. The low-priority ranking of environmental conservation suggested that within the machine-building industry, the development of techniques which economised on the forest resources was also given low priority. Thus if the development of low-waste technology, which made it possible to improve the utilisation of by-products after felling, had a low-priority status in the timber industry in the shortage economy, then acquisition was unlikely.

Hence, in the presence of shortage the timber enterprise had neither the incentives nor the means to promote technological progress which would have improved the use of forest resources. Empirical data show that much of the machinery in the timber industry was obsolete because of low replacement rates; the technological level of cutting machines and equipment was low by international standards. In some areas the Soviet Union achieved technological levels and rates of progress that were closer to Western standards.[113] It may therefore be the case that the technological deficiencies in felling were the result of low-priority status amplifying the general processes outlined in the shortage model.

8.3.3 Forced Substitution

The enterprise in a resource-constrained economy often encounters difficulties in acquiring all the inputs called for by its production plan.[114] As a result, certain input constraints become binding earlier than scheduled, production bottlenecks develop, and the enterprise has to engage in alteration in the composition of output, reduction in quantity or quality of output, and forced substitution of inputs.[115] In the case of the timber industry, when resource constraints on forest raw materials were not binding, while the resource constraints on most other inputs were relatively hard, the enterprise was likely to substitute forest raw material for other inputs whenever this was possible. Moreover, it was likely to substitute obsolete cutting machines for modern ones. If labour was scarcer than capital, it would have been forced to substitute capital for labour.[116]

The experiences of the Soviet timber industry appear to have been consistent with Kornai's hypothesis about production. The relative cost of labour in the production cost was decreasing in 1970–88. At the same time wages increased. This implies that the central planners were not willing to increase the wage fund allocated to the timber industry. The increase in wages should be seen as a result of market forces, rather than as an indication of increasing priority. The reduced number of workers in the timber industry indicates that manpower has been substituted by other inputs.[117]

8.3.4 Conclusions

Empirical evidence suggests that the quantity drive within the timber industry has been selective, which means that the use of some inputs have increased more than others depending on the 'hardness' of budget constraints.

The development of manpower has not been consistent with the shortage model. Increases in production have not been matched by corresponding increases in the use of labour. Market forces have instead played an important role in the allocation of labour. The relatively high wages in the timber industry might indicate that high wages were necessary to attract labour to this sector. Improvements in labour productivity have been achieved by reducing the number of workers. This might indicate that the timber industry had problems of labour recruitment. The constraint on labour has, in effect, been binding. Therefore, investment should have been oriented towards labour-saving investments.

However, because in the case of forestry resources there was no resource constraint as there was on other inputs, the enterprise could simply have violated restrictions and laws concerning the use of these. In order to fulfil the production plan the rational enterprise director therefore tended to substitute forestry resources for other inputs.

The profitability indicator did not stimulate the enterprise to increasing profits, an observation which supports the hypothesis that profitability has little effect on enterprise behaviour in the shortage economy. On the contrary, this indicator seems to have been beyond the control of the enterprise. Similarly, development of technology is consistent with the shortage model. The fund-forming indicators did not stimulate technological development. However, as shortage of manpower created obstacles to plan fulfilment, the enterprise should have been interested in labour-saving technical developments. On the other hand, the strict adherence to the annual plan stimulated the opposite behaviour. There was as a result no incentive to save on forestry resources.

8.4 THE BEHAVIOUR OF MINLESPROM

The Ministry did not merely administer the enterprises under its control in accordance with the wishes of central planners. The sheer volume of work and decisions in Gosplan also placed considerable powers in the hands of the ministries. The Minister and his deputies were super-directors, they were formally in charge of the production within the Ministry.[118] Under conditions of relative scarcity, and with investment allocation virtually free, the rational Minister should have seen good reasons for more resources to be allocated to the sector for which he was responsible.

Timber was the responsibility of Minlesprom. But Minlesprom was not in charge of the numerous enterprises which came under the control of other ministries involved in the timber complex, whose collaboration was essential if the projects were to be completed. These other ministries had other urgent tasks, and were answerable for their overall plan objective to the central planners. Whatever success criteria they had for their enterprises, they were not related to the timber project, and contractual relationships played a subordinate role.[119] Hence, as the production of timber might have suffered from disturbances in the supply of inputs,[120] Minlesprom would have been motivated to expand in order to provide its timber enterprises with inputs.

For the Ministry, the overall target figures were the most important task. If an enterprise failed to fulfil its quota, the fulfilment of the target for the sector as a whole was consequently threatened. In order to compensate for such a failure at one enterprise the Ministry would have had to place additional obligations on other enterprises. Moreover, as the Ministry wanted to report not only that it had fulfilled the sectoral plan, but that most of its enterprises had also, this, in turn, induced the Ministry to level out differences in performance concerning plan fulfilment. On the other hand, as levelling out provided the enterprise with a disincentive to more than fulfil its plans, it would not have done so unless overall plan fulfilment was seriously threatened.

Thus, the Ministry should have been interested in most of its enterprises fulfilling their own plans in order to avoid trouble that would have arisen if it had interfered. The Ministry should therefore have been interested in making sure that the enterprises obtained inputs necessary for plan fulfilment. Hence it should have tried to allocate resources in a rational manner. Moreover, it should have tried to avoid levying on its enterprises tasks that could threaten their plan fulfilment. As new technology, for instance, usually caused immediate disturbances at the enterprise,[121] it should not have promoted technological development. In other words, the Ministry should not have been interested in promoting technological development even though this would have reduced costs in the long run if it disturbed production performance in the short run.

The Ministry did not know the exact productive potential, the amount of hoarded stocks of materials and the degree of tautness of past and present plans. This made it rely primarily on its knowledge of the past performance of its enterprises.

Given that the timber industry could not be classified as a high-priority sector,[122] an attempt is made to outline a strategy for Soviet forestry development policy. Operating in a shortage economy, the Ministry would have perceived resource constraints on scarce inputs as binding. Some input constraints might even become binding earlier than scheduled. On the other hand, resource constraints on inputs which were not scarce would not have been considered binding. Non-priority implied that the overall plan might have been difficult to fulfil. The Ministry should have known this, and therefore tried where possible to use inputs which were not scarce. As the forest resources it managed were largely considered to be abundant, it would at ministerial level have been rational to substitute other inputs for forest raw material. Hence the Ministry had no incentive to encourage its enterprises to save on the use of forest resources.

Non-priority implied that the Ministry could not expect any major increase in the allocation of resources whatever good arguments it provided. On the other hand, in the presence of vast shortages throughout the economy, it should have been aware of the possibility that those resources allocated to the Ministry by central authorities in the plan, might be reallocated to high-priority production. Hence, the Ministry had every incentive to try to get as many inputs as possible in the first stage of the planning process. Then when it came to implementation, it would have been induced to choose the most beneficial strategy, given that plans were to be fulfilled in the very near future, as the annual plan was most important. As the most urgent task was the fulfilment of the annual plan, it could not have had a long-term perspective.

The rational Ministry might be assumed to have chosen the easiest way of fulfilling the overall plan targets.[123] A limited wage fund in the presence of labour shortage would have reinforced problems to recruit labour to the Siberian forests. The further away forest felling took place from existing social infrastructure, the higher the cost for labour, as it was necessary to pay higher wages in order to get labour to work under what were sometimes extremely hard working conditions in the Siberian forests. The regional coefficient in the Soviet Far North was 1.5–2.0, that is, a timber cutter could get up to 100 per cent extra in addition to his tariff wage.[124] As the spread in tariff wages in the timber industry was relatively high,[125] it was relatively costly to have skilled labour work in the distant forests of Siberia. It would also have been easier to recruit labour if housing was already available. Then, for a given wage fund, the farther away the areas were that the Ministry chose to exploit, the less labour it was able to employ. With respect to labour the Ministry should thus have preferred development of the timber industry in the western part of the Soviet Union to that in Siberia.

As regards investment policy, the Ministry would have behaved in a similar manner. It would have preferred development in areas where infrastructure, housing and so on already existed, and where there were factories nearby in order to avoid transportation problems. Thus with a given central allocation of capital resources, the rational Ministry should have preferred development in the accessible parts of the Soviet Union, in other words primarily in the Western parts of the country. The fact that Siberian enterprises obtained obsolete equipment from timber enterprises in the western part of the Soviet Union strengthens this hypothesis.[126]

When it comes to technological development, the Ministry would not have been interested in promoting new technology as this might have had a negative impact on plan fulfilment in the short run. Hence it would not have been interested in increasing the use of broad-leaved trees, as this would have required the introduction of new technology. All these factors made it advantageous for the Ministry to choose a strategy of development which favoured felling in the most easily available forests.

8.4.1 Conclusions

The incentive structure of Minlesprom appears to have been compatible with that of the timber enterprise. As the focus was on the annual plan, the Ministry had no incentive to encourage its enterprises to save on the use of forest resources. The Ministry was perhaps more interested than the enterprise in expansion, as it wanted to secure overall supply of inputs. Non-priority contributed in making the supply of inputs at ministerial level even more uncertain as this implied a risk that the central planners reallocated resources to branches of higher priority. Therefore, non-priority might have stimulated the Ministry to expand and develop its own supplies in order to become more independent from the central planners. Thus, the effect of priorities was probably more important at the ministerial level, than at the level of the enterprise.

8.5 CONCLUSIONS

The priority-revised shortage-economy approach was used to analyse the behaviour of the timber-procurement enterprise. It was shown that development of production in the timber industry has taken place through an expanded use of material inputs. It was argued that timber production has been restricted by a shortage of inputs. However, while the resource constraints on investment resources, labour and material inputs would have been relatively binding, Minlesprom had good reason to consider the forestry resource as abundant. Therefore there should have been a tendency for forestry resources to be substituted for other more scarce inputs at ministerial level.

The same would apply at enterprise level. On the input side, the timber enterprise experienced the consequences of shortages as a buyer. The relative scarcity of inputs affected its demand for technology. Problems in the recruitment of labour would have provided an incentive to concentrate on labour-saving machines in cutting.

Not only were the resource-saving incentives of the enterprise poor, but also it could not cut down on its use of resources for technological reasons because of their low priority in the machine-building industry.

The low level of technology was a general problem connected with the incentive structure of the Soviet economic system. Enterprise innovation might have had negative impacts on some important performance indicator, or it might have been impossible to obtain or reshuffle the necessary inputs without prior authorisation from higher planning organs. As management was primarily judged by its ability to fulfil the annual plan, it could not afford disruptions in the short run, which innovations are likely to cause. Innovations entail some element of risk, and risk-taking as such was not rewarded. The problems of recruiting labour to the timber-cutting industry might possibly have motivated the enterprise to invest in labour-saving technology. However, if it perceived forest resources to be abundant it had little reason to invest in forest-saving technology.

NOTES

1   While plans for timber production were generally fulfilled in the period 1965–75, they were consistently not fulfilled in 1976–88 (see various editions of *SSSR i Soyuznye Respubliki*). The non-fulfilment of plans for transporting timber by rail and river presumably exacerbated the shortage in the supply of timber (ibid.).
2   See *Narkhoz* (1989), pp. 401, 638.
3   See *Narkhoz* (1989), pp. 121–2, 401.
4   For instance, the Swedish firm, Johnson, was trying to buy timber for more than twelve years with little success; there was simply no timber to buy.
5   See Barr and Braden (1988), p. 65. The sale of timber has helped to finance the transfer of technology from the West to the Soviet Union.
6   See p. 44 of this study.
7   *Narkhoz* (1988), p. 608.
8   *Narkhoz* (1988), p. 609.
9   Kornai (1980), Chapter 3.
10   Davis (1989), p. 445.
11   In 1971–75 the capital investments amounted to 6,400 million roubles and in 1981–85 they amounted to 7,400 million roubles, *Narkhoz* (1986), p. 368.
12   See *Narkhoz* (1988), pp. 142–5. In the forestry products industry as a whole, capital investments increased by 28 per cent between the ninth and eleventh Five Year Plans (*Promyshlennost SSSR* (1988), p. 78).
13   By 1989 timber production had fallen back to the level of 1960 (*Narkhoz* (1990), pp. 396–7).
14   *Promyshlennost SSSR* (1988), pp. 50–51.
15   *Narkhoz* (1984), pp. 140, (1986), pp. 118–19, (1988), pp. 102–3.
16   Blandon (1983), p. 188.
17   Ibid. This explains why, in the longer term, areas of forests were cleared of coniferous species and the other species were left standing.
18   Barr and Braden (1988), pp. 201–2; Blandon (1983), Chapters 4 and 5.
19   Blandon (1983), p. 188.
20   Barr and Braden (1988), p. 87.
21   Blandon (1983), p. 187. For a general discussion of the success-indicator problem in the Soviet industry, see Nove (1982), pp. 96–102 and Gregory and Stuart (1981), pp. 178–80.
22   Ibid.
23   Kornai (1980), p. 63.

24   Blandon (1983), p. 193. According to Professor Mudretsov, a Forestry specialist at CEMI, the most important plan-indicators remained the same in the period 1966–88. Personal interview, CEMI, Moscow, 12 March, 1991.

25   Blandon (1983), p. 192. See also Freris (1984), Chapter 6, for a discussion of incentive funds and bonuses, and Oxenstierna (1987) and (1990), Chapters 5 and 6.

26   Blandon (1983), p. 193. Since 1982 a sum equal to eight per cent of the wage fund has been deducted from profits to the 'social insurance' (*sotsialnoe strakhovanie*), including payments to MIF (Morozov (1986), pp. 189 and 198). In most branches, however, MIF was expressed as a percentage of planned profits (Freris (1984), p. 138). For the light industries the 1980 wages fund was used instead. In the case of the timber enterprise the MIF was equal to about ten per cent of the wages fund. As the norm was given as a percentage of the wages bill, there was a direct incentive for the enterprise to maximise rather than minimise the wages fund. The enterprise would have been motivated to increase rather than decrease its staff. If profits went up as a result of a reduction in the number of workers employed, the wages bill went down. Therefore, since the MIF was calculated as a percentage of the wages bill, the payments into the incentive fund would have fallen as a result of the economy. See Nove (1986), pp. 91–2.

27   For the timber enterprise it was 30 per cent of the MIF.

28   Blandon (1983), p. 192. See also Freris (1984), pp. 21–2 for the general use of this fund.

29   Nove (1986), p. 79.

30   Blandon (1983), p. 192. See also Freris (1984), p. 21 for the general rules concerning the formation and use of this fund.

31   See Morozov (1986), pp. 89–90.

32   Blandon (1983), p. 192.

33   Blandon (1983), p. 193.

34   This was the case provided that the costs were included in the prices at which output was computed. The principal idea for calculating the price of timber per cubic metre was that it should be based on the average costs of production for the branch as a whole (see Blandon (1983), p. 196). Hence, there should at least have been an incentive to propose expensive variants at the ministerial level.

35   See footnote 25.

36   Kozhin et al. (1981), p. 48; see also Freris (1984), p. 20.

37   Kornai (1980), pp. 317–19, 345.

38   Kornai (1980), p. 309.

39   Nove (1982), p. 14. The timber enterprise has been working on the basis of *khozraschet* since 1966 (Blandon (1983), p. 188).

40   Blandon (1983), p. 188.

41   Timber enterprises which were surplus units had to pay a sum into the state budget before calculating their operating profitability while those making a loss received a subsidy (Blandon (1983), p. 192).

42   In cases where net profitability is used, the fixed capital in the denominator of the expression included only the capital funds on which the enterprise paid charges or interest rates. It excluded capital financed from the enterprise's own Development and Production Fund.

43   See Nove (1982), p. 93.

44   See Nove (1982), p. 96.

45   The discussion in this section is based primarily on Nove (1982), pp. 102–15; Gregory and Stuart (1981), pp. 177–86; and Blandon (1983).

46   Nove (1982), p. 107.

47   See Nove (1982), p. 105.

48   Nove (1982), p. 99.

49   Ibid.

50   Nove (1982), p. 105.

51   Nove (1982), p. 106; Blandon (1983), p. 187.

52   Nove (1982), p. 106,

53 See also Blandon (1983), p. 191.
54 Nove (1982), p. 107.
55 See Litwack (1991) for a discussion of the consequences of discretionary behaviour (*uravnilovka*) at ministerial and central levels in the Soviet Union.
56 Nove (1982), p. 107.
57 Kornai (1980), Chapter 2.
58 Ibid.
59 *Trud v SSSR* (1988), pp. 50 and 193; *Promyshlennost' SSSR* (1988), p. 51.
60 Davis (1989), pp. 438 and 448.
61 Ibid.
62 Blandon (1983), Chapter 3.
63 Production costs increased by 77 per cent between 1970 and 1980, and by 118 per cent between 1970 and 1985. This might be calculated from the statistics on wage costs in *Trud v SSSR* (1988), pp. 49 and 189, combined with statistics over the percentage distribution of costs of production in various editions of *Narkhoz*. See also Petrov et al. (1986), p. 154. Production costs were generally higher in Siberia and lower in the north-western part (Turkevich (1977), p. 25).
64 *Narkhoz* (1985), p. 161.
65 Various editions of *Narkhoz*.
66 *Trud v SSSR* (1988), pp. 50 and 193.
67 Apart from unspecified costs, which increased by 27 per cent under the period considered.
68 *Narkhoz* (1988), p. 99.
69 *Trud v SSSR* (1988), p. 193.
70 *Trud v SSSR* (1988), p. 50.
71 1970–87 wage costs have increased by 43 per cent in the timber industry, by 62 per cent in the forestry products industry and by 101 per cent in industry as a whole. *Trud v SSSR* (1988), pp. 189 and 193.
72 *Trud v SSSR* (1988), p. 189.
73 *Narkhoz* (1986), p. 368.
74 *Promyshlennost SSSR* (1988), p. 78. The corresponding increase in industry as a whole was 91 per cent.
75 Kozhukov (1984), p. 327.
76 *Promyshlennost SSSR* (1988), pp. 50–51. The corresponding increase for the whole of Minlesprom was 177 per cent, while that of industry as a whole was equal to 230 per cent.
77 *Narkhoz* (1988), p. 101.
78 Davis (1989), p. 437.
79 Kozhin et al. (1981), pp. 45–6.
80 Kornai (1980, Chapter 9.
81 Kornai (1980, p. 201.
82 See *Narkhoz* (1986), p. 123; *Narkhoz* (1988), p. 106; *Promyshlennost SSSR* (1988), p. 84.
83 See *Narkhoz* (1986), pp. 115 and 366–8; *Promyshlennost SSSR* (1988), pp. 50–51.
84 Davis (1989), pp. 450–51.
85 Kornai (1980), Chapter 6.
86 Ibid.
87 Gregory and Stuart (1981), p. 181.
88 Morozov (1986), pp. 89–91.
89 See Blandon (1983), Chapter 5.
90 See Gregory and Stuart (1981), pp. 377–81 and 399; Amann and Cooper (1986).
91 Gregory and Stuart (1981), p. 180; Blandon (1983), p. 91.
92 Gregory and Stuart (1981), p. 181; Davis (1989).
93 Blandon (1983), Chapter 5. It might also have been the case that lack of technical development was the cause of a slower rate of productivity than expected (p. 144), or that results appeared after a considerable time lag (p. 94).
94 See *Narkhoz* (1984), p. 138; *Promyshlennost SSSR* (1988).
95 *SSSR i Soyuznye Respubliki*, various editions.

96 In 1987, the plans for putting capacity into service were fulfilled to 71 per cent only in the chemical–forestry complex as a whole (SSSR i *Soyuznye Respubliki v 1987 gody* (1988), p. 30). As the chemical industry by most criteria (plan fulfilment for output, budget allocations of capital, relative wage rates) appears to have had a higher priority than the forestry products industry, it seems likely that most of the above-mentioned under-fulfilments may be attributed to Minlesprom.

97 Barr and Braden (1988), p. 201; and Blandon (1983), pp. 127 and 139.

98 Barr and Braden (1988), pp. 199–208.

99 *Narkhoz* (1988), p. 106; and *Narkhoz* (1989), p. 359.

100 Blandon (1983), Chapter 6 and p. 190.

101 Labour productivity is defined as gross output divided by the number of workers: $q = Q/L$, where q is labour productivity, Q is gross output and L is the number of workers. *Narkhoz* (1988), p. 686.

102 Compare the figures in *Narkhoz* (1984), p. 134; *Trud v SSSR* (1988), p. 237; and *Narkhoz* (1988). Between 1970 and 1987 labour productivity in the forestry products industry increased by 82 per cent, while it increased by 98 per cent in industry as a whole (ibid.).

103 In 1960–75 labour productivity in logging increased by 49 per cent as compared with the all-economy average, which increased by 122 per cent (Blandon (1983), p. 92). However, the increase in labour productivity was more rapid in logging in the 1950s (Blandon (1983), p. 114). In 1950–63, labour productivity rose by 8.1 per cent per year (Blandon (1983), p. 90), which was higher than the industrial average (*Trud v SSSR* (1988), p. 234). This might reflect a lagged response to the rapid increase in capital intensity in logging after the war (Blandon (1983), pp. 92–4).

104 *Trud v SSSR* (1988), p. 50.

105 *Narkhoz* (1984), p. 138.

106 Voevoda and Petrov (1987), p. 193.

107 Kornai (1980), Chapter 14.

108 *Narkhoz* (1986), p. 122; and *Narkhoz* (1988), p. 112.

109 *Narkhoz* (1984), p. 559.

110 *Lesnaya Promyshlennost*, No. 3, 1987, p. 31; *Lesnaya Promyshlennost*, No. 10, 1987, p. 24; Petrov et al. (1986), pp. 223–4. See, for instance, Kozhin et al. (1981), pp. 49–50 and 52 for a comparison between three production associations: Sverdlesprom, Tiumenlesprom and Irkutsklesprom. In 1978–79 some units within these associations were profitable while other enterprises made heavy losses. In 1979, profitability varied between 26.6 per cent at one of the production units within Irkutsklesprom and −21.2 per cent at one unit of Sverdlesprom. Also within the same production associations, variations in profitability between various units were sometimes considerable. For instance in Irkutsklesprom, where the profitability of one unit was 26.6 per cent that of another unit was −3.4 per cent in the same year (ibid.). In the Karpat production association, in 1984, profitability varied between 8.2 per cent at Chernovitsles and −15.2 per cent at Prikarpatles (Voevoda and Petrov (1987), pp. 177–78). While all the seven units within Prikarpatles worked with a loss with respect to cutting, they were all profitable as regards wood-working (ibid., pp. 275–7).

111 Davis (1989), pp. 436–7.

112 Gregory and Stuart (1981), p. 181.

113 See Cooper (1986).

114 Kornai (1980), Chapter 2.

115 Kornai (1980), pp. 36–8.

116 Blandon (1983), p. 94.

117 There is an upward trend in the share of costs of production going to amortization, indicating that the relative share of capital has increased. The proportional share of costs for raw materials and basic materials has increased as well.

118 Nove (1982), p. 62.

119 Gregory and Stuart (1981), pp. 179–80.

120 Blandon (1983), pp. 91, 127 and 139.

121 Blandon (1983), pp. 189–90.

122 Barr and Braden (1988), p. 65.

123 Nove (1982), pp. 106–7.

124 Morozov (1986), p. 170. This might be compared to that of the southern and central regions of Siberia and the Far East. In these areas the regional coefficient varied between 1.15 and 1.30. In the forest-deficient regions the coefficient was 1.0. The tariff wage was determined by the basic rate for the jobs involving the lowest skills together with the skill scale established for the branch. In the timber industry there were six skill scales. See also Oxenstierna (1990), pp. 126–30 for tariff wages and skill scales in Soviet industry.

125 In the timber industry the tariff coefficient was 1:87 (Morozov (1986), p. 169), implying that work in the highest skill group should have been paid 87 per cent more than work in the lowest skill group. The maximum spread in tariff wages in extractive industries was larger than other branches of the Soviet industry (see Oxenstierna (1990), Figure 5.1, p. 127).

126 *Ekonomicheskaya Gazeta*, No. 14, 1989, p. 11. In the Irkutsk region, for instance, about 25 per cent of the equipment had previously been used at European enterprises (ibid.).

9. The Ineffectiveness of Priority Changes in the Forestry Sector

In this chapter the shortage model is used to analyse the effect of changing priorities within forestry. An improved efficiency in the use of the forestry resources clearly presupposes an increased production efficiency in the felling of timber. The first step towards achieving this were the organisational changes which took place within the forestry sector in 1988. In this chapter an investigation is made into the effect of these changes in the presence of other alterations which occurred within the framework of the general reconstruction of the Soviet economy, on the use of forestry resources. For an improved production efficiency to take place it was thus necessary that the incentive structure facing the Ministry and its enterprises was also changed. This would largely have become a question of changing the criteria by which performance was evaluated and resources were allocated, changes which were not in line with the interests of Minlesprom as this would have threatened its position in resource allocation. Therefore, in order to implement a difference in priorities in the case of forestry, the monopolistic power of Minlesprom would have had to be broken.

By the end of 1988, the Gorbachevian reforms had instituted three types of changes aimed at reducing ministerial power and making mismanagement of forestry resources costly.[1] These were further changes in organisational structures, changes in the role of central planning and the transition of Soviet state enterprises to full cost-accountability. The shortage model is used to investigate the implications of these changes on the use of forestry resources.

In the first section of this chapter measures of reorganisation are discussed. Then, in Section 9.2, the effect of self-accountability in state enterprises, cooperatives and leasehold is investigated. The effect of a forestry charge is analysed in Section 9.3, with relation to the traditional Soviet economic system as well as in the context of Gorbachev's reform package.

9.1 REORGANISATIONAL MEASURES WITHIN THE FORESTRY SECTOR

In order to make the production of forestry products more efficient Minlesprom underwent some reorganisation in 1988. The reorganisation was the first actual step in an attempt to replace a path of development of the timber industry based on the mobilisation of resources by one based on improvements in productivity, which was a general ambition of the overall reconstruction of the Soviet economy. One easily identifiable 'measure' is that the name of the ministry was changed from the Ministry of Timber, Wood-Processing and Pulp and Paper Industry, Minlesbumprom, to the Ministry of Timber and Wood-Processing Industry, Minlesprom. This can be taken to indicate a down-grading in priority of the pulp and paper industry. It might also be a sign that the Ministry had been reorganised. Since the Ministry was first established in 1932, its name has been changed from time to time to reflect a reorganisation, however small.[2]

A signicant measure is probably that the staff numbers at the Ministry were cut by 40 per cent.[3] This might seem to be a rather drastic way to reduce bureaucracy. Soviet economists have expressed the view that such staff cuts would have caused great disturbances in production as the system still relied on administrative allocation of resources.[4] It might be argued that little was achieved through such mechanical cuts in staff if the role of the Ministry was left unchanged. As long as the Ministry was responsible for plan fulfilment it would continue to interfere in the functioning of the enterprise, and as long as it was in charge of the administrative allocation of resources, it would have used its power to allocate these in a way which made sure that plans were fulfilled. If a cut in staff thus implied that the Ministry could not perform its function of allocating resources, plan fulfilment was threatened.[5] Enterprises might not have been able to fulfil their plans if they did not receive the necessary inputs previously obtained through the administrative system and there was still no market where they could obtain them through wholesale trade.

Some changes within the organisational structure can also be seen. A coordinating body for the chemical and forestry industries was created in 1986 as part of the general attempt to curtail central bureaucracy. This was intended to reduce the power of the ministries, which were supposed to engage themselves in the general outline of development and not in detailed administration of enterprises' day-to-day activities. In the case of forestry, however, an extra layer was added to the hierarchy instead, just as during the general campaign against the bureaucracy, Minlesprom, despite strong criticism, retained its position in the management of forestry production. There were 40 forestry products production associations directly under Minlesprom,[6] below which the timber industrial enterprises, *lespromkhozy*, would be operating as before. The difference was that the *lespromkhozy* would be working mainly in Siberia, while a new type of complex timber enterprise, *kompleksnye lesnye predpriyatye*, would be operating in those areas in the western part of the Soviet Union where wood-cutting possibilities were still favourable.[7] Apart from being situated in different areas, the main difference between *lespromkhozy* and the 'complex timber enterprise' was that while the former were to move continuously from site to site as these were cleared, the latter would be permanently situated in one place. As is indicated by the name, the 'complex timber enterprise' was a more complex institution than the *lespromkhoz*.[8] The intention with these new types of enterprises was that, as they would be permanently based in the same place, they would be motivated to economise on forestry resources and concern themselves with forestry conservation. If, however, plan targets continued to be expressed in tons of timber procurement, it is not likely that these types of organisational changes would have accomplished the desired effects, especially as it required a technology which might not have been available.[9] As such changes would not have been in the interest of Minlesprom, to which the 'complex timber enterprises' belonged, an improved use of forestry resources was even more unlikely.

As a general rule, after cutting, 'complex timber enterprises' as well as *lespromkhozy* were required to tidy up the plot which had been vacated and carry out the requisite afforestation. They were assigned plan-indicators for the regeneration of forests. In practice the reforestation that was accomplished in Siberia had taken place through natural self-generation, since planting measures were rare.[10] Most of the replanting measures undertaken have been carried out in the south-western part of the Soviet Union.[11]

9.1.1 The State Committee for Forests – Goskomles

A second measure of reorganisation is that Goskomles, which was established in 1988, replaced the earlier State Committee for Forestry, Gosleskhoz.[12] This meant that Goskomles took over some of the tasks of Gosleskhoz, such as managing forest funds, which involved management of all types of forest utilisation. In as far as Goskomles took over the tasks of Gosleskhoz, the reorganisation seems to have been a change comparable with the changes in the names of the Ministry noted above. Just as before, forestry organs dealt with the protection and management of forests as such, and were not supposed to carry out timber procurement for economic reasons. The main forestry institutions at local level, the forestry enterprises, *leskhozy*, were still assigned plan targets for regeneration, protection and cutting of forests in poorly forested regions, in other words, in regions where cutting was not the principal activity. This included afforestation and the protection of forests against unwarranted fellings, fires and insect pests.

Goskomles was also responsible for controlling the use of forests. The forestry enterprise was obliged to see that the timber procurement enterprise observed established rules of forest utilisation within its own land area. Goskomles did not have any directly subordinated enterprises. The forestry enterprises which were formerly subordinate to Gosleskhoz operated under the republican ministries or state committees for forestry. Directly below the RSFSR Ministry of Forestry, for instance, there were in 1988 seven forestry associations. The forestry enterprises were formally subordinate to these.

Goskomles also took over the scientific role of Gosleskhoz, which meant that it was responsible for working out recommendations concerning the location of cutting, optimal cutting areas, the volume of cutting and so on for the whole country and for all types of forest utilisation. But apart from the tasks that Gosleskhoz had been in charge of, it was also responsible for duties which were more in tune with the general ambitions of *perestroika*. It was assigned the issue of developing economic tools for managing timber enterprises and of working out conditions for introducing full cost accounting in the timber industry and for self-financing of forestry measures.[13]

According to our model, increased priority to forestry would have meant that budget constraints for measures of forestry would have become softer. In the case of labour, the allocated wage fund was increased, indicating that wages as well as the allocated manpower would have increased.[14] However, due to the inflexibility of upward changes in priority, shortage intensity remains and quantity drive continues. Accordingly, increasing priority to forestry would thus only have been of minor importance to the *leskhozy*, who actually planted forests.

In principle, Goskomles should have had the same power as Minlesprom. That is, it was supposed to have the power to enforce its tasks and, in particular, it should have been able to decide when forestry measures were to be carried out. However, economic incentives did not work as long as the traditional system remained largely intact within which plan targets were to be fulfilled. Substantial power was given to Minlesprom during the Stalinist period and ever since then it defended its position over resource allocation. It would therefore have been difficult to implement any changes in priorities. Minlesprom would simply not have followed instructions from Goskomles, which had no power to enforce them. As long as the legal system did not function,[15] the respect for laws and regulations remained arbitrary. Moreover, it was not even possible to comply with such restrictions if the required materials were not provided. While production plans were accompanied by plans for investments and supplies, laws and regulations were not.

9.2 A CHANGE IN THE ROLE OF PLANNING

The Gorbachev reform proposed a significant shift from administrative to market resource allocation. Reducing administrative planning might have undermined the power of Minlesprom. The strategy of reform under Gorbachev centred around a flow of new decrees and laws.[16] Three important changes that could have contributed in breaking the monopoly of Minlesprom were the law on state enterprise and the decisions to allow cooperatives and leasehold. This section discusses the effect of these changes on the use of forestry resources.

9.2.1 The Law on State Enterprises and Wholesale Trade

One important ingredient in the Gorbachevian attempts at reform was the changed role of central planning. The emphasis was to be transferred from the annual plan to the Five Year Plan.[17] One intention with such a change was to remove the conflict between plan fulfilment and technical development discussed above.[18] In practice production would not be based on central directives to the same extent as earlier.[19] Enterprises would work out their own plans and confirm these plans themselves. While, in 1987, 100 per cent of timber procurement was based on state orders, plans were drawn up so that in 1989 it would have been reduced to 40 per cent.[20] Thus 60 per cent of production would be sold to wholesale trade between enterprises without the interference of central planners. However, this was not realised in practice.[21] There was still no domestic market where enterprises could buy the required materials and sell their products.[22]

A decreasing role of directives in production meant that there was less of an emphasis on output performance. The official document that opened the possibility for economic accounting, self-financing and decentralised decision-making was the law on state enterprises, which has been in force since January 1988.[23] One important aim with the law was that the enterprise would be guided by economic incentives, rather than by administrative rules. The work of the enterprise would be evaluated by means of earned profits as well as by output performance. The law stated that the net profit after necessary deductions to the state budget would be left to the enterprise for the benefit of its staff, and was not to be confiscated by the state, as was the case up to 1987.[24] However, in officially adopted documents on the distribution of profits, its allocation was strictly regulated.[25]

By January 1989 all timber enterprises were to run on full economic accounting.[26] However, as long as the seller's market prevailed neither the timber enterprises, nor Minlesprom would have been motivated to consider costs.

9.2.2 Cooperatives and Leasehold

The law on the right to form cooperatives, which was adopted in 1988, is another document which was aimed at reducing the power of ministries.[27] While state orders, *goszakazy*, were to be gradually reduced, the bulk of production was to be sold through wholesale trade. However, the reduction in central orders implied that the administrative allocation of inputs was to be reduced as well.[28] Thus, in order not to reduce production a market would have had to be created whereby the enterprise could obtain the needed inputs. One intention of central reform makers was that such a market would be created by the cooperatives. Although the idea of cooperatives appeared to be promising when it was first introduced, few of the expectations connected with this idea were, however, realised in practice.[29] Cooperatives had difficulties operating in a shortage economy, as it was not easy for them to get hold of the required inputs, and it appears as though many cooperatives became corrupt.[30] Another problem was that the cooperative sector was subject to numerous rapid policy reversals in the Gorbachev period. As new problems emerged, existing decrees were revoked and replaced by additional legislation.[31] The expectation of discretionary changes in the rules governing the activity would have impeded their development. Nevertheless, cooperatives have played quite an important role in forestry. In Krosnoyarsk, for instance, a forestry cooperative bought low-quality timber, which had been discarded during production.[32]

In 1988, many Soviet economists expected that the new possibility of leasing state enterprises would become more important for the economic development in the Soviet Union than the law on state enterprises itself. Under long-term lease arrangements in industry, a workers' collective was given the opportunity to rent land from the state or from a state enterprise.[33] In 1987 the first industrial enterprise in Moscow started to operate on the leasehold basis, and by 1988 a few hundred state enterprises were working on the same principle.[34] In the absence of a clear law on leasing there was much confusion about the nature of leasing arrangements.[35] A law stating the rules for leasehold was adopted in 1989.[36] Goskomles was in charge of working out a proposal of the terms for leasing timber enterprises.[37] However, because of the weak role of money in the shortage economy, Minlesprom would not have been interested in earning rent from leasing out enterprises. Therefore, Minlesprom would only have been willing to lease out enterprises which did not work well. As long as the legal system was not working, it might even have reclaimed the enterprise in question. This in effect meant that the possibility of leasing or even buying enterprises from the state did not threaten the power of Minlesprom. The incentives to engage in leasing among the population have also been undermined by a discretionary change in the conditions regulating leasehold.[38] Nevertheless, it might have contributed to the improvement of forestry, especially if foreign assistance had been available.[39]

9.2.3 Conclusions

It has been seen here that the reform measures discussed did not seem to generate a development which would have threatened the monopolistic power of Minlesprom. As Minlesprom continued to decide how much the timber enterprise was to produce, it obtained no real autonomy. The reform measures did not lead to the development of a market and competition in the forestry sector. Their development was held back by supply problems and by problems of inconsistent and unstable government regulation. The fact that the Soviet economy remained unreformed in 1991, despite the adoption of many reform measures, suggests that the effect of policy changes was likely to be weak.

9.3 THE EFFECT OF INCREASED FOREST CHARGES

In the traditional Soviet economic system, it was only increases in the fund-forming plan-indicators that led to extra bonus payments in the timber industry.[40] This meant that a change in relative input prices would have influenced the enterprise's financial account only if the price changes were of importance to the fulfilment of plan-indicators.

In 1982, the forest tax (*lesnykh taks*) as well as the rental payment for the use of forests (*popennaya plata*) were increased by 100 per cent as an ingredient of the general price revision.[41] The increase in the forest payment did not have any effect on three of the four fund-forming plan-indicators at the timber enterprise. It affected neither the planned nor the actual level of the indicators of timber production, nor the sales or labour productivity as none of these were related to the use of forestry resources.

However, the rental payment might have had an impact on the indicator of profitability. If the enterprise saved on the use of forestry resources in relation to the plan, it would then have saved on its payments for it as well. If actual forest payments were less than planned, *ceteris paribus*, it would have meant that actual profits had exceeded their planned level. This suggested that actual profitability would have exceeded planned profitability, which was one requirement for extra payments into the Material Incentives Fund.[42] However, as argued above, the rational enterprise director was likely to maximise rather than minimise costs of production, as performance was rewarded in relation to the figures which had been settled in the plan. If the planned level of profits was high the planned value of the profitability would be set high as well, and the risk that the enterprise would be unable to fulfil it increased. As the director was deprived of all bonuses if a fund-forming plan-indicator was not fulfilled the incentive to strive for modest plan-indicators in the planning stage was strong. This incentive was further strengthened by the fact that the enterprise operated in an environment with permanent shortage.

Thus, the rational director was likely to maximise the planned budget for forestry resources rather than minimise it, and hence, the incentive for the enterprise to reduce its use of forestry resources in the traditional Soviet economic system was weak. If the director considered the forestry resources to be abundant he should have tried to obtain a generous budget for them as he had to expect the budgets for other scarce production factors to be tighter in both the planning and implementation stage. The incentive effect of an increase in the payments would have been stronger if the planned value of the profitability indicator was not adjusted to take into account such an increase in the costs of production.

Another factor which contributed to the weakening of the effect of forest payments in the traditional Soviet economic system was that existing payments were paid out of the fixed percentage of the profit which went to taxes without affecting the part of the profit which was left at the timber enterprise.[43] As it did not matter to the enterprise if the amount of money it paid to the state for its use of forestry resources was called taxes or rental payments, such payments did not provide the enterprise with any economic incentive to save for its own use of resources. If this was to work it would have been necessary for the payment to be taken out of profits which the enterprise otherwise could have disposed of.

It seems clear from this discussion that an increase in the rental payment would not have stimulated the timber enterprise in the traditional Soviet economic system to reduce its use of forestry resources. The question is then whether a charge would have affected behaviour in the presence of Gorbachev's *perestroika*. The law on state enterprises from 1988 included a paragraph on the introduction of charges for the use of natural resources.[44] A forest charge was introduced in the autumn of 1991.[45]

The primary aim of the forest charge was to adhere to changes in Soviet economic policies towards complete self-accountability, which meant that the enterprise itself was to finance its costs of production.[46] The existing payments for forest use were substantially lower than a charge equal to the average cost of reforestation.[47] A second reason for this charge was that the prospect of saving on payments for the use of forest resources should have provided the enterprise with an incentive to economise. If charges were added to the production costs of the timber enterprise, the enterprise should in principle have had as much, or as little of an incentive to save on these as on other costs of production.

But the effectiveness of a charge did not only depend on its size. It also depended on the actual use of resources. This was acknowledged by Soviet economists who suggested that the charge should be paid per unit of used resource, and not as existing rental payment which was paid per unit of natural resource output, and thus did not reflect losses during the extraction process.[48] In the case of forestry resources, it was decided that the charge be paid per hectare of utilised forest land, and that it be differentiated with respect to quality.[49] In effect, increased priority to forestry should have implied that the budget constraint on the use of forestry resources became hard, meaning that Minlesprom and its subordinates would have felt an incentive to use it more efficiently. This was, however, not likely to be the case as Goskomles had not acquired the power to enforce such a hard budget constraint.

9.4 CONCLUSIONS

The so-called reform measures that have been undertaken were not likely to improve the use of forestry resources. It has been shown here that priority changes within the forestry industry have been ineffective. As the priority change has not led to a corresponding change in the incentive structure, the behavioural pattern of the shortage economy was left unchanged. Goskomles did not have the power to prevent Minlesprom and its subordinates from continuing their policy of extensive growth. And the laws on state enterprises, cooperatives or leasehold have not threatened the monopolistic power of Minlesprom either. Relative to Minlesprom, the economic activities that resulted from these laws did not become competitive as they suffered badly from shortages on the input side. There was no market where the new establishments could buy the required materials and sell their product. In addition, the expectations of discretionary changes in the rules governing these activities would have impeded their development. Nevertheless, they might have been beneficial to forestry as they made use of the forestry waste and low-quality timber that Minlesprom had discarded.

One conclusion to be drawn from this is that it would have been very difficult to implement any changes in priorities with respect to environmental protection if this were to affect the ministerial bureaucracy.

NOTES

1   Professor Ivan Voevoda, personal interview, 18 November 1988. Ivan Voevoda is a forestry specialist at the Institute of Economics and Industrial Organisation in Akademgorodok, at the Siberian branch of the Soviet Academy of Science.

2   See Blandon (1983), pp. 51–61, for a description of the organisational changes which took place in 1971 and 1981. See also Barr and Braden (1988), Chapter 2.

3   Personal interview. The average staff cut in the bureaucracy by the spring of 1990 was 24 per cent (Gregory (1991), p. 862).

4   The staff were transferred to forestry institutes which were attached to the Ministry (Professor Ivan Voevoda, personal interview, Akademgorodok, 18 November 1988).

5   Timber production decreased by 15 per cent in the period 1988–90 (*Narkhoz* (1991), p. 413).

6   *Lesnaya Promyshlennost*, 28 May 1988, pp. 1–2.

7   G.I. Grzhrozhnoi, Goskomles, personal interview, Moscow, 25 November 1988.

8   Complex timber enterprises were enterprises with a varying degree of cutting, wood-processing and forestry activities, while *lespromkhozy* were in charge only of timber cutting.

9   Barr and Braden (1988), pp. 199–208.

10   Voevoda (1980), pp. 30–32.

11   Barr and Braden (1988), Chapter 3.

12   Gosleskhoz was established in 1966. The duties for Gosleskhoz included conducting forest inventories, carrying out reforestation, and protecting forests from fires, insects and disease. It supervised 20 research institutes (Barr and Braden (1988), pp. 20–21).

13   *Sotsialnaya Industriya*, 2 February 1988.

14   Petrov (1986), p. 160; *Trud v SSSR* (1988), pp. 158–9.

15 This was an important obstacle to the successful implementation of reforms in Russia even in 1992 (Åslund (1992), p. 12). See also Capelik (1992) for the ineffectiveness of the antimonopoly legislation which was passed in 1991.

16 Litwack (1991), p. 165.

17 One aspect of this was the use of norms which remained stable for at least five years (Litwack (1991), p. 166).

18 See Goldberg (1992).

19 Filtzer (1991), p. 991.

20 Abalkin (1989), p. 9.

21 Noren (1990), p. 26.

22 See Filtzer (1991) for a discussion of the contradictions of the marketless market. See Schroeder (1991), pp. 5–9 for a discussion of reform measures in 1990–91 and for the small effect of Gorbachev's reform package. See Burawoy and Hendley (1992) for the effects of *perestroika* on the functioning of a Soviet enterprise in Moscow.

23 *Zakon SSSR o gosudarstvennom predpriyatii/obedinenie*. The decision on the law was taken at a Plenum on 25 June 1987. This law replaced the 1965 enterprise statute (*Polozhenie o sotsialisticheskom gosudarstvennom proizvodstvennom predpriyatii), Ekonomichskaya Gazeta*, 42, October 1965. The law was published in *Pravda* on 1 July 1987. For a discussion of the law, see Oxenstierna (1990), Chapter 10. See also Ericson (1988). This law was amended in 1989, and was replaced by a new 1990 law 'On the Enterprises in the USSR' (*Zakon Soyuza Sovetskikh Sotsialisticheskikh Respublik o predpriyatiyakh v SSSR*, 4 June 1990), reprinted in *Ekonomika i zhizn*, June 1990, No. 25, pp. 19–21. The law of 1990 meant that the right of workers to be consulted over the selection of the enterprise director was invalidated (Teage (1992), p. 6).

24 On 1 January 1989, 15 per cent of workers in forestry were transferred to the new salary system (*RSFSR v 1988 gody* (1989), p. 282).

25 'Tipovoe polozhenie o normativnom metode raspredelenia pribyli na 1988–1990 godi', *Ekonomicheskaya Gazeta*, 1987, No. 50, p. 16.

26 Professor Ivan Voevoda, personal interview, Akademgorodok, 18 November 1988.

27 *Zakon Soyuza Sovetskikh Sotsialisticheskikh Respublik o kooperatsii v SSSR, Ekonomika i zhizn*, June 1988, No. 24, pp. 3–18.

28 Filtzer (1991), p. 991.

29 Slider (1991); Litwack (1991), p. 269.

30 See Litwack (1991), pp. 267–8. In 1989 the Supreme Soviet passed a law on changes in and amendments of the law on cooperation (*Ekonomicheskaya Gazeta*, 1989, No. 44, p. 3). Another law with an identical title was passed in 1990 (*Zakon Soyuza Sovetskikh Sotsialisticheskikh Respublik o vneseni izmenenii i dopolnenii v Zakon SSSR 'O kooperatsii v SSSR', Izvestiya*, 24 June 1990).

31 See Litwack (1991), pp. 267–9 and Slider (1991), p. 817, Table 5.

32 Yurii Shubaev, Goskomles, personal interview, Moscow, 25 November 1988.

33 Litwack (1991), p. 269.

34 Personal interview.

35 For instance, questions on who will be leasing from whom, to whom is the rent to be paid, how shall the rent be determined, to whom will the funds that the enterprise itself accumulates belong, how are the shares of the workers to be determined, will a worker who leaves the enterprise be able to obtain his share of the enterprise, were issues that still remained to be solved.

36 *Ob Arende. Osnovy zakonodatelstva soyuza SSR i soyuznykh respublik, Pravda*, 1 December 1989.

37 Proekt *Polozheniya ob arende lesov v SSSR, Lesnaya Promyshlennost*, 13 April 1988.

38 Litwack (1991), pp. 269–70.

39 One example is that of Geli Motkin, who told me that he bought a wood-working enterprise in the Ukraine which was in a very bad state. With the help of financial assistance from Germany, he could have it renovated enough to increase production, personal interview, CEMI, Moscow, 12 March 1991 (Motkin is a natural resource economist at CEMI, and he also runs a firm of consultants in the field together with Gofman).

40   See Chapter 8.

41   Morozov (1986), pp. 186–7. The forest tax was paid by the timber enterprise per tree for the allocated forest fund (*lesfond*) and depended neither on planned felling nor on actual felling. This is not discussed further here. It was paid from profits to be used for regeneration. The rental payment was paid from the allocated tree-felling fund (*lesosechnyi fond*). The size of these payments corresponded to 5 to 10 per cent of the cost for felling (*Lesnaya Promyshlennost*, No. 10, 1986, p. 24). They were payments for the raw material, to the state budget. Neither of these payments depended on the actual amount of felled timber, and their size varied considerably between different regions (Shkatov (1974)).

42   See Chapter 8.

43   Morozov (1986), pp. 186–7.

44   Paragraph 17.

45   Personal interview, Sergei Kutukov, Goskompriroda, 15 March 1991.

46   Personal interview, Professor Ivan Voevoda, Akademgorodok, 22 November 1988.

47   Gorstvo and Khaiter (1991), p. 522.

48   Gofman and Vitt (1987), *Ekonomicheskaya Gazeta*, No. 37, p. 4.

49   *Doklad...* (1990), p. 127.

10. Conclusions

In this study an attempt has been made to show how and why the environmental situation in the Soviet Union deteriorated. The scattered facts presented in Chapter 2 suggest that environmental disruption has been considerable. Just as in market economies there have been problems of environmental pollution from industrial production, agriculture, road transport and so on. However, although environmental problems in the Soviet Union were similar to those recognised in the West, they were of a somewhat different character. It was basically the development strategy drawn up by Stalin that was in many ways responsible for the severe environmental situation. In the strive for rapid industrial expansion, the leadership pursued an extractionist policy in the use of natural resources. There was little room for environmental concerns as over-ambitious plans and the focus of the annual plan implied a short-sighted policy. As this policy resulted in the creation of massive industrial conglomerates, based on the exploitation of local natural resources, several types of environmentally harmful activities were concentrated in some regions. Particularly badly off were the Donbass area in the Ukraine, the Kuzbass area in Siberia, and the eastern Urals. With population density being high in these industrial areas, a large proportion of the Soviet population were affected by high levels of pollution. The fact that heavy industries were situated within residential areas and the policy of having child-care centres within factory areas contributed to the seriousness of illnesses. Despite ambitious environmental programmes, there was a general backlog in the implementation of measures aimed at preserving the environment.

Large-scale industrial undertakings have changed the environment. One example is the great efforts expended by central planners to redistribute water supplies by means of huge dams, channels and river diversions. Another example is how the leadership has attempted to change the natural conditions of soil. Large-scale irrigation and disproportionately high amounts of mineral fertilisers, herbicides and pesticides have been used in order to facilitate the fulfilment of politically determined production targets within farming.

It has been appropriate to distinguish between two main approaches used to explain environmental disruption in the Soviet Union as they constitute two alternative views as to how the Soviet system actually worked. According to the first approach, environmental problems were related to an inability of the system to allocate resources in an 'optimal' way. Lack of information would have caused problems of evaluation, which in turn explained the 'inoptimal' allocation of resources for environmental purposes. In both Western and Soviet literature environmental disruption has been viewed as a result of some kind of divergence from an ideal model. This view is compatible with approaches to analyses of centrally planned economies in which optimal-planning models, neoclassical models and input–output models are used.

The other approach views problems as consequences of a conscious policy of neglect by planners who were simply more concerned with other matters. The perceived abundance of natural resources made a policy of neglect possible, while the 'man-could-master-nature' attitude motivated it.

An alternative to analysing the Soviet economic system in terms of divergences from ideal models is to analyse it on the basis of observed features which is one of a conscious policy of environmental neglect. It is felt that such an approach provides a more plausible framework for analysis. This approach is used in the shortage and the priority models on which the present study has been based.

In seeking an explanation of the environmental disruption in the Soviet Union, the view of the Soviet economy as a shortage economy was applied, adapted to take into account the low priority of environmental protection. The priority-revised shortage-economy approach offers an explanation of the ineffectiveness of environmental programmes as well as of the mismanagement of natural resources. With the low priority given to environmental protection implying that the budget constraint was hard for such measures, actual expenditures were generally less than planned. This explains why in the early 1990s substantial amounts of pollutants were emitted without prior treatment. It also explains why pollution charges and fines for environmental violations should have had a stronger effect in low-priority sectors than in branches of higher priority. As the budget constraint seems to have been soft for natural resources, regardless of priority, this was in conflict with the priority-revised shortage-economy approach.

The high shortage intensity implied that the quantity drive took place at the expense of the quality of environmental equipment, developments in environmental technology and environment-saving production and use of by-products. This explains why high-priority sectors appear to have achieved a higher degree of fulfilment of quality norms than low-priority sectors. The pattern for resource allocation to environmental protection is another factor which might have contributed to the ineffectiveness of measures. Planners have reacted to the violations of norms by allocating more resources to the worst polluters and/or to high-priority sectors rather than to the most seriously affected regions.

This approach also offers an explanation as to why high-priority activities as well as sectors of lower priority might have been important contributors to pollution. As environmental equipment was allocated to high-priority sectors first, low-priority sectors were not able to do much about their pollution. The high shortage intensity in low-priority sectors would further have implied that, even if environmental equipment had been allocated to these sectors, its quality would have been particularly low. However, as high-priority sectors were less efficient, even though they received the required environmental equipment, it would not have been used efficiently. Similarly, the high shortage of inputs in low-priority branches could have been detrimental to the use of natural resources as these might have been substituted for other more scarce inputs whenever this was possible. In the case of high-priority branches the low shortage intensity would not have incited such a forced substitution. Nevertheless, their low efficiency in production might have implied a wasteful use of natural resources.

The above explanation shows how there were two contributing factors in the Stalinist strategy for development which caused problems of air and water pollution and the depletion of natural resources in the Soviet Union. On the one hand there was the low priority to environmental protection that this strategy has encouraged, and on the other there was the behavioural pattern of Soviet enterprises that it generated. This approach suggests that low priority to environmental concerns would have ensured that any measure to improve the environmental situation was likely to be ineffective. The signs of an increased priority to environmental protection were not matched by similar improvements in quality. On the contrary, evidence indicates that in the case of water purification, quality has actually decreased.

When it comes to air protection, the increased investment has not resulted in more than a marginal increase in the purification of emissions. This suggests that investments have been ineffective and that quality of purification equipment has been low. It might also imply that the reduced emissions were the result of an improved quality of purification, an observation which was in conflict with the approach used in this study. However, the closing of factories might also have contributed to the reduction in emissions. The increased priority to air protection seemed to have suggested more resources to heavy polluters within heavy industry, while the worst-polluting industries within low-priority sectors have been shut down. This might explain why the high-priority energy sector as well as the low-priority pulp and paper industry have decreased their emissions of air pollutants.

This approach further explains why high-priority sectors appear to have been more responsive to central directives than have low-priority sectors. As high-priority sectors have generally been favoured in the central allocation of resources, they would have had stronger incentives as well as better opportunities to follow these.

That measures have actually been taken seems to reflect the fact that environmental disruption had become an impediment to development even for high-priority sectors. It also suggests that, even if priority to environmental protection had been radically increased, its effect on the environment might have been minimal due to the power of shortage economic processes.

This explanation is compatible with those offered in other Soviet and Western studies which indicate the importance of the emphasis on material production. It especially highlights why the priority of material production appears to have been particularly detrimental in the Soviet economic system. Environmental programmes were more likely to suffer from the general shortage of resources as these were allocated to more important tasks first. However, the explanation advocated here is compatible with those approaches which emphasise the importance of the Soviet price system, but only in the case of low-priority activities.

The changes in environmental policy which took place within the framework of Gorbachev's reform package were not likely to have improved the environmental situation. One such change was the use of cost-benefit analysis in decision-making, which might have contributed to the adoption by Goskompriroda of the ambitious environmental programme for the 1990s. Other changes were the introduction of charges for the use of natural resources, pollution charges and regional environmental funds. However, as Goskompriroda did not acquire the power to change the plans of other ministries, the changes in environmental policy amounted to just another attempt to administer an increased environmental awareness. For the changes to have been effective it was required that necessary inputs and technical equipment would be available. Thus, the vast environmental problems to have been solved required first a change in the economic system alongside a strengthening of environmental policies, and second, massive international assistance with technology and finance.

To get further insight into the impact of the shortage economy on the management of natural resources, this book focused on a case study of the use of forestry resources which provided an example of how the Soviet leadership, in its strive towards rapid industrial development, has pursued an extractionist policy when it came to natural resources and labour. It illustrates how central policy ensured that the use of natural resources was maximised rather than optimised. There was no room for environmental concerns as over-ambitious plans and the focus on the annual plan implied a short-term policy. It also provides an illustration of how the high targets for the extraction of natural resources, which led to a heavy demand for manpower, led to the introduction of compulsory methods as it was no longer possible to recruit enough workers on a voluntary basis, which in turn contributed to the low labour productivity. This further implies that low-priority environmental protection activities would have been affected by labour shortage. The case study also provided an example of how the low priority to environmental concerns emerged as the logical result of the rapid industrialisation policy which was drawn up by Stalin in the first Five Year Plan.

An investigation into central forestry policy further illustrates how technical change has been planned at higher levels. If the centre decided to implement an idea developed at one of its research institutes, it did so on a large scale. The fact that technical change has been planned at a high level suggests that if developments in environmental technology were ever implemented, it would have been on a large scale with a considerable timelag. There was then the risk that the technology would have been obsolete before it was even adopted, and that it was ill-suited to existing plants.

The development of the timber industry appears to have been consistent with the priority-revised shortage-economy approach although the effect of priorities seems to have been more important at the ministerial level than at the level of the enterprise. The risk that planners would have reallocated resources to branches of higher priority might have motivated the Ministry to expand and develop its own supplies.

It has been seen how the quantity drive has played an important role in the production of timber. It was shown that to the extent that bonuses affected the behaviour of the timber enterprise they tended to strengthen this quantity drive. Empirical evidence suggests however, that the quantity drive has been selective, which means that the use of some inputs increased more than others depending on the 'hardness' of budget constraints.

The constraint on labour has in effect been binding. Therefore the 'urge to invest' in the Soviet Union should have been oriented towards labour-saving investments. In the case of forestry resources there has been no resource constraint as has generally been the case for other inputs, and the enterprise could simply have violated restrictions and laws concerning their use. In order to fulfil the plan for timber production the enterprise director would therefore have tried to substitute forestry resources for other inputs.

The profitability indicator has not stimulated the enterprise to increase profits. On the contrary, this indicator seems to have been beyond the control of the enterprise. Similarly, development of technology is consistent with the shortage-economy approach used in this study. The fund-forming indicators did not stimulate technological development. As shortage of labour, however, implies problems in fulfilling plans for timber production, the enterprise should have been interested in labour-saving technical developments. On the other hand, the intense focus on the annual plan stimulated the opposite behaviour. There was as a result no incentive to save on forestry resources.

One conclusion of the case study is that as the most abundant natural resources were exhausted, a continuation of such a policy required heavier and heavier investments. The longer it continued, the greater the problems would have become. The case study thus gives an illustration of how the strategy for development based on sheer expansion led to a dead end, as it placed heavy demands on investment if it was to be continued, regardless of whether development was concentrated in Siberia or in the European

Soviet. It suggests that the extensive Soviet policy for development was made possible by the enormous riches in natural resources. The efforts expended to change policy suggest that the point had been reached when resources had been depleted to the extent that they were no longer easily mobilised and that their depletion started to affect priority branches.

The case study also illustrates how the Stalinist priority on growth had become embedded in institutions which have impeded attempts by central decision-makers to change the strategy for development. It provides an example of how the Soviet strategy for development drawn up by Stalin in the first Five Year Plan has created a managerial system which permitted and even promoted the waste and destruction of natural resources. In addition it provides an example of how the institutions which were once created to impose effectively the central priorities, developed their own objectives and resisted changes that could jeopardise their interests. One important conclusion to be drawn from this is that it would have been very difficult to implement changes in priorities with respect to environmental protection if this were to affect the ministerial bureaucracy.

The strategy of reform under Gorbachev centred around a flow of new decrees and laws. Three important documents were adopted, aimed at breaking the ministerial power and improving the efficiency of the use of resources. Very few of the hopes linked to these laws seem to have been realised in practice. The introduction of charges for the use of natural resources, which was one component of the enterprise law, has proven not to have been effective. The charges have not even affected the use of natural resources in low-priority branches as soft budgets were most likely in extracting branches. As the legal system did not function, the respect for laws and regulations remained arbitrary. The development of cooperatives and leasehold was held back by supply problems and problems of inconsistent and unstable government regulation. The incentive structure resulting from Gorbachev's reform package has not promoted the development of cooperatives in this field.

Reform in the Soviet context is a rather difficult concept. Although the leadership legislated on far-reaching reforms, it has often been the case that nothing really changed. The situation as regards environmental protection has been of precisely this nature. The leadership has passed on decree after decree without achieving the desired reactions.

Although much has happened since the demise of the Soviet Union, a fundamental change in the economic system, analysed in this study, has not taken place. In Russia the reforms have just got under way, and in the other former Soviet republics they have generally not even come this far. As long as the seller's market prevails against the reform measures a fundamental change in the behavioural pattern is not likely to take place. The branch ministries have been replaced by other monopolies. As long as the legal system is not working, state agencies are not able to enforce hard budget constraints and the uncertainty as to whether new rules will be changed or

156

replaced by others remains. Discretionary behaviour of the leadership in particular would hamper long-term adjustment, which is especially important in the case of environmental protection. The present analysis is therefore still relevant.

References*

Abalkin, L. (1989), 'Perestroika ekonomiki: sovetskaya tochka zreniya', *Voprosy Ekonomiki*, No. 4, pp. 3–10.

Aganbegyan, A.G. (1988), 'Ekonomicheskie aspekty programmy biosfernykh i ekologicheskikh issledovanii', *Vestnik Akademiya Nauk SSSR*, No. 11, pp. 64–7.

Aleksandrov, I.A. (1986), 'Effektivnost obshchestvennogo proizvodstva regiona i voprosy ekonomicheskogo stimulirovaniya okhrany okruzhayushchei sredy', presented at Vtoraya Vsesoyuznaya Koferentsiya Sovershenstvovanie Metodologii Upravleniya Sotsialisticheskim Prirodopolzovaniem, in Moscow, 13–16 May.

Altshuler, Igor I. and Golubchikov, Yuri N. (1990), 'Ecological Semiglasnost: On the Publication of the First Three Official Documents on the State of the Environment in the USSR', *Environmental Policy Review*, Vol. 3, No. 2.

Amann, R. and Cooper, J.M. (1986), *Technical Progress and Soviet Economic Development*, Oxford: Blackwell.

Ames, E. (1965), *Soviet Economic Processes*, Homewood, Ill.: Irwin.

'Aralskaya Katastrofa', *Novyi Mir*, No. 5, 1989, pp. 182–241.

Åslund, A. (1988), 'How small is the Soviet national income?', Paper presented at the Hoover–Rand Conference on the Defense Sector in the Soviet Economy, Stanford University, 23–24 March .

Åslund, A. (1992), 'Det ryska systemskiftet', *Nordisk Östforum*, 2, pp. 5–13.

Bajt, A. (1971), 'Investment cycles in European socialist economies: A review article', *Journal of Economic Literature*, Vol. 9, pp. 53–63.

Barr, B. (1983), 'Regional dilemmas and international prospects in the Soviet timber industry', in Jensen, K.G., *Soviet Natural Resources in the World Economy*, Chicago and London: University of Chicago Press.

Barr, B.M. and Braden, E.B. (1988), *The Disappearing Russian Forest - A Dilemma in Soviet Resource Management*, London: Rowman & Littlefield, Hutchinson.

Bechuk, B.Ts., Varlamova, O.S. and Gusev, A.A. (1991), 'Voprosy ekologo-ekonomicheskogo obosnovaniya strategii NTP v oblasti

---

* This list does not include official materials and newspaper articles. These are referred to in the text only.

159

prirodopolzovaniya', *Ekonomika i Matematicheskie Metody*, Vol. 27, No. 5, pp. 904–16.

Belkin, V.D. (1987), 'Vmesto fondirovaniya', *EKO*, No. 6.

Bergson, A. (1953), *Soviet National Income and Product in 1937*, New York: Columbia University Press.

Berliner, J. (1957), *Factory and Manager in the USSR*, Cambridge, MA: MIT Press.

Berliner, J. (1976), *The Innovation Decision in Soviet Industry*, Cambridge, MA: MIT Press.

Birman, I. (1978), 'From the achieved level', *Soviet Studies*, Vol. 30, No. 2, pp. 153–73.

Blam, Yu.Sh. (1983), *Optimizatsionnye modeli v perspektivnom planirovanii lesnogo kompleksa*, Novosibirsk: Nauka, Sibirskoe otdelenie.

Blam, Yu.Sh., Babenko, T.I. and Arzumanyan, E.A. (1982), 'Ekonomicheskaya otsenka lesnykh resursov v modelyakh optimizatsii plana razvitya lesnoi i lesopererabatyvayushchei promyshlennosti', in Mkrtchyan, G.M. and Suspitsyn, S.A. (eds) (1982), pp. 128–49.

Blandon, P. (1983), *Soviet Forest Industries*, Boulder, Colo.: Westview Press.

Boiko, P. (1987), 'Ecologicheskie problemy povysheniya ustoichivosti selskokhozyaistvennogo proizvodstva', *Vestnik Leningrad Gu*, Series 5, No. 3, pp. 59–65.

Bowles, W.D. (1958), 'Economics of the Soviet Logging Industry', PhD Thesis, University of Columbia.

Burawoy, M. and Hendley, K. (1992), 'Between *perestroika* and privatisation: divided strategies and political crisis in a Soviet enterprise', *Soviet Studies*, Vol. 44, No. 3, pp. 371–402.

Bystritskaya, N. and Mikhura, V. (1983), 'O plata za vodu i khozyaistvennyi raschet v selskom khozyaistve', *Planovoe Khozyaistvo*, No. 1, pp. 123–5.

Byullentin No. 1 (1990), 'O deyatelnosti Goskomprirody SSSR v 1989 godu', Goskompriroda i Press-Tsentr Vsesoyuznoe Obshchestvo 'Znanie', Moskva.

Capelik, V. (1992), 'The Development of Antimonopoly Policy in Russia', *RFE/RL Research Report*, Vol. 1, No. 34, 28 August.

Carr, E.H. and Davies, R.W. (1969), *Foundations of a Planned Economy, 1926–1929 (Vol. 1)*, London: Macmillan.

Cave, M., McAuley A. and Thornton, J. (1982), *New Trends in Soviet Economics*, New York and London: M.E. Sharpe, Inc., Armonk.

Chapman, J. (1963), *Real Wages in Soviet Russia since 1928*, Cambridge: Harvard University Press.

Cooper, J.M. (1986), 'The civilian production of the Soviet defense industry', in Amann and Cooper (1986).

Dallin, D.J. and Nikolaevsky B.I. (1948), *Forced Labour in Soviet Russia*, New Haven, Conn.: Yale University Press.

Davies, R.W. (1980), *The Socialist Offensive. The Collectivization of Soviet Agriculture, 1929–1930*, London: Macmillan.

Davis, C. (1988), 'The high priority defense industry in the Soviet shortage economy', Paper presented at the Hoover–Rand Conference, Stanford University, 23–24 March.

Davis, C. (1989), 'Priority and the shortage model: the medical system in the socialist economy', in Davis and Charemza (eds) (1989).

Davis, C. and Charemza, W. (1989), 'Introduction to models of disequilibrium and shortage in centrally planned economies', in Davis and Charemza (eds) (1989).

Davis, C. and Charemza, W. (eds) (1989), *Models of Disequilibrium and Shortage in Centrally Planned Economies*, London: Chapman & Hall.

DeBardeleben, J. (1983), 'Marxism–Leninism and economic policy: Natural resource pricing in the USSR and the GDR', *Soviet Studies*, Vol. 35, No. 1, pp. 36–52.

DeBardeleben, J. (1985), *The Environment and Marxism–Leninism*, Boulder, Colo.: Westview Press, Inc.

Doklad: Sostoyanie prirodnoi sredy v SSSR v 1988 godu (1990), Goskompriroda, Moskva: Lesnaya Promyshlennost.

Dreifelds, Juris (1983), 'Participation in pollution control in Latvia, 1955–1977', *Journal of Baltic Studies*, Vol. 14, No. 4, pp. 273–95.

Dumnov, A. and Pospelov, (1991), 'Prirodookhrannyi Kontrol i Statistika', *Vestnik Statistiki*, No. 2, pp. 65–7.

Dyker, D. (1983), 'The process of investment in the Soviet Union', Cambridge: Cambridge University Press.

Ellman, M. (1971), *Soviet Planning Today*, Cambridge: Cambridge University Press.

Ericson, R.E. (1988), 'Priority, duality, and penetration in the Soviet command economy', *Rand Note*, December.

Eronen, J. (1982), 'Soviet Pulp and Paper Industry: factors explaining its areal expansion', *Silva Fennica*, No. 3, pp. 267–85.

Fedorenko, N.P. and Petrakov, N. Ya. (eds) (1985), *Khozyaistvennyi mekhanizm v sisteme optimalnogo funktsionirovaniya sotsialisticheskoi ekonomiki*, Moskva: Nauka.

Feiwel, G.R. (1965), *The Economics of a Socialist Enterprise*, New York: Praeger.

Feshbach, M. and Friendly, A. (1992), *Ecocide in the USSR*, New York: Basic Books.

Filtzer, D. (1991), 'The Contradictions of the Marketless Market: Self-financing in the Soviet Industrial Enterprise, 1986–90', *Soviet Studies*, Vol. 43, No. 6, pp. 989–1009.

Freris, A. (1984), *The Soviet Industrial Enterprise: Theory and Practice*, London and Sydney: Croom Helm Ltd.

Fuller, E. (1987), 'Armenian journalist links air pollution and infant mortality', *Radio Liberty Research*, RL 275/87, 14 July.

Fuller, E. and Mikaeli, M. (1987), 'Azerbaijan belatedly discovers environmental pollution', *Radio Liberty Research*, RL 2/88, 30 December.

Gaidar, E. (1988), 'Kursom ozdorovleniya – ekonomicheskoe obozrenie', *Kommunist*, No. 2, pp. 41–50.

Gallik, D., Heneimeier, M., Kostinsky, B., Treml, V. and Tretyakova, A. (1984), 'Construction of a 1977 Soviet input–output table', *CIR Staff paper*, US Bureau of Census, Washington DC.

Gerner, K. (1988), 'Glasnost och miljödebatten i Sovjetunionen', in Ignats and Hammar (eds) (1988), pp. 80–87.

Gerner, K. and Lundgren, L. (1978), *Planhushållning och miljöproblem – Sovjetsisk debatt om natur och samhälle 1960–1976*, Stockholm: Liber Förlag.

Gofman, K.N. (1977), *Ekonomicheskaya otsenka prirodnykh resursov v usloviiakh sotsialisticheskoi ekonomiki*, Moskva: Nauka.

Gofman, K.N. (1982), *Okhrana okruzhayushchei sredy: modeli sotsialno-ekonomicheskogo prognoza*, Moskva: Ekonomika.

Gofman, K.N. (1985a), 'Ekonomicheskaya otsenka prirodnykh i problemy platnosti prirodopolzovaniya', in Fedorenko and Petrakov (eds) (1985), pp. 151–65.

Gofman, K.N. (1985b), 'Prirodopolzovanie i makroekonomicheskie pokazateli razvitiya narodnogo khozyaistva', in Gofman and Motkin (eds) (1985), pp. 3–9.

Gofman, K.N. (1988a), 'Khozyastvennyi mekhanizm prirodopolzovanyia: puti perestroiki', *Ekonomika i Matematicheskie Metody*, Vol. 24, No. 3, pp. 389–99.

Gofman, K.N. (1988b), 'The Payments for Consumption of Natural Resources and Environmental Pollution – New Approaches in Soviet Economy', Paper presented at the Conference on Environmental Affairs at the Swedish Institute of International Affairs, Stockholm, 9–10 June 1988.

Gofman, K.N., Dunaevskii, L.V., Krechetov, L.I. and Lvovskaya, K.B. (1991), 'O formirovanii regionalnykh rynochnykh sistem regulirovaniya kachestva okrazhayushchei prirodnoi sredy', *Ekonomika i Matematicheskie Metody*, Vol. 27, No. 5, pp. 894–903.

Gofman, K.N. and Fedorenko, N.P. (eds) (1987), *Tipovaya metodika opredeleniya ekonomicheskoi effektivnosti stimulirovaniya osuchestvleniya prirodookhrannykh meropriyatii i ekonomicheskoi otsenki ucherba ot zagrizneniya okruzhayushchei sredy*, proekt, Moskva: Akademiya Hauk – Tsentralnyi Ekonomiko-Matematicheskii Institut.

Gofman, K.N. and Gusev, A.A. (1981), 'Ekologicheskie izderzhki i kontseptsiya ekonomicheskogo optimuma kachestva okruzhayushchei prirodnoi sredy', *Ekonomika i Matematicheskie Metody*, Vol. 17, No. 3, pp. 515–27.

Gofman, K.N. and Gusev, A.A. (1985), 'O nekotorykh diskussionnykh voprosakh metodologii optimizatsii prirodopolzovaniya', *Ekonomika i Matematicheskie Metody*, Vol. 21, No. 4, pp. 604–9.

Gofman, K.N. and Motkin, G.A. (eds) (1983), *Upravlenie Sotsialisticheskim Prirodopolzovaniem*, Moskva: Akademiya Nauk, Tsemi.

Gofman, K.N. and Motkin, G.A. (eds) (1985), *Ekonomicheskie problemy pripodopolzovaniya*, Moskva: Nauka.

Gofman, K.N. and Motkin, G.A (1991), 'Ob imushchestvennoi otvetstvennosti predpriyatii za zagryaznenie okrazhayushchei prirodnoi sredy i sozdanii v SSSR sistemy ekologicheskogo strakhovaniya', *Ekonomika i Matematicheskie Metody*, Vol. 27, No. 6, pp. 1005–12.

Gofman, K.N. and Vitt, M.B. (1987), 'Platezhi za prirodnye resursy', *Ekonomicheskaya Gazeta*, No. 37, p. 4.

Gofman, K.N. and Vitt, M.B. (1990), 'Platezhi za prirodopolzovanie', *EKO*, No. 2, pp. 19–31.

Goldberg, P. (1992), 'Economic Reform and Product Quality Improvement Efforts in the Soviet Union', *Soviet Studies*, Vol. 44, No. 1, pp. 113–22.

Goldman, Marshall (1972), *The Spoils of Progress*, London: MIT Press.

Gomulka, S. (1985), 'Kornai's soft budget constraint and the shortage phenomenon: A criticism and restatement', *Economics of Planning*, Vol. 19, No. 1, pp. 1–11.

Gorstvo, A.B. and Khaiter, P.A. (1991), 'K voprosy ob ekonomicheskoi otsenke lesnykh resursov', *Ekonomika i Matematicheskie Metody*, Vol. 27, No. 3, pp. 522–7.

Granick, D. (1954), *Management of the Industrial Firm in the USSR*, New York: Columbia University Press.

Granick, D. (1960), *The Red Manager*, New York: Doubleday.

Gregory, P.R. (1991), 'The Impact of *Perestroika* on the Soviet Planned Economy: Results of a Survey of Moscow Economic Officials', *Soviet Studies*, Vol. 43, No. 5, pp. 859–73.

Gregory, Paul R. and Stuart, Robert C. (1981), *Soviet Economic Structure and Performance*, New York: Harper & Row.

Grossman, G. (1953), 'Scarce capital and Soviet doctrine', *Quarterly Journal of Economics*, August.

Gusev, A.A. (1985), 'Problemy sovershenstvovaniya upravleniya kachestvom vozdyshnogo baseina', in Gofman and Motkin (eds) (1985), pp. 21–33.

Gusev, A.A. (1988), *Sotsialisticheskoe prirodopolzovanie – Ekonomicheskii Aspekt*, Moskva: Akademiya Nauk, Tsemi.

Gusev, A.A. and Mustafaev, A.M. (1983), 'Isledovanie diapazona statisticheskikh otsenok effektivnosti atmosfernykh meropriyatii', in Gofman and Motkin (eds) (1983), pp. 117–22.

Gusev, A.A and Varlamova, O.S. (1988), 'Dinamicheskie aspekty ekonomicheskogo optimuma kachestva okruzhayushchei prirodnoi sredy', *Ekonomika i Matematicheskie Metody*, Vol. 24, No. 3, pp. 447–57.

Gustafson, Thane (1980), 'Environmental Policy under Breznev: Do the Soviets really mean business', in Kelley (ed.) (1980), pp. 129–49.

Gustafson, Thane (1981), *Reform In Soviet Politics: Lessons of Recent Policies on Land and Water*, Cambridge: Cambridge University Press.

Hare, P. (1988), 'The economics of shortage in the centrally planned economies', in Davis and Charemza (eds) (1989).

Harrison, M. (1993), 'Soviet Economic Growth Since 1928: The Alternative Statistics of G.I. Khanin', *Europe–Asia Studies*, Vol. 45, No. 1, pp. 141–67.

Heal, Geoffrey Martin (1973), *The Theory of Economic Planning*, Amsterdam: North Holland.

Hedlund, Stefan (1984), *Crisis in Soviet Agriculture*, London and Sydney: Croom Helm, New York: St Martin's.

Hedlund, Stefan (1989), *Private Agriculture in the Soviet Union*, London & New York: Routledge.

Hedlund, Stefan (1990), *Östeuropas Kris*, Stockholm: Nordstedts.

Holzman, F. (1960), 'Soviet inflationary pressures, 1928–1957: Causes and cures', *Quarterly Journal of Economics*, Vol. 74, No. 2, pp. 167–87.

Hunter, H. (1961), 'Optimum tautness in developmental planning', *Economic Development and Cultural Change*, Vol. 9, No. 4.

Ignats, Ulo (1988), *Fosforitbrytningen i Estland*, Göteborg: MH Publishing.

Ignats, U. and Hammar, M. (eds) (1988), *Sovjet under Glasnost*, Göteborg: MH Publishing.

Ilic, M. (1986), 'The Development of the Soviet Timber Industry, 1926–40', M.Phil. Thesis, University of Birmingham.

Izdelis, A. (1977), 'Institutional response to environmental problems in Lithuania', *Journal of Baltic Studies*, Vol. 15, No. 4, pp. 296–306.

Jackson, W.A. (ed.) (1978), *Soviet Resource Management and the Environment*, Columbus, Ohio: Anchor Press.

Jancar, B. (1987), *Environmental Management in the Soviet Union and Yugoslavia*, Durham, NC: Duke University Press.

Jasnay, N. (1962), *Essays on the Soviet Economy*, New York: Praeger.

Jensen, R.G. (ed.) (1983), *Soviet Natural Resources in the World Economy*, Chicago and London: University of Chicago Press.

Kaganovich, I. (1986), 'Economic estimation of distant consequences of nature management', *Izvestiya Akademii Nauk Estonskoi SSR*, No. 35, pp. 248–56.

Kallaste, Tiit (1987), 'O nekotorykh zadachakh po okhrane okruzhayushchei sredy Estonskoi SSR na nerspektivy', *Izvestiya Akademii Nauk Estonskoi SSR*, No. 36, pp. 320–23.

Kallaste, Tiit (1988), 'Composite estimates of environmental pollution as a part of environmental planning', *Izvestiya Akademii Nauk Estonskoi SSR*, No. 37, pp. 225–31.

Kallaste, Tiit (1989), 'How to assess the level of air pollution', *Fennia*, Vol. 167, No. 1, pp. 73–85.

Kazannik, A.I. (1985), 'Plata za prirodopolzovanie', *Zemlya Sibirskaya Dalnevostochnaya*, No. 12, pp. 47–9.

Kelley, D.R. (1976), 'Environmental policy-making in the USSR: The role of industrial and environmental interest groups', *Soviet Studies*, Vol. 28, No. 4, pp. 570–89.

Kelley, D.R. (ed.) (1980), *Soviet Politics in the Brezhnev Era*, New York: Praeger.

Kemme, D.M. (1988), 'The chronic excess demand hypothesis', in Davis and Charemza (eds) (1989).

Keren, M., Miller J. and Thornton, J.R. (1983), 'The Ratchet: A Dynamic Managerial Incentive Model of the Soviet Enterprise', *Journal of Comparative Economics*, No. 7, pp. 347–67.

Khachaturov, T. (1987), 'Khozraschetnye interesy i ekologiya', *Ekonomicheskaya Gazeta*, No. 7, p. 4.

Kisilev, A.M. (1983), 'Plata za prirodnye resursy v sisteme ekonomicheskikh normativov (na primere lesnykh resursov)', in Gofman and Motkin (eds) (1983), pp. 106–11.

Kisilev, A.M. (1985), 'Zamykayushchie zatraty v sisteme optimizatsii prirodopolzovaniya', in Gofman and Motkin (eds) (1985), pp. 71–80.

Kornai, J. (1959), *Overcentralisation of Economic Administration*, Oxford: Oxford University Press.

Kornai, J. (1971), *Anti-Equilibrium*, Amsterdam: North Holland.

Kornai, J. (1979), 'Resource-constrained versus demand-constrained economics', *Econometrica*, Vol. 47, No. 4, pp. 801–19.

Kornai, J. (1980), *Economics of Shortage*, Amsterdam: North Holland.

Kornai, J. (1982a), 'Adjustment to price and quantity signals in a socialist economy', *Economie Appliquée*, Vol. 35, No. 3.

Kornai, J. (1982b), *Growth, Shortage and Efficiency*, Oxford: Basil Blackwell.

Kornai, J. (1986), 'The soft budget constraint', *Kyklos*, Vol. 39, No. 1, pp. 3–30.

Kornai, J. (1992), *The Socialist System. The Political Economy of Communism*, Princeton, NJ.: Princeton University Press.

Koutaissoff, E. (1987), 'A survey of Soviet published material on environmental problems', 3rd World Congress for Soviet and East

European Studies, Washington DC, Nov. 1985, published in Singleton (ed.) (1987).

Kozhin, V.M., Novikov, A.B. and Morozov, A.N. (1981), *Analiz khozyaistvennoi deyatelnosti obedinenii i predpriyatii lesnoi promyshlennosti*, Moskva: VNIPIEI – Minlesbumprom SSSR.

Kozhukhov, N.I. (1978), *Ekonomika Lesnogo Khozyaistva*, Moskva: Lesnaya promyshlennost.

Kozhukhov, N.I. (1984), *Osnovy upravleniya v lesnom khozyaistve i lesnoi promyshlennosti*, Moskva: Lesnaya promyshlennost.

Kramer, J. (1973), 'Prices and the conservation of natural resources in the Soviet Union', *Soviet Studies*, No. 3, pp. 364–73.

Kukushkin, G (1985), 'Planirovaniya ratsionalnogo ispolzovaniya prirodnykh resursov', *Planovoe Khozyaistvo*, No. 3, pp 64–70.

Lacko, M. (1988), 'Sectoral change models in Hungary', in Davis and Charemza (eds) (1989).

Lemeshev, M.Ya. and Ushakov, E.P. (eds) (1982), *Ekonomicheskie problemy prirodopolzovaniya*, Moskva: Nauka.

Lesnoi Kodeks RSFSR (1986), Moskva: Yuridicheskaya Literatura.

Levina, I.G. (1983), 'Ekonomicheskie otsenka kompleksnoi effektivnosti vodookhrannykh meropriyatii v tselyulozno-bumazhnoi promyshlennosti', in Gofman and Motkin (eds) (1983), pp. 173–81.

Linz, S.J. and Martin, R.E. (1982), 'Soviet Enterprise Behaviour under Uncertainty', *Journal of Comparative Economics*, Vol. 6, No. 1, pp. 24–36.

Litwack, J.M. (1991), 'Discretionary Behaviour and Soviet Economic Reform', *Soviet Studies*, Vol. 43, No. 2, pp. 255–79.

Liu, C. (1982), 'Managerial Objectives and Equilibrium Outputs in the Socialist Firm', *Journal of Comparative Economics*, No. 6, pp. 204–12.

Lobov, S.S. (1932), *Puti Razvitya Lesnoi Promyshlennosti v Borbe za Plan*, Moskva: Lesnaya Promyshlennost.

Lvovskaya, K.B. (1985), 'Metodologicheskie printsipy ekologo-ekonomicheskogo obosnovaniya meropriyatii po okhrane okruzhayushchei sredy goroda', *Izvestiya Akademii Nauk SSSR – Seriya Ekonomicheskaya*, No. 6, pp. 81–90.

Lvovskaya, K.B. (1988), 'O vliyanii sredozashchitnoi strategii na ekologo-ekonomicheskoe razvitie', *Ekonomika i Matematicheskie Metody*, Vol. 24, No. 3, pp. 438–46.

Lvovskaya, K.B. and Ronkin, P.S. (1990), *Regionalnoe Upravlenie Kachestvom Okruzhayushchei Sredy: Sotsialno-ekonomicheskii aspekt*, preprint, Moskva: Akademiya Nauk, Tsemi.

Lvovskaya, K.B. and Ronkin, P.S. (1991), 'Okruzhayushchei Sreda i Rynochnaya Ekonomika: Problemy Regionalnogo Upravleniya', *Ekonomika i Matematicheskie Metody*, Vol. 27, No. 4, pp. 674–85.

References

Mallin, V.N. and Korobov, A.V. (eds) (1957), *Direktivy KPSS i Sovetskogo Pravitelstva po Khozyaistvennom Voprosam*, Moskva: Ekonomika.

Mamin, P. (1992), 'Ekonomicheskie Vozdeistvie na Kachestvo Prirodnoi Sredy', *Ekonomist*, No. 7, pp. 81–5.

Marples, D. (1988), 'In defense of the Danube–Dnieper canal', *Radio Liberty Research*, RL 488/88, 27 October.

Marrese, M. and Mitchell, J.L. (1984), 'Kornai's Resource-Constrained Economy: A Survey and an Appraisal', *Journal of Comparative Economics*, No. 8, pp. 74–84.

Mcintyre, Robert J. and Thornton, James, R. (1978), 'On the environmental efficiency of economic systems', *Soviet Studies*, Vol. 30, No. 2, April, pp. 173–92.

Mcintyre, Robert J. and Thornton, James R. (1980), 'Environmental policy formulation and current Soviet management: a reply to Ziegler', *Soviet Studies*, Vol. 32, No. 1, January, pp. 146–9.

Medvedev, N.A. (1970), *Ekonomika Lesnoi Promyshlennosti*, Moskva: Lenaya Promyshlennost.

Medvedev, Zh. (1991), 'Limity industrialnoi ekonomiki', *EKO*, No. 6, pp. 147–63.

Mikhailisko, M. and Tovstink, (1988), 'Questions about semiconductor plants and thallium poisoning in Chernovtsy', *Radio Liberty Research*, 24 November, pp. 1–5.

Mkrtchyan, G.M. and Ponomareva, V.V. (1987), 'Sistemnoe modelirovanie razvitiya otraslei v regione', in Mkrtchyan and Rozin (eds) (1987), pp. 114–31.

Mkrtchyan, G.M. and Rozin, B.B. (eds) (1987), *Sovershenstvovanie Razrabotki Planov Razvitiya Otraslevykh Kompleksov*, Novosibirsk: Nauka, Sibirskoe Otdelenie.

Mkrtchyan, G.M. and Suspitsyn, S.A. (eds) (1982), *Prirodnye Resursy v Modelakh Territorialno-Proizvodstvennykh Sistem*, Novosibirsk: Nauka, Sibirskoe Otdelenie.

Monakhova, L.I. (1988), 'Rol tsen na vtorichnoe syre i produktsiyu iz nego v povyshenii urovnya ispozovaniya otkhodov', in Gusev (1988), pp. 166–72.

Morgun, F. (1989), 'Ekologiya i sisteme planirovaniya', *Planovoe Khozyaistvo*, No. 2, pp. 53–63.

Morozov, F.n. (1986), *Planirovanie Proizvodstvennoi Deyatelnosti Lesopromyshlennostykh Predpriyatii*, Moskva: Lesnaya Promyshlennost.

Motkin, G.A. (1983), 'Nekotorye printsipy klassifikatsii obektov pri ekonomiko-statisticheskom analize kachestva okruzhayushchei prirodnoi sredy', in Gofman and Motkin (eds) (1983), pp. 65–73.

Mudretsov, A.F. (1981), 'Ekonomicheskie problemy okhrany i ratsionalnogo ispolzovaiya lesnykh resursov', in Lemeshev and Ushakov (eds) (1982), pp. 128–37.

Mudretsov, A.F. (1982), 'Modeli prognoza ispolzovaniya zemelnykh i lesnykh resursov i meropriyatii po ikh okhrane', in Gofman (ed.) (1982), pp. 140–63.

Narkhoz (various years), *Narodnoe Khozyaistvo SSSR (Statistical Yearbook)*, Moskva: Finansy i Statistika.

Narodnoe Khozyaistvo Estonskoi SSR v 1986 godu (1987), Tallin: Eesti Paamat.

Narodnoe Khozyaistvo Kazakhstana v 1985 godu (1986), Moskva: Finansy i Statistika.

Narodnoe Khozyaistvo Latviiskoi SSR v 1986 godu (1987), Moskva: Finansy i Statistika.

Narodnoe Khozyaistvo RSFSR (various years), Moskva: Finansy i Statistika.

Narodnoe Khozyaistvo Ukrainskoi SSR v 1986 godu (1987), Moskva: Finansy i Statistika.

Norak, A.A. (1986), 'O respublikanskom fonde okhrany okruzhayushchei sredy i ratsionalnogo ispolzovaniya prirodnykh resursov v Estonskoi SSR', Paper presented at Vtoraya Bsesoyuznaya konferentsiya sovershenstvovanie Metodologii Upravleniya Sotsialisticheskim Prirodopolzovaniem, Moskva, 13–16 May.

Noren, J.H. (1990), 'The Soviet Economic Crisis: Another Perspective', *Soviet Economy*, No. 6, pp. 3–55.

Noren, J.H. (1992), 'The Russian Economic Reform: Progress and Prospects', *Soviet Economy*, No. 2, pp. 3–41.

Nove, Alec (1982), *The Soviet Economic System*, London: George Allen & Unwin.

Nove, Alec (1986), *The Soviet Economic System*, London: Unwin & Hyman.

O Korrenoi Perestroike dela Okhrany Prirody v Strane (1988), Tsentralnyi Komitet KPSS I Soviet Ministrov SSSR, postanovlenie, 7 yanvariya godu, No. 32, Moskva: Kreml.

Okhrana Okruzhayushchei Sredy i Ratsionalnoe Ispolzovanie Prirodnykh Resursov v SSSR (1989), Moskva: Finansy i Statistika.

Okhrana Zdorovya v SSSR (Statistical Yearbook) (1990), Moskva: Finansy i Statistika.

Oxenstierna, S. (1987), 'Bonuses, factor demand and technical efficiency in the Soviet enterprise', *Journal of Comparative Economics*, Vol. 11, No. 2, pp. 207–20.

Oxenstierna, S. (1990), *From Labour Shortage to Unemployment? The Soviet Labour Market in the 1980s*, Swedish Institute for Social Research – Dissertation Series.

Peterson, D.J. (1990a), 'The State of the Environment: An Overview', *Report on the USSR*, 23 February.

Peterson, D.J. (1990b), 'The State of the Environment: The Air', *Report on the USSR*, 2 March.

References

Peterson, D.J. (1990c), 'The State of the Environment: The Water', *Report on the USSR*, 16 March.

Peterson, D.J. (1990d), 'The State of the Environment: The Land", *Report on the USSR*, 1 June.

Petrov, A.P., Burdin, N.A. and Kozhukhov, N.I. (1986), *Lesnoi Kompleks*, Moskva: Lesnaya Promyshlennost.

Popov, V.A. (1957), *Lenaya Promyshlennost SSSR 1917–1957*, Moskva: Lesnaya Promyshlennost 3 vols.

Popov, Ya. P. (1985), "Operativnoe predotvrashchenie vysokikh urovnei zagryaznenii atmosfery i otsenka ekonomicheskoi effektivnosti etikh meropriyatii", in Gofman and Motkin (eds) (1985), pp. 90–97.

Portes, R.D. (1969), "The Enterprise under Central Planning", *Review of Economic Studies*, Vol. 36, No. 106, pp. 197–212.

Problemy okruzhayushchei spredy i prirodnykh resursov (1989), Moskva: VINITI.

Promyshlennost SSSR (1964), Moskva: Statistika.

Promyshlennost SSSR (1988), Moskva: Finansy i statistika.

Pryde, P.R. (1972), *Conservation in the Soviet Union*, Cambridge: Cambridge University Press.

Pyazok, R. (1984), "Metodologiya ekonomicheskoi otsenki ushcherba ot otchuzhdeniya i narusheniya zemel gornymi razrabotkami", *Izvestiya Akademii Nauk Estonskoi SSR*, No. 33, pp. 193–202.

Rabinovich, B. (1985), "Effektivnost prirodopolzovaniya", *Voprosy Ekonomiki*, No. ", pp. 85–97.

Rabinovich, B. (1991), "Zemelnaya sobstvennost i plata za zemlyu pri perekhode k pynku", *Voprosy Ekonomiki*, No. 3, pp. 98–115.

Reshenie (1990), "*O provedenii ekonomicheskogo eksperimenta po sovershenstvovaniyu khozyaistvennogo mekhanizma prirodopolzovaniya v g. Moskve*", Moskovskii Gorodskoi Sovet Narodnykh Deputatov Ispolnitelnyi Komitet, No. 840, 14 Aprelya.

Rotar G.V. and Stavrakova, N.E. (1988), "Voprosy postroeniya ekonomiko-matematicheskikh modelei sovershenstvovaniya khozyaistvennogo mekhanizma sredozashchitnoi deyadetnosti na urovne regiona", in Gusev (1988), pp. 33–9.

Sätre Åhlander, A-M. (1989), "Miljöproblemen i Sovjet", *Världspolitikens Dagsfrågor*, No. 8.

Sätre Åhlander, A-M. (1994), "Environmental policies in the former Soviet Union", in Sterner (ed.) (1994), pp. 68–81.

SCB, *Miljöstatistisk Årsbok*, 1986–87.

Schroeder, G.E. (1991), "*Perestroika* in the Aftermath of 1990", *Soviet Economy*, No. 7, pp. 3–13.

Sheinin, L.B. (1987), "Plata za vodu i khozyaistvennyi raschet v selskom khozyaistve", *Vestnik Selskogo Khozyaistvo Nauki*, No. 8, pp. 11–15.

Shkatov, V.K. (1974), *Popennaya Plata SSSR*, Moskava: Lesnaya Promyshlennost.

Shmelev, N. (1987), "Avansy i dolgi", *Novyi Mir*, No. 6.

Sinelshchikov, V.S. and Ushakov E.P. (1985), "K probleme cotsiolno-ekonomicheskogo obosnovaniya zadanii pyatiletnikh planov no okhrane vod s uchetom dolgosrochnoi perspektivy", in Gofman and Motkin (eds) (1985), pp. 127–39.

Singleton, F. (1986), "Eastern Europe: do the Greens threaten the Reds?", *The World Today*, August/September, pp. 159–62.

Slider, D. (1991), "Embattled Entrepreneurs: Soviet Cooperatives in an Unreformed Economy", *Soviet Studies*, No. 5, pp. 797–821.

SSSR i Soyuznye Respubliki (various years), Moskva: Finansy i Statistika.

SSSR v tsiffrakh (various years), Moskva: Finansy i Statistika.

Sterner, T. (ed.) (1994), *Economic Policies for Sustainable Development*, Dordrecht: Kluwer Academic Publishers.

Sutela, P. (1984), *Socialism, Planning an Optimality: A Study in Economic Thought*, Helsinki: The Finnish Council of Sciences and Letters.

Swianiewicz, S. (1965), *Forced Labour and Economic Development*, London.

Syrodoroyev, N. (1975), *Soviet Land Legislation*, Moscow: Progress Publishers.

Teage, E. (1992), 'Russia's Industrial Lobby Takes the Offensive', *RFE/RL Research Report*, Vol. 1, No. 32, 14 August, pp. 1–6.

Thornton, Judith (1978a), 'Resources and property rights in the Soviet Union', in Jackson (ed.) (1978), pp. 1–12.

Thornton, Judith (1978b), 'Soviet Methodology for the valuation of natural resources', *Journal of Comparative Economics*, No. 2, pp. 321–33.

Thornton, Judith (1983), 'Resource valuation and efficiency of Soviet resource production and use', in Jensen (ed.) (1983), pp. 597–613.

Trehub, A. (1988), 'The USSR state committee for environmental protection', *Radio Liberty Research*, RL 27/88, 21 January.

Treml, V.G., Kostinsky, B.L. and Gallik, D.M. (1973), 'Interindustry structure of the Soviet economy: 1959 and 1966', in US Congress, Joint Economic Committee, *Soviet Economic Prospects for the Seventies*, Washington DC: USGPO.

Tretyakova, A. (1991), 'Energy crisis in the USSR', Paper presented at the Conference on the Soviet Economy in Crisis and Transition at the Stockholm School of Economics, 11–12 June.

Tretyakova, A. and Birman, I. (1976), 'Input–output analysis in the USSR', *Soviet Studies*, Vol. 37, No. 2, April, pp. 157–86.

Trud v SSSR, (1988), Moskva: Finansy i Statistika.

Turkevitch, I.V. (1977), *Kadastrovaya Otsenka Lesov*, Moskva: Lesnaya Promyshlennost.

Turnball, M. (1990), *Soviet Environmental Policies and Practices – The Most Critical Investment*, Aldershot, Brookfield USA, Hong Kong, Singapore and Sydney: Dartmouth.

Ushakov, E.P. (1983), 'Dolgosrochnye aspekty sotsialno-ekonomicheskoi optimizatsii ispolzovaniya prirodnykh resursov', in Gofman and Motkin (eds) (1983), pp. 3–16.

Ushakov, E.P. (1985), 'Prirodookhrannaya deyatelnost kak obekt optimizatsii', in Gofman and Motkin (eds) (1985), pp. 9–21.

Voevoda, I.N. (1980), *Lesnaya i lesopererabatyvayushchaya promyshlennost Sibiri*, Novosibirsk: Nauka, Sibirskoe Otdelenie.

Voevoda, I.N. and Petrov, A.P. (1987), *Territorialnye otraslevye kompleksy*, Novosibirsk: Nauka, Sibirskoe Otdelenie.

Volkov, N.A. (1959), *Puti Povysheniya Proizvoditelnosti Truda v Lesozagotovitelnoi Promyshlennosti*, Ioshkar-Ola.

Vremennaya tipovaya metodika opredeleniya ekonomicheskoi effektivnosti stimulirovaniya osushchestvleniya prirodookhrannykh meropriyatii i otsenki ekonomicheskogo ushcherba prichinyaemogo narodnomu khozyaistvu zagryazneniem okruzhayushchei sredy (1986), Gosplan, Gosstroi i Prezidium Akademii Nauk, Moskva: Ekonomika.

Ward, B. (1967), *The Socialist Economy*, New York: Random House.

Weissenburger, Ulrich (1984), 'Umweltprobleme und Umweltschutz in der Sowjetunion, Teil I: Umweltverschmutzung und -zerstörung als Problem der Wirtschaftpolitik', *Berichte des Bundesinstituts fur Ostwissenschaftliche und International Studien*, Teil 1, Köln, No. 52.

Weissenburger, Ulrich (1988), 'Umweltschutz in der Sowjetunion: Zwang zum Handeln', Deutsches Institut fur Wirtschaftsforschung, *Wochenbericht*, No. 44, pp. 595–9.

Weitzman, M.L. (1976), 'The New Soviet Incentive Model', *Bell Journal of Economics*, Vol. 7, No. 1, pp. 251–7.

Wolfson, Z. (1986), 'The Soviet Environment in the Early 1980s: More Concern, Fewer Allocations', *Russia*, No. 12, pp. 31–40.

Wolfson, Z. (1989), 'Dangerous Levels of Pesticides and other Chemicals in Food', *Environmental Policy Review*, Vol. 3, No. 1, pp. 7–11.

Yablokov, A. (1988), 'Pestitsidy, Ekologiya, Selskoe Khozyaistvo', *Kommunist*, No. 15, pp. 34–42.

Yablokov, A. (1990) 'The Current State of the Soviet Environment', *Environmental Policy Review*, Vol. 4, No. 1.

Zaikov, G. (1985), 'Politiko-ekonomicheskie problemy ucheta ekologicheskikh faktorov v sotsialisticheskom proizvodstve', *Ekonomicheskie Nauki*, No. 1, pp. 59–67.

Zaleski, E. (1971), *Planning for Economic Growth in the Soviet Union, 1918–1932*, Chapel Hill: University of North Carolina Press.

Zaleski, E. (1980), *Stalinist Planning for Economic Growth, 1933–1952*, Chapel Hill: University of North Carolina Press.

Ziegler, Charles E. (1980), 'Soviet environmental policy and Soviet central planning', *Soviet Studies*, Vol. 32, No. 1, pp. 124–34.

Ziegler, Charles E. (1982), 'Centrally planned economies and environmental information: a rejoinder', *Soviet Studies*, Vol. 34, No. 2, pp. 296–9.

Ziegler, Charles E. (1987), *Environmental Policy in the USSR*, Amherst: University of Massachusetts Press.

ZumBrunnen, Craig (1987), 'Soviet water, air, and nature preservation problems of the Gorbachev era and beyond', Paper presented at Conference on the Soviet Economy: A New Course?, NATO – Economics Directorate, Brussels, 1–3 April.

Index